Just Sex is the book I have been longing for in my ministry for many years – one that does not merely delineate an orthodox view on sexual ethics, but provides a persuasive apologetic for the watching world. The relevance, goodness and transforming power of the Christian world-view is painted in stark contrast to the rootless, shallow and corrosive individualism that masquerades as modern-day morality.

Just Sex is an important book for the twenty-first-century church since it provides us with the categories, approach and evidence to speak persuasively and prophetically to our dying culture. I doubt I will read a more important or impressive book this year – compulsory reading for all serious-minded Christians.
Revd Richard Cunningham, Director of UCCF –
The Christian Unions

Just Sex articulately grapples with the psychology and cultural conditions required for mature, healing sex. As a result it plumbs at a deeper and wider level than most other books you will read on this topic. Through its pages you will learn about yourself and your place in this relational world; from this vision your understanding of sex will fall into place in a new way which will be profoundly counter-cultural. Brandon meticulously unwraps why God's ideal is good, setting sex in a relational and societal context that challenges the accepted framework of 'what consenting adults do in private is none of anyone else's business'. A must-read to contextualize your thinking on sex.
Maggie Ellis, Psychosexual Therapist and Agony Aunt for Christianity *magazine.*

Dare we believe society could wake up to the chaos that sex without responsibility is causing to our social fabric? Dare we hope for a turnaround in public opinion about sex and relationships? It happened with slavery in the nineteenth century, and with ecology and smoking in more recent years.

This watershed book raises hopes that our hypersexualized culture could be convinced that it has got it wrong about sex. Its logic, evidence and relational perspective, while written in a British context, deserve to be studied and discussed throughout Europe and the West. May it spark a quiet revolution to restore a future for our children – and our culture.

Jeff Fountain, YWAM Europe field director

Just Sex is a thought-provoking book, packed with startling facts and figures, effective quotes and lively personal stories. Guy Brandon has tackled a crucial issue, bringing clear biblical thinking to bear on postmodern culture in a robust and very readable fashion. Not content simply to diagnose the problems, Guy suggests practical and compassionate solutions. His book deserves to be placed in the hands of all Christian leaders, pastors and youthworkers. It would also be challenging and interesting to those who don't share the Christian faith yet are concerned by the state of sexual mores in Britain today and are looking for humane and thoughtful wisdom.

Steve and Anna Griffiths, International Directors for Personnel, OMF

A good book that exposes many of the double standards in Christian ethical thinking about sexuality, and has some wonderful 'quotable quotes' that challenged and amused me.

Martin Hallet, Director, True Freedom Trust

Swapping the 'r-World' for the 'i-World' is the central theme of this compelling book. It is an excellent explication of how 'throughout the Bible, strong relationships are a currency of well-being and a barometer of social health'. In his emphasis on sexual behaviour as a key indicator of so much else about how people treat each other, Guy Brandon goes well beyond the usual truisms and provides a well-argued case for a societal, as well as an individual, change of heart and mind.

Canon Ann Holt OBE, Executive Director of Bible Society (England & Wales)

An exceptionally important and well-written study which should be on every church bookstall. It is right up to date and urgently needed.

Peter Lewis, author, and senior minister of Cornerstone Church, Nottingham.

The central theme of this book is that sexual relationships affect a much wider group of people than just those immediately involved in them. There is thus a social, as well as personal, aspect to them. This means that we, as citizens, and society as a whole, should be concerned about the social fallout of family breakdown in particular. The book provides us with a clear analysis of the economic costs involved but points also to the emotional and personal costs. It calls for a re-evaluation of the goods of marriage in our society, for support in terms of education and preparation for marriage, favourable tax arrangements and employment policies which are family friendly.

This is an important intervention at a time when it is appropriate to reconsider national values and priorities. The Jubilee Centre has, once again, put us in its debt by addressing directly one of the central issues facing our society.

The Rt Revd Dr Michael Nazir-Ali, Bishop of Rochester

Unquestionably stands out as the most enlightened work on human sexual behaviour which provokes intelligent thinking. Guy Brandon writes on this subject with much passionate enthusiasm giving biblical clarity, whether he secures assent or controversy.

Men and women are made in the image of God and their sexual behaviour in some manner participates in the divine likeness. Sadly, our world has distorted God's concept of sexuality. Even sadder is the confusion in the church about godly sex. This work is seasonal at an age when social structures, including the nucleus of the family, have collapsed, leaving many young people to find out for themselves what 'feels right' for them. As a result, many, including those in the Christian church, are living a life of guilt. Many believers lack biblical teaching on the subject of sex. Many believers fall into the lie of the world that sex is just for fun. It is merely another commodity with no strings attached – it is 'just sex'.

The lie of our time is that it is about me and my choices, and whatever I choose and whomever I have sex with is nobody's business as long as no-one gets hurt. The result of those private choices? Too many people carrying around lifetime emotional scars.

Promiscuous sexual choices of high-profile people become everybody's business. Societies are disrupted by the lack of trust and confidence in those who lead.

The examples and statistics cited in the book are mainly from the UK and other Western nations, but the devil is just as active here in South Africa. Those who take time to read this excellent work will be informed and enlightened. They will know that sex is God's idea and that when enjoyed within the boundaries he has set nobody gets hurt, nobody feels used, nobody becomes just a service provider. It is NOT just sex!

Revd Edwin Ngubane, Rector of Holy Trinity, Benoni, Gauteng, South Africa

Guy Brandon's *Just Sex* compellingly argues from both social and theological sciences the truth that most of us in the West are blind to – sex is never just about sex, or mere consent, it's about community. Noting our iPod culture has morphed into an iWorld culture, Brandon's analysis exposes our Western individualism and reveals our nakedness and lostness, and records in unrelenting detail the high price our cities and nations pay for what they term 'free sex'. *Just Sex* not only presents critical analysis of our problem, but winsomely offers a better way forward through recovering a richness in relationships that are less about 'me' and more about 'we'.

Revd Dr Alfred J. Poirier, author, The Peacemaking Pastor

Just Sex makes clear that, in the intimidating culture of selfish secular hedonism in Western society, to place sexual intercourse on 'special reserve' for marriage between a husband and wife meaning lifelong commitment and responsibility for children conceived is the cutting edge of obedience to God, respect for others and witness to life abundant in Western culture. Guy Brandon carefully sets out teaching from the Bible with acute documentation of the social and financial costs of sexual disorder. Are you ready for today's counter-cultural challenge?

Canon Dr Chris Sugden, Anglican Mainstream

Guy Brandon

Just Sex

Is it ever just sex?

ivp

INTER-VARSITY PRESS
Norton Street, Nottingham NG7 3HR, England
Email: ivp@ivpbooks.com
Website: www.ivpbooks.com

First published 2009
Reprinted 2009

British Library Cataloguing-in-Publication Data

A catalogue record for this book is available from the British Library.

ISBN: 978–1–84474–371–1

Set in Monotype Garamond 11/13pt
Typeset in Great Britain by Servis Filmsetting Ltd, Stockport, Cheshire
Printed and bound in Great Britain by Ashford Colour Press Ltd, Gosport,
Hampshire

Inter-Varsity Press publishes Christian books that are true to the Bible and that
communicate the gospel, develop discipleship and strengthen the church for its
mission in the world.

Inter-Varsity Press is closely linked with the Universities and Colleges Christian
Fellowship, a student movement connecting Christian Unions in universities and
colleges throughout Great Britain, and a member movement of the International
Fellowship of Evangelical Students. Website: *www.uccf.org.uk*

TABLE OF CONTENTS

ACKNOWLEDGMENTS

Although this book has a single name on the cover, its contents are the result of many months and years of careful thought and discussion by far more people than it is possible to thank in these acknowledgments.

The origins of *Just Sex* began long before my own involvement, as the Jubilee Centre turned its collective mind to the question of how our understanding of sex both reflects our honour for God and impacts our broader relationships with one another across our families, friendships and society as a whole. Christopher Ash, Mario Bergner, Jonathan Burnside, Robert Gagnon, Patricia Morgan, Julian Rivers, Jeffrey Satinover, James Skillen, Gordon Wenham and others provided important foundations at this stage, and their work has continued to be crucial. Similarly, we are grateful to the 500 private donors whose generous contributions to the Jubilee Centre made work on this book possible.

Michael Schluter has been closely involved with the project from its inception and throughout my own work on the book, which draws on several of his key concepts. Rose Lynas has also given much of her time to it, and her research and critique have been invaluable. John Ashcroft has frequently suggested fresh perspectives on much of the subject matter. Simon Burton and James Williams have both provided substantial pieces of supporting research. Overall, Jason Fletcher's warm encouragement and focus has been greatly appreciated, followed by John Hayward's when he took over as executive director of the Jubilee Centre in 2008.

Particular thanks go to Dale Kuehne, one of the only ordained politics professors in New England, for his concept and language of the 'iWorld' and other ideas that will appear more fully in his forthcoming book, *Sex and the iWorld: Rethinking Relationship Beyond an Age of Individualism*,[1] and to Sharon Willmer, Professor of Developmental Psychology at the University of California, for her expertise in the areas of child development and relational order. Those who responded to our invitation to provide case studies also deserve special mention for their willingness to show vulnerability and lend personal insight to material that could otherwise risk becoming cold and academic. To maintain privacy, names have been changed throughout.

Kate Byrom and the IVP team have offered helpful feedback on the later drafts, as have the many readers, whose attention has addressed numerous errors and oversights.

Finally, for all the help I have received, any mistakes are mine.

Guy Brandon
Jubilee Centre
Cambridge
July 2008

Note

1. Baker, 2009.

FOREWORD

A teenage lad once told me that sex was just another big disappointment in his life. 'I was really happy about losing my virginity but when I did I thought, "It ain't all it's cracked up to be".'

A female friend of mine recently confessed to feeling the same. 'I know that I am young and supposed to have it all and not care, but I can't just keep doing sex like this. I want more but don't know how to ask for it. I don't think I deserve to fall in love.'

The whole point about sex is that it isn't just sex.

Because when it is – we are left craving something more.

In her book *Unhooked*, Washington Post journalist Laura Session argues that more and more people are replacing relationships with casual sexual encounters. '. . . love . . . is being put on hold or seen as impossible [and] sex is becoming the primary currency of social interaction.'

Most of us are confused about relationships and/or sex at some point in our lives. Some of us might have been hurt by a broken promise, a one-night stand, a past relationship, an unrequited love. As a youth worker I find myself daily in conversations with teenagers about these very things. I love it when I can give young people space to make some sense of the confusion of hormones, emotions, desires, pressures and expectations and to be able to stand back and take in a bigger view. To explore some of the possibilities for godly intimacy that being made in the image of an intimate and loving Creator gives us.

That's why this book is essential.

It isn't preachy or judgmental, but neither does it fudge the
tricky issues or pretend that there aren't differing ideas. Guy
Brandon offers us the chance to take in a bigger view of sex and
to see the benefits of 'doing sex' a different way – God's way.
Painfully aware that he writes this in the context of a broken and
hurting world, he offers a pastorally-sensitive Christian response.
And in today's climate of tension in both the church and society,
that's a remarkable thing to do.

In my work with Romance Academy I constantly see the
amazing effects of teenagers discovering for themselves the benefits of 'doing sex' a different way. Although not usually from
church backgrounds, the young people commit to following biblical principles for a period of time to see what difference it makes
to them. Time after time we meet young people who feel the pain
and regret of unhappy and unfulfilling relationships. Many feel
they have lost the chance to make the right decisions about their
own lives. Romance Academy offers them an invitation to build a
new future with the support and care of a loving community.

As Romance Academy asks people to *try out* God's way, Guy
Brandon explores *why* we should. He provides a clear and balanced
view of contemporary attitudes to sex and explores where it's
failing us. And, by contrast, puts flesh on the bones of why God's
intention for sex is better. In particular he scrutinizes whether the
much-loved myth of 'it's OK if it's between consenting adults' is a
sufficient marker for negotiating sexual morality.

So take a deep breath. This is vital stuff.

Rachel Gardner
Creative Director of the Romance Academy
September 2008

INTRODUCTION

Boris Johnson complained, 'It is a wretched and lamentable day when people's private lives can become used in political machinations', after being sacked from the Conservative shadow cabinet over an extramarital affair, yet later went on to become London's mayor. Similarly a newspaper report that Max Mosley, the president of the FIA, motorsport's governing body, took part in a 'Nazi-style orgy' with prostitutes threatened to split the world of motorsport – the Germans suspended its FIA activities, the Americans considered doing the same, and a break-off body was possibly to be formed – yet Mosely survived a vote of confidence. Sex is supposed to be no one else's business, but at times its effects seem to be significant enough that we ignore that golden principle. Our culture certainly has strong opinions about sex; it's just that, at times, it struggles to know exactly what they are.

At the same time, sex has also become a big issue for Christians, with the threatened split in the FIA being paralleled in the worldwide Anglican Communion. Faced with a barrage of messages from a sexually permissive environment and lacking a clear rationale for biblical teaching, many Christians are unsure of what they think – uncertain whether an ancient text has anything to say to our Brave New World and, if it does, unconvinced of whether they really want to pay it any attention. Church leaders are divided over key issues like sex before marriage, divorce and homosexuality.

One reason for the confusion is that people find themselves walking a narrow line between, on the one hand, affirming traditional standards of sexual conduct and, on the other, showing grace and forgiveness to those who have chosen alternative forms of sexual expression. It is understandable and right that we should seek to comfort an individual who has been hurt by their own actions and those of another in a sexual relationship. Equally, in an age that extols diversity and multiculturalism, few people want to risk being accused of intolerance or prejudice. However, such desires and fears can obscure the need to uphold the biblical standards that this book argues can prevent so much pain – particularly when the reasons for these standards are poorly understood.

The days are long gone when 'Because the Bible says so' was a good enough reason by itself to decide a person's behaviour. Nowadays, people want more than what they see as an arbitrary appeal to authority. They want to know *why* it is wrong to act in a particular way – specifically, what harm their actions do to others. If as Christians we want to be heard today – if our views are to be acknowledged and respected by people who do not share them in the first instance – then it is down to us to explain why our beliefs are relevant. If our reasons are deficient or unconvincing then they will fail; the choices we each face can no longer be decided by reference to an unsupported appeal to divine authority.

Just Sex supports a Christian worldview, and we expect that many readers will be Christians, but it does not presuppose faith on the part of the reader. It seeks to provide clear reasons – social, psychological and financial – why the Bible has a better vision for human sexuality than the confusion of our present culture. These reasons, rather than a simple appeal to 'what the Bible says' alone, are the grounds on which we expect this book to stand or fall, and those on which we hope it will be judged.

This book is different to many other recent treatments of sexual ethics in that it does not offer a comprehensive exposition of the familiar biblical texts. Neither does it seek to lay out systematically a theological framework for sexual behaviour. Many other books have already covered this ground. Instead *Just Sex* examines the reasons *behind* the biblical injunctions that so many people have found so difficult to understand, or even, at times, intrusive and offensive. These reasons are explained in terms of the impacts of the sexual relationship on third parties: people who may be deeply affected but who, unlike the couple themselves, did not consent to the sex act. 'Immaturity, short-sightedness, worldly philosophies, ignorance, abuse, injury and our sinful nature can . . . easily converge into torrents of destructive behaviours. The 21st century's emphasis on unbridled pleasing of the sexual Self too easily obscures the inevitable, tragic consequences of such actions. While it may be more acceptable and easier to see the consequences to the Self, it is not always so acceptable or easy to see the consequences to others.'[1] 'Consenting adults' as the sole criterion for sex barely begins to tell us who might be harmed by a couple's 'private' decision. Our hope is that this book will guide our readers into a deeper understanding of the wisdom and love that are embedded in God's word.

This research grows out of a long-term commitment by the Jubilee Centre to explore the relevance of the Bible for the challenges faced by Britain and the world today. Its findings are in keeping with the framework, founded upon Jesus' insight that the whole of Scripture hangs on the twin commandments to love the Lord our God and to love our neighbour as ourselves, of a society held together by close personal, social, political and economic relationships. To explore the full extent of this relational framework, we hope readers will visit our website, www.jubilee-centre.org.

John Hayward
Executive Director
Jubilee Centre
Cambridge 2008

Note

1. Sharon Willmer, personal correspondence, 17 May 2008.

1. RELATIONAL PERSPECTIVES

Seeing the world differently

There is not a sexual relationship, an improper sexual relationship or any other kind of improper relationship . . . it depends on what the meaning of the word 'is' is.

Bill Clinton, during the 'Lewinsky scandal'

A climate of confusion

People today are hopelessly confused about sex. On the one hand, sex is supposed to be routine, normal, natural. More people are having more sex before, after, and outside of marriage than at probably any point in the past. Sex has become increasingly separated from marriage, with many people keeping their options open rather than pinning themselves down to one long-term, stable relationship. At the same time, sex is also supposed to be something special. Many of the same people who keep their options open regard this as part of the process of finding that perfect relationship that will last forever. The cost of the average wedding is now £20,000 (up £5,000 in five years) indicating the increasing importance that people place on their Big Day.[1] And yet around a fifth

of those who do choose marriage will have parted ways within just
ten years.[2]

We are also confused about the effects of our sexual choices on
others. We often say that sex is a private matter between consenting adults.

> *I've got five kids by three women . . . but no one in this city cares what consenting*
> *adults do as long as you don't involve children, animals or vegetables.*
>
> Ken Livingstone, former mayor of London

Ken Livingstone, when mayor of London, could claim that the
fact he had five children by three women was of no relevance
to his public career.[3] And yet, in the same week, one of the
country's most senior judges warned that family breakdown had
reached catastrophic levels, that the courts are overstretched to
the point of collapse as a result, and that 'almost all of society's
social ills can be traced back to the collapse in family stability'.[4]
Which view is correct? Do 'private' actions have 'public' consequences, or not?

The confusion about the significance of sex is nothing new,
especially for Christians. The Apostle Paul spent considerable
time explaining to the Corinthian church why, having accepted
Christ, they should be different in their sexual practices. That was
nearly two thousand years ago, but many of the same questions
and doubts still surface amongst Christians today. Faced with
a sexually permissive culture, probably not so very different in
some ways from the Corinthians' own, many of us are lost for
guidance.

Just Sex seeks to explain the goodness of the Christian world-
view of sex in terms that our culture understands and accepts,
without relying solely on the theological arguments that have
lost traction with many people. In doing so, it also addresses the
inconsistency and inadequacy of the prevailing idea that consent
alone is enough to legitimate a sexual relationship, and argues
that if we have truly accepted the concern for justice inherent in
the gospel, we have to question the assumption that 'just sex' is
really just.

Sex and the iWorld

I am always looking for meaningful one night stands.

Dudley Moore, actor and comedian

Although the focus of the book is on sex and sexuality, these are only really pointers to far deeper changes in our culture. If sexual chaos is the symptom, then the 'me-culture' is the disease we see in the West today. Whether we know it as postmodernity, individualism, what Dale Kuehne calls the iWorld, or by any other label, the guiding belief of our time is that I can live my life on my own terms, without reference to other people. 'Steven Jobs and Apple Computer have brilliantly understood the spirit of our age, a spirit of unfettered individualism and freedom, by marketing many of their products by using the prefix "i". The iPhone, the iPod, the iMac are names that capture the essence of the age in which we live. The t[raditional]World has been replaced by the iWorld.'[5]

So long as it doesn't hurt anyone else, I can be whoever I want to be and express myself however I see fit, which includes having sex with whoever I want to have sex with. My choices are my own; I don't judge anyone else for theirs and I expect – in fact, I demand – that they extend me the same courtesy.

This me-centred philosophy shows itself in many different ways: in a mass of symptoms besides rapidly shifting attitudes towards sex. In some cases, they are as much a cause as an effect, interdependent patterns of behaviour that are reinforcing and circular. One is the rise in consumerism and the resulting debt which, at over £1.5 trillion in the UK (£238 billion excluding mortgages; over $2.5 trillion excluding mortgages in the US), is currently running at the highest level ever recorded. Others are the job opportunities that enable and even encourage people to move away from the communities into which they are born, weakening family ties and leaving children living on the opposite side of the country – or world – to their parents and wider networks of belonging. Relationships in this new world have become stretched, confused and ultimately redefined according to the individual's situation. My relationships – my friends, my family and my sexual partners – are now whatever I want and need them to be. Later in this book we will argue that in recent decades intimacy has been seriously damaged in families, friendships and other relationships, and that sexual relationship is now used as a kind of catch-all pseudo-intimacy to fill that gap.

What changed?
Human nature hasn't changed in millennia, but over the last fifty years cultural attitudes have shifted on an unprecedented scale. In this respect, the 'sexual revolution' was not sexual at all. Medical and technological advances were catalysts for a change in sexual behaviour that simply enabled people to live the lives they have always wanted to, but that formerly had socially and financially damaging consequences. These consequences are still serious, but they have been rendered acceptable by the widespread belief that we can now circumvent them altogether: nice in theory but, as the evidence suggests, another matter in practice.

The real revolution was not that contraception allowed sex without the risk of a child, but that the sexual relationship itself could then be redefined to *mean* something different. Instead of bringing with it the usual expectation of childbirth and raising a family, the intimacy of the sexual relationship was sought in isolation and sex became about something else. The me-culture appropriated it for its own purposes, even as this new-found sexual choice reinforced the me-culture. Sex no longer entailed responsibility for family and others but increasingly became about expressing 'me' – a part of my identity. Divorced from family, sex has been recast to serve the me-culture's pursuit of pleasure and need for self-identity. With the advent of the iWorld, the traditional values of Dale Kuehne's 'tWorld' all but vanished.

'Consenting adults'

This me-centred mindset is reflected in our laws about sex, which focus heavily on the idea of consent. The Sexual Offences Act 2003 (the first major overhaul of sexual law in nearly fifty years) replaced older legislation which was felt to reflect nineteenth-century attitudes about men and women. In keeping with modern thinking, protection of society as a whole was emphasized over personal morality, thus permitting most consensual acts that take place in private.[6] This reflects the idea that private, consensual acts are harmless to others. Typically, a sexual act is only illegal where consent is not given, or where it is deemed invalid – for example, on the grounds of young age or mental disorder, or incapacity through alcohol or drugs. Further protection for those under 18 was provided through an 'abuse of a position of trust' category, which covers adults who look after children in, for example, hospitals, schools and children's homes. The Act also brought a greater measure of protection to families by considering a wider range of relationships, reflecting more complex family forms, rather than restricting 'incest' to blood relations.

The Sex Offences Review Group began from the point of view that 'Respect for private life means that any regulation which is proposed must be limited to what is necessary in a democratic society and proportionate to the problem. Such a concept of the criminal law does not condone or advocate any particular form of sexual behaviour, but is based on principles of preventing harm and promoting public good.'[7] Although the Act shifted the focus away from personal morality and towards consent, it is worth noting that it is still forced to make moral assumptions. In some cases, it is valid to outlaw consensual sex, for example in the case of intercourse in public: there are limits to individuals' sexual autonomy. It is also worth noting that, although the principle of harm to others is paramount in the Act, 'harm' is difficult to define, often meaning direct, physical harm, but also extending to moral or psychological harm.[8]

The relational lens

Although the Sexual Offences Act 2003 is more concerned with consent and harm with regards to the individual, it has so far proved impossible to ignore at least some wider implications of the harm principle. This is a theme we will develop and use at length in this book: that sexual acts have consequences beyond those directly involved. Ultimately, the relational values of the rWorld provide an antidote to the isolating and relationally shallow individualism of the iWorld.

'Consenting adults in private' is a necessary starting point: it is the absolute minimum requirement to determine whether a sexual act is valid. All too often, however, this principle on its own is hopelessly inadequate in restricting the harm that can result from a sexual relationship – to the individuals themselves, to their immediate families, to wider networks of friends and relatives, to communities and to society as a whole.

We are not here advocating a form of collectivism, in which the individual's desires and actions are sacrificed for the good of the group. But the problem is that, like it or not, we do all live in relationship to others. To add insult to injury in this climate of individualism, it is our relationships more than our consumption that truly affect our wellbeing. As the philosopher Emmanuel Mounier said, 'the adult only finds himself in his relationships to others and to things, in his work and comradeship, in friendship and in love, in action and encounter, and not in his relationship to himself.'[9]

Tragically, our culture has lost this relational perspective. Our values have moved sharply over the last half-century and we now define success and happiness heavily in terms of financial outcomes and material prosperity: keeping up with the Joneses has become more important than maintaining a strong relationship with them.

People in the West have got no happier over the last 50 years. They have become much richer, they work much less, they have longer holidays, they travel more, they live longer, and they are healthier. But they are no happier.

Richard Layard, London School of Economics

Put simply, our culture often appears to know the cost of everything and the value of nothing. However, the goal of healthy relationships provides a framework to express a positive vision for society in which relationships matter more than individual rights, personal choice and materialism.

Christianity: a relational religion

Christianity is, strikingly, a relational religion.[10] In Matthew 22:37–40, Jesus summarized Scripture in terms of relationships:

'Love the Lord your God with all your heart and with all your soul and with all your mind . . . Love your neighbour as yourself.'

This includes relationships involved in business, worship, fellowship between believers, and within the family. It even encompasses the environment, the stewardship of which reflects our attitudes to its Creator, and the others who live in it.[11] And, of course, it applies to sexual relationships.

Then God said, 'Let us make man in our image, in our likeness . . .' (Gen. 1:26)

The Christian God is Trinity, and relational by nature. Humans are made in the image of this relational God; we are God's image-bearers on earth, and our capacities to form and sustain relationships are a core aspect of our identity. There is clarity in the relationship; the persons of the Trinity are distinct and defined: Father, Son and Holy Spirit. There is equality, and there is stability; no person of the Trinity is more or less important than another, and the relationship is eternal. These characteristics are significant when we come to consider the qualities that mark our own relationships, and in the concept of Relational Order (see below and in chapter 4).

The Trinity is a relationship of love, something which led to our own relationship with God, and with each other. 'And here's why we exist: Love, by its nature, desires to expand its own communion. God certainly didn't *need* anyone else. The love of the Trinity is perfect and complete in itself. Yet out of sheer goodness and generosity, God wanted to create a great multitude of other persons to share in his own eternal, ecstatic "exchange of love."'[12]

The Bible describes the result of this outward-looking act of love: two relationships between humans and God, maintained first through the old covenant and then enabled through Jesus and the new covenant. A covenant is a relationship based on a promise, so the purpose of the Bible is to shape our response to the Lord as our covenant Lord.[13] This obviously has enormous significance in how the people of God should live and relate to one another.

The Lord God said, 'It is not good for the man to be alone. I will make a helper suitable for him.' . . . The man and his wife were both naked, and they felt no shame. (Gen. 2:18, 25)

Throughout the Bible, strong relationships are the currency of wellbeing and a barometer of social health. In Genesis 2, the human creature's lack of relationship was the first feature of creation that God declared was 'not good', and promptly addressed with the creation of Eve (Gen. 2:18–25). In this ideal setting, humanity enjoys both perfect relationship with God and perfect relationship between its members. One chapter on, a ruptured relationship between humans and God is immediately followed by ruptured relationships between humans; Cain and Abel's tragedy swiftly follows Adam and Eve's offence and is replicated through society, culminating in the corporate sin of the Babel story (Gen. 11) with its long-term consequences of scattering and difficulty in communicating.

Later in the Bible, punishment is often seen in terms of a loss of relationship. In Exodus, Leviticus and Numbers, certain sins are punished by the offender being 'cut off' (Hebrew *karet*) – generally understood to be premature death at God's hands, but stated in terms of separation from the community.[14] The psalmist highlights his belief that death leads to the loss of relationship with God, asking, 'No-one remembers you when he is dead. Who praises you from his grave?' (Ps. 6:5). There is every indication that heaven is relational – not just between humans and God but between humans too. John 17:3 states that 'this is eternal life: that they may know you, the only true God, and Jesus Christ, whom you have sent'. At the Transfiguration in Mark 9:2–7, Elijah and Moses talk with Jesus. In Matthew 22:23–33, Jesus explains that in heaven people will be 'like the angels'. Although this means that there will be no marriage in heaven, angels are nevertheless capable of communicating with each other and with humans, as in Genesis 18 – in fact, the word angel means 'messenger', and this is their role throughout both Testaments.

Relational wellbeing, or *shalom*

Asked which was the greatest commandment, 'Jesus replied, "Love the Lord your God with all your heart and with all your soul and with all your mind." This is the first and greatest commandment.

And the second is like it: "Love your neighbour as yourself." All
the Law and the Prophets hang on these two commandments'
(Matt. 22:37–40). Love is not a term of finance and economics, but
describes a quality of relationships. The two great commandments
which are the basis of Christian ethics are relational, whilst the
crucifixion was God's ultimate answer for the broken relationships
that followed the 'relational rupture' in Eden.

The Bible calls the intended result of these principles *shalom*:
relational wholeness, wellbeing, completeness and prosperity – a
far richer and more nuanced concept than the usual translation,
'peace'.[15] The 'peace' of shalom is not merely a passive peace, the
absence of evil and danger. It is an active enjoyment of relationships, health and prosperity. It encompasses not only how things
appear on the surface, but the values on which society is rooted.
Shalom is more than an absence of crime and fear; it is the outworking of justice at all levels of society and in all relationships. It
is relational wholeness.[16]

Isaiah relates a vision of this shalom:

Justice will dwell in the desert
and righteousness live in the fertile field.
The fruit of righteousness will be peace;
the effect of righteousness will be quietness and confidence forever.
My people will live in peaceful dwelling places,
in secure homes,
in undisturbed places of rest.
Though hail flattens the forest and the city is levelled completely,
how blessed you will be,
sowing your seed by every stream,
and letting your cattle and donkeys range free. (Isa. 32:16–20)

There are many implications of God having relational priorities for
the ordering of human society. There is no sacred-secular divide;
all aspects of human life – including business, justice, health, education and finance – are ultimately about relationships between
individuals, organizations or nations. God's concern with sexual
behaviour, too, is concerned with the relational context in which
the sexual act takes place, and the relational 'knock-on' effects

to third parties. In eternity, God will not be asking us specifically about the bank accounts we left behind on earth, or about the kind of car we owned, but will want to know about the quality of our relationships in every sphere of our lives – home, work, church, neighbourhood and society. (The way we spend our money has implications for our relationships, however, so we cannot assume that such issues are entirely irrelevant.)

Reading from right to left

Many people today, including some Christians, express doubt that the Bible could have anything to say about the way we approach sexual relationship in twenty-first-century Western society. The often unspoken argument is that the Bible is a product of another era; it comes from another world, or other worlds, since the Bible's books span many centuries and numerous cultures – none of which seem to have much of use to say to our enlightened times.

It is true that we have to be careful when we look to the Bible for guidance today on any matter, not least this one. We cannot lift its teachings out of their setting and blindly apply them to our own. The Bible, like the Hebrew language, has to be read 'from right to left', to use one commentator's phrase. Its message must be understood in its own context before it can be transferred to ours; if we impose our own cultural norms and points of view onto it from the start we can hardly expect to gain a coherent result – any more than a copy of the Highway Code (which, being designed for British roads, states that you should keep to the left-hand lane wherever possible) will help you when driving in America. We are looking for the underlying principles expressed by the laws and narratives of the Bible – not just what God wants for the world, but why. Once we know that, hopefully we can then apply the same principles to our own circumstances.

The laws of the Bible are not arbitrary, though some of them seem so strange to us that they can appear so. Why, for example, were Israelite men forbidden from trimming the sides of their beards (Lev. 19:27)? Why were they not to plant two different kinds of seed in the same field (Lev. 19:19)? And what was so terrible about cooking a young calf in its mother's milk (Exod. 23:19)? Without the relevant context, we often have little chance of understanding the point of much of the Old Testament. (For an answer to these questions in the more general context of how we understand and apply different types of Old Testament laws as Christians, see Appendix #18.)

Right relationships: what constitutes shalom?

Intimacy and relational wholeness are dependent on psychological health. That is to say, healthy relationships (sexual or otherwise) are grounded in emotional maturation. Developmental psychologist Erik Erikson famously saw maturity in terms of different life stages, and the successful negotiation of 'crises' or crucial psychological tasks associated with each.[17] These include learning trust and then autonomy – establishing independence and freedom; initiative and planning, and understanding the appropriate role of guilt; learning responsibility and correct motivations for success; confidence in one's own identity; intimacy and isolation, commitment and both how to carry out an intimate relationship and exist apart from this where necessary. Later stages involve guiding the next generation, and accepting life with a sense of fulfilment rather than despair.

> *Early love is when you love the way the other person makes you feel. Mature love is when you love the person as he or she is. It is the difference between passionate and compassionate love. It's Bon Jovi vs. Beethoven.*
>
> Mark Goulston, psychiatrist[18]

Although each 'task' is generally associated with a different age or stage of life, each remains important and may surface at different times. It is possible to go through life never having properly learned even the earliest skills. For example, establishing a healthy identity as an individual is a prerequisite for forming intimate relationships. All development is an interpersonal and relational process, and it is only with reference to others that we understand ourselves.

> *There is no 'self' outside of relationship.*
>
> Sharon Willmer, Professor of Developmental Psychology

Sex takes place within and as a part of this ongoing psychological development. For example, the biblical idea of 'leaving and

cleaving' in marriage requires 'autonomy' (Gen. 2:24). That is, individuals need to know who they are and how to regulate their own
emotions – managing anxiety and its underlying causes – before
they are able to separate from their parents. It also requires a
healthy understanding of intimacy to be able to share your life with
another person. However, the way our society typically detaches
sex from the setting of overall personal and relational development, treating it as isolated from other aspects of these processes,
has the effect of arresting and distorting development. This inevitably impacts the next generation, who are reliant on the last to
guide them in healthy development of their own.

Relational order

As Jesus implied when he summarized Scripture as 'love God
and love your neighbour' in Matthew 22:37–40, concern for right
relationships runs through both Testaments and all of God's interactions with humans. Biblical laws are concerned with maintaining
the 'relational order' of society – the templates that enable relationships to flourish as God intended. 'The Lord commanded us to
obey all these decrees and to fear the Lord our God, so that we
might always prosper and be kept alive, as is the case today. And if
we are careful to obey all this law before the Lord our God, as he
has commanded us, that will be our righteousness' (Deut. 6:24–25).

The relational order of a society can be articulated as a measure
of the health of its relationships. One broken marriage or a few
single parents – or a failed friendship or a fall-out between business partners, for that matter – doesn't destroy the relational
framework upon which our society rests, any more than cutting
down a single tree threatens the entire natural order, including
every woodland and forest. But there are general norms for relationships, ideal patterns that God has built into creation, and when
we stray too far from these the result for society is akin to that of
deforestation for the environment. The balance is disturbed, with
unwelcome and sometimes unpredictable consequences. There is,
broadly speaking, a right way to approach relationships, as there is
a right way to interact with the environment.

The eighteenth-century political philosopher Edmund Burke
famously said that to love the 'little platoons' of society – families
and other small groups of belonging – was the first step we take
towards loving our country and wider humanity.[19] Time and again
we find that those whose adult relationships are broken or dysfunctional have learnt from faulty templates; the children of broken
homes are more likely to divorce later in life and children of single
parents are more likely to become single parents themselves. One
third of prisoners and over half of young offenders were in local
authority care, although the national average is 0.6% of children in
care at any given time. Seventy percent of young offenders come
from single-parent families.[20] Relationship breakdown can trap
families in cycles of poverty.[21]

The Apostle Paul makes the point that the commandment to
honour our parents is 'the first commandment to come with a
promise' (Eph. 6:2–3). The promise is given in both versions of
the Commandments, tersely in Exodus 20:12 and more fully in
Deuteronomy 5:16: 'so that you may live long and that it may
go well with you in the land the Lord your God is giving you.'
From the earliest stages of Israelite history, respect for parents
was associated with prosperity and the health of society. This
may be because there is a close connection between family and
property. Inheritance (of both property and culture) is bound up
with respect for preceding generations. In addition, the family is
or should be primarily responsible for children's religious teaching,
'secular' education and discipline. The roots of civilized life are
found in the family. This does not mean that every strong family
will produce prosperous, happy children who have strong families
of their own; the world is fallen and the general promise of the
fifth commandment does not follow so directly and specifically as
this. But it is the overall order of things that a healthy, prosperous
society follows from strong families.

Relational order does not begin and end with the nuclear family
– in a series of strong, structured but isolated and limited relationships of love and respect. The fifth commandment's promise of
life and prosperity reflects the more general respect for elders
found in the Bible. Leviticus 19:32 reads, 'Rise in the presence
of the aged, show respect for the elderly and revere your God. I

am the Lord.' Respecting the older generation is here framed as an obligation that goes alongside fearing God. Another way of looking at it is this: how can we respect God if we do not respect our parents? The broader principle seems to be that human beings should show honour and respect for the source of life, both towards God as the ultimate source and parents as the proximate one. This principle even extends to how we treat wider creation. As it says in Deuteronomy 22:6–7, in a rather different context, 'If you come across a bird's nest beside the road, either in a tree or on the ground, and the mother is sitting on the young or on the eggs, do not take the mother with the young. You may take the young, but be sure to let the mother go, so that it may go well with you and you may have a long life.' This concern and honour for the source of life is also seen in Leviticus 22:28: 'Do not slaughter a cow or a sheep and its young on the same day.'

The Bible sees this honour as a two-way commandment. Parents had a responsibility to look after children and it was their duty to educate them in the law (see Deut. 4:9; 6:6–7). This meant more than simply teaching them dry facts, like learning multiplication tables by rote; they were to provide them with an education in wisdom, positive and life-giving principles which had implications for the whole of their lives. 'The proverbs of Solomon son of David, king of Israel: for attaining wisdom and discipline; for understanding words of insight; for acquiring a disciplined and prudent life, doing what is right and just and fair . . . Listen, my son, to your father's instruction and do not forsake your mother's teaching' (Prov. 1:1–3, 8).

By the same token, children had a responsibility to provide for their parents in old age. Jesus made arrangements for his own mother on the cross. Elsewhere he criticized the Pharisees who gave to God at the expense of their parents (Mark 7:6–13). The main heir was the one to care for the parents and any unmarried sisters – responsibilities that explain the allotment of a 'double portion' in inheritance (Deut. 21:15–17). This, too, is seen as part of the godly order. It is certainly counter-cultural in today's welfare-based society.

Relational order was inherent in God's creation, as family and other patterns of relating were a part of God's original design. It is within creation that we exist and relate to each another and to God, and our stewardship of it is a part of how we do this – for others around the world now and for later generations. God put humankind in Eden 'to work it and take care of it' (Gen. 2:15), but stewardship for stewardship's own sake was surely not the sole point. You do not maintain your car for the sake of maintaining your car, but to enable you to travel from A to B: to visit friends and family, go to work, attend church – to cultivate and enjoy networks of relationships. Aside from the inherent spiritual value of tending God's good creation, honouring the Creator in our care of the created, it is in and through creation that we relate to others.

Although this argument has focused on one (arguably the most important) aspect of relational order, respect for parents, a fuller discussion would include our relationships and duty of care in other areas: marriage, the three-generational and extended family, neighbours and the wider community. If we take seriously Jesus' instruction of treating others like ourselves then we cannot ignore these.

A relational 'highway code'

> The family is where the vast majority of us learn the fundamental skills for life; physically, emotionally and socially it is the context from which the rest of life flows.
> Iain Duncan Smith, former leader of the Conservative Party[22]

When it is said that the family is the smallest and most fundamental unit of society, this is because the early interactions in the family provide the basis for all other later interactions outside the family: the child's first attachment, education, discipline and relational skills originate here. But it is also true that parental authority was subject to divine authority: it was not arbitrary. We are also to assume that parental authority comes second to divine authority, and that we are to obey the former within the constraints of the latter. Jesus himself had to choose between obeying his earthly family and his heavenly Father (Mark 3:31–35).

Viewed in these terms, relational order is something between a set of rules God has given us and an observation of the way the world works best – what the Bible calls wisdom (for example, throughout Proverbs). When we follow this wisdom, right relationships and strong foundations for life are more likely to be the result: in terms of marriages and families, but also in terms of the principles we learn and apply to every other sphere of life – business, education, religion and others. Relational order is like the Highway Code, to return to this analogy. So long as everyone follows it, there is a framework in place and everyone knows what to expect. Accidents still happen, but they are vastly reduced. But where significant numbers of people disregard the Highway Code, chaos ensues – for everyone, not just for negligent drivers.

Roles: who is responsible to whom, and for what?[23]

With different roles (child, parent, student, friend, spouse, work colleague, boss) come different expectations and responsibilities. Attachment – relationship – is the most basic human need; roles and boundaries secure and protect attachments, enabling them to function as intended. God and culture both ascribe power to people so that they can carry out their various roles. From both a divine and cultural perspective, it is important that we utilize the power associated with the roles we have. There is something chaotic and destructive about a child who rules a house, or a teacher who is subject to a student. Roles have four important components:

1) Responsibilities
2) Prohibitions
3) Privileges
4) Entitlements

The role of a married person, for example, entails the responsibility to care for the spouse as well as the prohibition of having any other sexual partner. It also includes the privilege of sex and the entitlement to exclusivity. So, too, the privileges of parenthood come with the responsibilities; they cannot be held in isolation – at least, not by a good parent. Abuse of a role is not so much the *mis*use of the power given to it, but the *failure* to take it up in these areas – an absent father, an unfaithful spouse, a cheating student, an ungrateful child. Proverbs 30:21–23 alludes to the awful abuse of power in different roles: 'Under three things the earth trembles, under four it cannot bear up: a servant who becomes king, a fool who is full of food, an unloved woman who is married, and a maidservant who displaces her mistress.' This ideal of roles and what they entail is crucial in understanding the concept of Relational Order, which poses the question, 'Who is responsible to whom for what?'

Understanding the responsibilities, prohibitions, privileges and entitlements of different roles is vital to maintaining relational order. Acknowledging the 'presence of the divine imprint' – the requirements of our roles – aligns our lives with God's pattern. This understanding is a result of healthy psychological development. Hence 'the health of the social system is maturation-dependent'.[24] It is only when people understand the nature of the roles they are in, along with the purposes, responsibilities and boundaries that those entail, that they can sustain working networks of relationships.

Maturation – healthy psychological development – is indispensible for mutual intimacy between two people. Sex is neither a condition of intimacy nor a guaranteed route to it. Sex on its own, divorced from this overall context which makes possible 'nakedness of the soul', offers a false intimacy which cannot contribute to relational and emotional wholeness. In fact, it tends to do exactly the opposite, because the most intimate physical act of which humans are capable is removed from the broader context of intimacy, undermining individuals' expectations and understanding of what intimacy really means. The goal of public policy that deals with attitudes and behaviour surrounding sex and relationships should therefore be maturation: enabling and nurturing healthy psychological development and ensuring that sex is understood within that framework.

The golden rule

The so-called 'golden rule', or 'ethic of reciprocity', reflected in almost every religion, is that we should treat others in the way in which we wish to be treated ourselves. In the Judaeo-Christian tradition, this is first seen in Leviticus 19:18. This, and Jesus' reiteration of it in Matthew 7:12, are active, positively stated expressions: 'do to others what you would have them do to you.' Our society's consent-only approach to sex reflects a subtly different and negatively stated form of the fundamental moral principle: 'don't do anything you wouldn't want others doing to you.' There may be moral grey areas between the two versions, positive and negative, but the starting point is essentially that behaviour is valid if it does not hurt anyone else.

Tort

> *There is nothing safe about sex. There never will be.*
>
>   Norman Mailer, writer and film-maker

This moral principle is embodied in our legal system under the law of tort. Torts are civil wrongs that consist of some kind of harm to another person. Although some torts involve criminal actions which may result in imprisonment or other punishment, the wrongs are primarily recognized as grounds for lawsuits with the aim of compensating the harmed party. This compensation may cover a number of areas, including pain and suffering, medical bills, and past and future loss of earnings. It can even cover loss of reputation, for example in the case of defamation, or the infliction of emotional distress. Harm may be intentional, as in the case of assault, or accidental, as in the case of a car crash. For the tort of negligence to be established, three conditions must be fulfilled. There must be a duty of care; this duty must have been breached; and damage must have been caused by the breach.

The general principle for duty of care was formulated in 1932 and was based on the parable of the Good Samaritan (Luke 10): 'The rule that you are to love your neighbour becomes in law you must not injure your neighbour; and the lawyer's question: Who is my neighbour? receives a restricted reply. You must take reasonable care to avoid acts or omissions which you can reasonably foresee would be likely to injure your neighbour. Who, then, in law, is my neighbour? The answer seems to be – persons who are so closely and directly affected by my act that I ought reasonably to have them in contemplation as being so affected when I am directing my mind to the acts or omissions that are called in question.'[25]

The modern definition was laid down in 1990: 'What emerges is that, in addition to the foreseeability of damage, necessary ingredients in any situation giving rise to a duty of care are that there should exist between the party owing the duty and the party to whom it is owed a relationship characterized by the law as one of "proximity" or "neighbourhood" and that the situation should be one in which the court considers it fair, just and reasonable that the law should impose a duty of a given scope upon the one party for the benefit of the other.'[26]

One defence to a tort is *volenti non fit injuria*: 'to the willing, no injury is done'. This simply means that someone who consents to an action that is likely to be harmful cannot then sue for damages. Sometimes this 'consent' may be carefully defined; for example, a professional boxer consents to the type of harm he is likely to sustain in a boxing match. However, if he is attacked in between rounds, or outside the strict rules of the sport, this is grounds for a case. When Mike Tyson bit Evander Holyfield's ears in their 1997 World Heavyweight bout in Las Vegas, this was so far outside the rules and normal events of boxing that he risked civil tort proceedings.

Our society's assumption is that consensual sex fulfils the golden rule and that it therefore does not violate the principles of tort. There is no legal recognition that a sexual relationship entails a duty of care, either between the couple themselves or towards others who are closely involved – for example, the children of a family which is broken up by an affair.[27] Neither do we typically consider any harm to our relationship with God – although 1 Corinthians 6 and Ephesians 5 make it clear that there is a strong spiritual dimension to sex. If neither of the two adults are harmed by an act that is agreed by them alone, then there is therefore little or no reason to prevent it. In most cases, consent is the sole and sufficient condition for sex to take place.

Whether or not we would want or expect sexual standards to be upheld by civil law, we will argue in the following chapters that sex outside of marriage (as well, of course, as destructive patterns

within marriage) does violate the golden rule because there are significant third-party effects to so-called personal and private sexual
behaviour. The consent is only between the two people directly
involved, whereas the harm can stretch to many others, who may
bear the consequences for a lifetime.

Why does it not seem curious to us – and unjust – that both our
legal system and our prevailing cultural attitudes completely fail to
take into account the harm that is done in these circumstances? Is
'consenting adults' really enough, or do we need something more
before we can say that 'just' sex is really just?

Notes

1. 'Wedding costs soar to more than £20,000', *The Telegraph*, 9 June 2008.
2. Office of National Statistics (ONS).
3. *Metro*, 4 April 2008.
4. 'Breakdown in families "as harmful as global warming"', *The Telegraph*,
   7 April 2008.
5. We are indebted to Dale Kuehne and his forthcoming book, *Sex and the
   iWorld: Rethinking Relationship Beyond an Age of Individualism* (Baker, 2009,
   but unpublished at the time of writing), for developing the concept of the
   iWorld.
6. See Jonathan Burnside, *Consent versus Community* (Jubilee Centre, 2006),
   p. 3. Available from <http://www.jubilee-centre.org>.
7. *Setting the Boundaries: Reforming the Law on Sex Offences* (Sex Offences Review
   Group, 2000), p. 98. Available at <http://www.homeoffice.gov.uk/
   documents/vol1main.pdf> (accessed 22 July 2008).
8. See Burnside, *Consent versus Community*, p. 2.
9. Emmanuel Mounier, *The Personalist Manifesto*, 1938. Quoted in Graham
   Cole and Michael Schluter, 'From Personalism to Relationism':
   Commonalities and Distinctives (Jubilee Centre, 2004). Available from
   <http://www.jubilee-centre.org>.
10. Christopher Wright, *Old Testament Ethics for the People of God* (IVP, 2004),
    pp. 18–19, and throughout.
11. See Nick Spencer and Robert White, *Christianity, Climate Change and
    Sustainable Living* (SPCK, 2007).

12. Christopher West, *Theology of the Body for Beginners* (Ascension Press, 2004), p. 8.

13. Wright, *Ethics*, p. 19.

14. Sometimes, as in Leviticus 20:1–5, *karet* is combined with immediate human punishment such as death by stoning – a 'double whammy' that 'indicates that these offences are seen as the most serious offences in Lev. 20'. See Burnside, *Consent versus Community*, p. 31 note 31.

15. For complete definitions see F. Brown, S. Driver and C. Briggs, *Hebrew and English Lexicon* (Hendrickson, 1997, third printing).

16. Wright, *Ethics*, pp. 276–278.

17. Erik Erikson, *Childhood and Society* (Norton, 1950).

18. 'The Right Chemistry', *Time Magazine*, 15 February 1994.

19. Edmund Burke, *Reflections on the Revolution in France*, 1790.

20. In 'Fractured Families', *Breakdown Britain* (Centre for Social Justice, 2006), p. 11.

21. See Oliver Letwin, 'Why we have signed up to Labour's anti-poverty target', *The Guardian*, 11 April 2006; <http://www.guardian.co.uk/commentisfree/2006/apr/11/comment.politics2> (accessed 22 July 2008).

22. *Breakthrough Britain, vol. 1, Family Breakdown* (Centre for Social Justice, 2007), p. 3. Available at <http://www.centreforsocialjustice.org.uk/default.asp?pageRef=182> (accessed 22 July 2008).

23. For material in this section we are indebted to Sharon Willmer, Professor of Developmental Psychology at the University of California.

24. Sharon Willmer.

25. Lord Atkin, *Donoghue v. Stevenson (1932)*.

26. Lord Bridge, *Caparo Industries v. Dickman (1990)*.

27. Although duty of care has been accepted in several cases in which an STI has been negligently passed to a sexual partner.

2. RELATIONAL FOUNDATIONS

Is sex my choice, or everyone's business?

It is like people who were on a boat and one of them took an auger and started to bore a hole under him. His fellows said to him: 'What are you doing?' He said to them: 'What do you care? Am I not doing it underneath myself?'

Rabbi Shimon bar Yochai[1]

I don't remember the first time I had sex; a mixture of cocktails, beer and vodka made sure of that. It is a frightening reality that an act that I have no conscious recollection of still affects my life today. Although I didn't realize it at the time, I had turned a corner and there was no way back. It was not until I was married that the continuing effects of that transition became apparent, and I saw that the only way out was a painful journey through.

After my 'first time' it was surprisingly easy to have sex. It became an assumed, and enjoyable, part of my life, alongside eating and sleeping. I rarely questioned my actions; when I did analyse it, it was merely to allay my fears of getting pregnant.

My husband-to-be was a virgin who wholly accepted me despite my track record. Before we got married it seemed that we had left the actions of the past where they belonged – in the past. But it was not to be as easy as all *that. For one reason (excuse) or another we managed not to have sex on our honeymoon. Looking back I am amazed that we missed, or managed to ignore, the early warning signals. Needless to say the tension in our marriage mounted and presented itself in many deferred ways; it was only after several years that we were able to untangle the threads and discover what the real issue was. My lack of interest in, not to mention enjoyment of, sex I put down to tiredness. We put my husband's growing self-consciousness and insecurities down to his felt inadequacy to meet mounting work responsibilities.*

Why should my previous private actions between two consenting adults follow me into our marriage, and be able to cast such a dark shadow over it? This is the question that I have repeatedly asked myself. My answer may seem unsatisfactory – I don't know why, but I know that they did in a tangible way.

As I said earlier, the only way out is through. My husband and I attempted to reason our way through our increasingly turbulent marriage. Whilst listening to teaching on God's love for his physical creation the truth hit home – our physical and sexual distance had informed, and exacerbated, our emotional and even spiritual distance.

I realized that my previous sexual experiences, separated from a holistic committed emotional and spiritual relationship, had created a chasm within me. This division I had transported into our marriage, where it festered, and threatened to destroy my and my husband's sense of 'being', as well as any real chance of intimacy between us.

Needless to say the journey through was not completed in a day; indeed it continues. Healing of the rifts within and between us is ongoing. It is an un-learning, re-claiming, and new-discovering process. Our sexual life has improved, and with that our relationship as a whole, as well as my husband's sense of appropriate bodily pride, and my sense of wholeness. For the first time in our ten-year relationship, the possibility of discussing, and acting upon, our dreams of having children, has emerged.

I am extremely grateful for a husband who remains committed to me and us. I am humbled and excited by the possibilities that remain despite the choices I have made. Indeed, it is important to us not to reflect negatively on the past but to allow God's mercy and grace to redeem my sexual past and to present opportunities otherwise not possible.

– Kate, 28

How do we know who we are?

Our culture places me at the centre of my life. My rights, my freedoms, my choices and my desires are the most important factor to consider – whether I'm buying a car, choosing a job, starting a sexual relationship, or deciding on a new mobile phone contract. Advertisers play on this tendency all the time, with banking, food, technology and cosmetics companies offering us slogans like 'My life, my card' . . . 'Have it your way' . . . 'You're worth it' . . . 'Thousands of possibilities. Get yours' . . . 'Express yourself' . . . 'Just do it' . . . 'It's all about you'. The message is that life is about me and should meet my needs.

We consider ourselves individuals, unique and distinct from the six billion other unique individuals with whom we share the planet. We are more likely to define our identities by our outward appearance – what brand of clothes we wear, the deodorants, perfumes or aftershaves we buy, what vehicle we drive (or cycle), the music we like and the technology we use to listen to it – rather than by the people we know. It is difficult to consider the effect that our choices have on people we may never meet, and will probably never know in any depth. Many people, whether consciously or unconsciously, choose a car because it makes a statement about them; it's hard to connect that choice to the situation of a family in Bangladesh whose home may one day be swept away by flooding. We may talk about 'community', but our choices reflect concern for ourselves over and above our wider circles of relationships.

In biblical culture the opposite was true. People would define or 'place' themselves in the world with reference to their families, clans and tribes, and perhaps their home town or role within the wider community. Even the ways characters are introduced to us suggests this: 'Joshua son of Nun, Moses' assistant' (Josh. 1:1); 'a Benjamite, a man of standing, whose name was Kish son of Abiel, the son of Zeror, the son of Becorath, the son of Aphiah of Benjamin' (1 Sam. 9:1); 'Ehud, a left-handed man, the son of Gera the Benjamite' (Judg. 3:15); 'James son of Zebedee' (Matt. 4:21). Jesus' own genealogies in Matthew 1 and Luke 3 are extensive; the authors take great pains to trace his family roots, although this is partly to make the theological point that they are located within the Davidic line. The national designation 'Israelite' also said something about the person's relationship with God.

Today, the importance of community in our lives is much weaker than it was even fifty years ago. The 24/7 culture makes new demands on our time at the expense of those closest to us. Alongside easy travel and the requirement or wish to move repeatedly for university, work, and other reasons, our frames of reference have changed too. They are no longer rooted in the family or community, but increasingly in the self.

Psychotherapists see this as part of a desire for independence, tracing it to an increasing reluctance to rely on anyone else: an 'excessive psychological self-reliance or the impaired capacity for dependency'.[2] 'I am suggesting that this state is becoming endemic, and culturally dominant: an inability to lean on others, created by fear of emotional abandonment and deprivation, is being turned into a pseudo-virtue of illusory independence.'[3] In other words, we are terrified of admitting that we are reliant on others – and equally, that other people's actions affect us too. Instead, we stick our heads in the sand by pretending we are best off when we need no one.

It is through our responses to other persons that we become persons. It is others who challenge, enlighten and enrich us. There is no such thing as the isolated individual . . . all real life is meeting.

J. H. Oldham, missionary and author

In fact, the psychotherapist insists, mutual need and trust are vital for healthy relationships. Without them, we harm the thing on which we are desperately pretending not to be reliant. '*Inter*dependence is not only a crucial skill for personal relationships; it is also an essential way of understanding and relating to both the social sphere and the ecosphere. The illusion of *in*dependence damages the individual and those who come into contact with him or her. It also damages society as a whole, and the whole planetary biosphere, when people believe that they can take without giving, and that taking does not make them dependent on the sources from which they take.'[4] (Italics mine.) The 'illusion of independence' undermines relationships – with family, friends, partners, workmates and the environment – because the 'independent' person doesn't acknowledge the significance of his or her relationships.

Morality in the me-culture

It is important to understand that me-culture morality is not a coherent system of values. Postmodernism has been described as an 'incredulity towards metanarratives'[5] – a rejection of any systematic structure or coherent 'story' of belief, which itself is a kind of metanarrative. There is no one overarching philosophy for the me-culture; packages of beliefs are as unique as the individuals who adopt them. So, although consumerism and sexual licence are both evident in the twenty-first-century West, one does not require the other. In fact, people often choose to define themselves in ways that show a dissatisfaction with some aspect of the prevailing culture's norms. Many make ethical choices about what they eat, drive (or make a point of not driving) and purchase, knowing that they are part of a global community and that how they lead their lives does affect others. Fair Trade, Food Miles, Carbon Footprint; these are common phrases which show an awareness for those outside our immediate circles of relationships – but this awareness does not have to extend to other areas of life such as sexual choices. Morality may be coherent in the me-culture, but it doesn't have to be.

> *I have taken the pill. I have hoisted my skirts to my thighs, dropped them to my ankles, rebelled at university, abused the American Embassy, lived with two men, married one, earned my keep, kept my identity and, frankly . . . I'm lost.*
>   Cover of *Nova* women's magazine, 1968

Individualism has a long history in England. One author traces it back to economic changes that occurred in the thirteenth century, well before the Reformation or Industrial Revolution, and possibly to much earlier roots in Germanic tribes, which were described as having a concept of 'absolute individual property' as early as the time of the Roman historian, Tacitus.[6] The 'Protestant individualism' of the Reformation expressed the idea that a person's faith was a relationship between God and the individual, not mediated by the church. Whereas this particular expression of individualism may be seen in positive terms, individualistic thinking has now become unhelpful; first because it was extended from the individual's relationship with God to the individual's relationship with the rest of the world, taking the focus away from community and onto the self; and second because the faith out of which this individualism grew has largely been discarded. In other words, we have kept the Reformation idea that faith is about 'my' (not 'our') relationship with God, but substituted God with anything we choose. As Dale Kuehne writes, 'In many respects the iWorld is a product of the individualism of a liberalism that lost the ability to effectively limit individualism.'[7]

The emphasis on personal choice in the area of sexual ethics is an expression of social change in a wider context. However, the primacy of 'consumer choice' leads to problems when it is applied in all areas of life. Family structures are inevitably affected, and as relational skills are damaged, so too are other areas in which they are necessary. Business and education suffer, damaging the economy in the process (see chapter 5).

So individualism is partly to blame, but postmodernity has played a part in eroding moral boundaries, which are then subject to individualistic approaches (hence the definition of the 'iWorld' as a climate of 'postmodern individualism'). In terms of personal identity, we are more likely to talk about forging our own identities than accepting them – determining who we are in and of ourselves rather than belonging within existing families and communities. However, individualism does not just encompass the self. We are each able to make up our own minds about much bigger and more important issues such as Third World debt, the environment and what constitutes ethical business practices.

Postmodern/individualistic attitudes towards sex tend to fall into two conflicting categories. The first sees sex as part of the consumerist culture, a commodity to be separated out, sought after on its own terms and used without reference to those who engage in it. The sociologist Anthony Giddens discusses 'pure relationships' – relationships that are entirely self-referential and last only as long as they remain rewarding for its members.[8] These fit into this first category and are becoming increasingly common. Giddens acknowledges the problems with these, as well as suggesting some benefits. In terms of relational order, they appear completely isolated from any wider frame of reference. The problem, of course, is that relationships are never isolated: how we conduct a relationship affects not just the two parties directly involved, but many others, directly and indirectly. In Giddens's worldview, these relationships are also entirely selfish: as soon as the cost-benefit analysis comes up short for either party, the relationship is over.[9] As explored below, this attitude rewards and reinforces a lack of commitment, affecting a person's capacity to relate on a deeper level.

The second category does the opposite, placing too much emphasis on sex, which acquires an almost spiritual quality: an expression of the core personality. Both of these categories involve a distortion. Either the biological instinct is emphasized to the expense of any broader considerations, or the importance of sexual identity, and the right to express one's sexual nature, is stressed to the detriment of other markers of identity, such as family, community and faith. In Christian teaching, at least, people are more than their sexual identities and expressions.

A similar set of problems seems to have existed in the New Testament church in Corinth. In his first letter to the Corinthians, Paul writes to two different groups of people. One group have not realized how important sex is; they are visiting prostitutes and treating sex as if it were as trivial as eating and drinking (1 Cor. 6:12–20). The second group have decided that sex is inherently bad and are avoiding it even within marriage (1 Cor. 7:1–7). The inclusion in the canon of Song of Songs, a celebration of sexual and romantic love, shows that the Corinthian Christians were missing a vital biblical perspective. Comparatively few people today think that sex is wrong of itself, but they may attribute to sex an unwarranted influence over their identity, defining themselves by something God has created rather than by their relationship to the Creator himself. Today, many believe that life without sexual relationships is somehow unfulfilled and lacking a crucial ingredient. This is also a profound misunderstanding of the role that God intended for sex in human experience.

'Consequence-free' sex: all it's cracked up to be?

The media often depicts sex as consequence- and responsibility-free. Film and TV programmes show couples making and breaking attachments, often in one-night stands, often entirely devoid of lasting emotion, any desire for relationship, or the realities of pregnancy and sexually transmitted disease. The concept of recreational sex has become a part of our cultural mindset, even in programmes shown on daytime and prime-time TV. The frequent change of sexual partners was a common theme in the hugely popular and award-winning sitcom *Friends*, which ran for ten seasons. In general, new boyfriends and girlfriends came and went, but the core of six friends remained unchanged. And yet one of the reasons that *Friends* was so popular was precisely *because* it tapped into something deeper, a desire for lasting relationship in the broader sense. 'All you need is Friends' was one of the show's taglines. One suggestion of the series is that, in the modern world, platonic friendships can provide the stability and permanent intimacy that both traditional family and marriage so often fail to deliver (a theme that was somewhat blurred as four of the six friends paired off with each other by the final series).

> *C. J. Cregg, Press Secretary at the White House, returns from Washington, D.C. to her home town of Dayton, Ohio, to speak at a high school reunion. While she is there, she discovers that not only has her father's new wife left him, but that his Alzheimer's has progressed and his condition is rapidly deteriorating. At the airport she runs across an old classmate, Marco. Her brief fling with him appears to be little more than a night off amidst the emotional chaos and heartache, a throwaway line in the plot before they go their separate ways and she returns to the White House. He is never mentioned again.*
>
> – 'The Long Goodbye', *The West Wing*, series 4

The truth is that recreational sex is not consequence-free; the case study at the beginning of this chapter is just one example of the 'baggage' that is carried into future relationships but that extends far beyond the personal sphere. Think first of the consequences at a national level. In a very real sense, sex shapes our society. Our individual sexual choices are each a small part of the overall

mosaic of the culture we live in. Moreover, the culture itself
heavily influences those choices. Without the continual drip-feed
by certain adverts and magazines that sex is essential for intimate
relationship, expectations in many relationships would be very different. Sexual choices have serious implications for families, along
with the wellbeing of any children involved. For example, a widely
publicized statistic is that approximately 40% of marriages end in
divorce[10] – 50% in the US. One consequence of this is that every
year around 150,000 children in England and Wales will see the
separation of their parents and that about a quarter of all children
in the UK now live in single-parent households.[11] The economic
cost of this is enormous, even before any other factors are taken
into consideration.[12] This is one obvious, measurable way in which
'individual' sexual choices affect others.

Again, elements of the media and popular culture are partly to
blame for their tendency to idealize romantic love over all other
types of love, rather than recognizing the strengths in different
types of relationship. Strangely, this idealization of romantic love
and marriage has led to *increased* breakdown of relationships, as
one person is overloaded with the roles and expectations that
should be spread around many different relationships – friends,
family members and colleagues, for example, as well as a partner.[13]
This disproportionate burden on spouses and partners is further
explored in chapter 3. However, the principle serves to illustrate
the essentially inward-looking mentality of many relationships
today. They are expected to serve 'me', or at least 'the two of us'.
The outward-looking perspective has largely been lost; relationship is no longer seen as relevant to the wellbeing of others and the
community in general. People express surprise at the very idea that
marriage is any more than a personal choice about an arrangement
'evaluated on the basis of sexual and emotional satisfaction'.[14]

The Clinton factor
In his book *True Sexual Morality*, Daniel Heimbach discusses one
very public and contemporary example of how 'private' sexual
decisions affect the wider community. Early in 1998, allegations
of President Bill Clinton's sexual relationship with a White House
intern appeared in the media. Clinton vehemently and publicly

denied the rumours. Many people (including, at the start, his wife Hillary Clinton) demanded that, if they were true, he should resign his presidency.

As it turned out, despite attempts to cover it up, the 'Lewinsky Scandal' came to light. Many suggested that the president's reputation was indelibly tarnished, his integrity lost. But he did not resign and, writes Heimbach, 'Hillary, Congress, the media, and most Americans instead changed their minds on sexual morality. After getting over the initial shock, most simply decided that what Bill Clinton did sexually, even in the Oval Office, was not all that important. Some decided it might not even have been immoral. And even if it was, perhaps sexual morality was such a private thing that others should not believe it affects public dignity no matter what a president does, or where he may choose to do it.'[15]

Of course, American sexual morality does not hinge around Bill Clinton's indiscretions; the culture did not U-turn overnight from spotlessly high standards of chastity to a cesspool of rampant depravity when the scandal broke. Sexual morality has been changing on a grand scale, both in America and in Western Europe, for decades. Bill Clinton's actions were more a reflection of this reality than an influence upon it. However, his own response to the Lewinsky Scandal, as well as society's continuing rethink of its sexual morality in the light of the news, did affect real people. What was the indirect knock-on effect on millions of partners and children when society decided that what the president and everyone else did in private was none of their business?[16] Alternatively, what if he had resigned, giving the message that adultery and the lying it entailed – public and private – were still considered unacceptable? Might this have had an effect on those who take their cues for right and wrong behaviour from leading authority figures?

What happened – and why?

The change in thinking about the purpose of sex is relatively easy to trace. More-or-less effective means of mass-produced contraception has existed since the nineteenth century, but the turning point came when the contraceptive pill was introduced in the UK in 1960. In the following decade, this available contraception – along with newly legalized abortion – enabled the separation of sex from childbirth, and from marriage. This in turn led to divorce becoming more acceptable, as it did not necessarily affect children, and to a decline in marriage itself. Whilst contraception undoubtedly has a positive aspect, one additional side effect was that sex and marriage lost the outward-looking aim of creating and nurturing family, and became more about an inward-looking relationship between the couple themselves and serving personal desires.

We would never argue that the sole significance of sex is childbirth; it is also designed to reinforce an intimate marital relationship, as the Song of Songs demonstrates. One problem of this far-reaching sexual revolution was that this latter aspect was emphasized and distorted above the former. Sex before marriage lost its stigma and couples began to live together before getting married. As time went on, cohabitation gradually became a substitute for marriage; which was increasingly seen as a 'piece of paper', and became less privileged over living together. Then, as there was 'no difference', couples were less inclined to get married before having children. In Sweden and other Scandinavian countries, this shift of thinking has gone even further than in the UK, with even higher rates of cohabitation and the state's reluctance to distinguish this from marriage.

Ironically, then, the ability to have child-free sex outside of marriage has actually led to an increase in the number of children born outside of marriage. However, unmarried couples with children are even more likely to break up than those without.[17] No one wants to return to a (fictional, in any case) golden age of 1950s innocence; on the other hand, it is clear that sex outside of marriage has damaged marriage and, in the process, damaged the life chances of millions of children in terms of both health and educational outcomes.[18]

> *Stable marriages and families are essential to the survival, flourishing, and happiness of the greater commonwealths of church, state, and civil society. And a breakdown of marriage and the family will eventually have devastating consequences on these larger social institutions.*
>
> John Witte, religious historian and marriage expert[19]

It can be argued that, before reliable and readily available contraception, sex still did not always result in pregnancy. It can also be argued that men (predominantly) have always pursued responsibility-free sex, with prostitutes or other temporary partners, and that a huge variety of sexual practice has existed throughout history. However, the possibility that shaped the sexual relationship before effective contraceptives were freely available was that it very likely *would* result in pregnancy sooner or later. Similarly, although sexual liberty was practised, it was rarely viewed favourably, whereas in our present culture, the moral limits on sexual behaviour have been almost completely eroded.

In 2005, around 3.25 million women in the UK used the contraceptive pill – a quarter of 16- to 49-year-old women.[20] Amazingly, its ubiquitous availability has not reduced the number of unwanted pregnancies. Since the 1967 Abortion Act legalized abortion, rates have risen from around 8 to 18 per 1,000 women aged 15 to 44; and now over a fifth of conceptions in England and Wales are terminated: 193,737 in 2006.[21] Around a third of these are carried out on women who had previously had one or more abortions, and sometimes as many as five or more.[22] Instead of stemming the tide of accidental pregnancy, legislation that makes abortion so accessible means that it is now treated as another form of birth control.

So, in only the last forty years or so, the entire setting and expectation of sex has changed on a near-universal scale for the first time in human history. We cannot conceive of how this unprecedented development will affect society. The option to wait for the best time to have children is one beneficial outcome, and the ability to reduce the rate of childbirth in overcrowded countries. But increased promiscuity, abortion, adultery, and prostitution, and a sharp increase in sexually transmitted infections, are part of the picture too.

Of course, such a profound cultural shift cannot be laid exclusively at any one door. At root, it is the product of the me-society brought about by the retreat of religion and the replacement of the belief in 'what is right' by 'what is right for me'.

Melanie Phillips, columnist and author[23]

For Christians there is further unfinished business. Our culture's tendency to redefine its morality in terms of sexual norms, rather than to view sexual norms in the light of Christian morality, brings us to a crossroads: will Christians do the same? Once again, sexual confusion is an indicator of a deeper issue. Morality is becoming increasingly subjective – whatever is most acceptable for us by the standards of the times. If we redefine sin to mean something less inconvenient to us, we also redefine salvation as something less important. We imply that salvation is on our terms, not God's, denying the power of the Cross and the full extent of God's grace expressed in Jesus' sacrifice. The church's reaction to changes in sexual morality will strike to the heart of the Christian faith.[24]

Biblical sex

It is worth stating our first principles. Our understanding of the biblical texts that deal with sexual issues is that *the Bible allows sex only within permanent, faithful marriage, between a man and a woman and that every other sexual act outside of marriage falls short of God's ideal.*

As we have said, this book does not seek to provide a systematic interpretation of the biblical texts dealing with sexual ethics, but an explanation of *why* God's ideal is good: we hope to discern the reasons behind the biblical teaching. For this reason, a thorough examination of the texts is outside the scope of this book, and is, in any case, available elsewhere.

However, we equally recognize that not everyone will share our starting point – that sex is intended by God to take place only within marriage. There is a vast range of opinion on the Bible's treatment of different sexual acts, including sex before marriage, adultery, divorce and same-sex intercourse. Although it is not necessary that readers fully agree with us on this starting point to appreciate many of the arguments on which the book rests (indeed, we hope that they will be equally convincing to non-Christians), this book was written primarily for Christians. A broad agreement is likely to be helpful if our conclusions are not to appear arbitrary, or at least grounded in something other than biblical standards, even if those conclusions still seem valid. Rather than include a lengthy treatment of the relevant passages in the text, where they may interrupt the flow of the argument and prove a distraction to some readers who do share this point of view, we have included an appendix, addressing in some detail many of the questions and objections that are typically raised by these issues. Where necessary we will refer to this for fuller arguments.

'It's OK because it doesn't hurt anyone else . . .'

Our culture and laws in Britain are based on the view that sexual behaviour is legitimate as long as the participating adults have consented to the act. Although consent must be one unarguable factor for sex to be regarded as legitimate, by itself it leads to a narrow and unrealistic assessment of who is affected, whether in positive or negative ways. Consent needs to be a starting point, not the end point.

The couple
At the most local, personal level, the couple themselves are affected to a far greater extent than our culture realizes – the case study at the beginning of the chapter being just one example. A sexual act cannot be separated from every other aspect of our personalities, no matter how much the media gives this impression. Sex is not isolated from our overall emotional development, but both occurs within and contributes towards it. Sexual choices reflect and determine other facets of our behaviour and character. In biological terms, sex is intended for procreation; it is also designed to foster commitment to help fulfil this objective. The aim of permanent commitment is still an ideal for the majority of people today, despite the many marriages and partnerships which end in separation. But casual sex as part of short-term, disposable relationships affects our later chances of committed, stable partnerships by damaging our capacity for long-term bonding. Moving from partner to partner becomes a habit that is not easily altered.

Sex affects every subsequent sexual relationship that a person has. Even the most anonymous one-night stand, which appears in principle not to affect any other person, alters the assumptions and expectations on which future relationships are based, and arguably more so than a failed long-term sexual relationship, as there is never any intention of commitment.[25]

When sex becomes commodified, sexual partners become service providers rather than confidantes and life mates – which is not a mindset that leads people to invest in a relationship.[26] These attitudes tend to be reinforced by repeated break-ups, rather than diminished by them, which is why second and third marriages or cohabitations tend not to be a 'fresh start' and are progressively less likely to succeed than first ones. It is also one of the reasons why those who have had many sexual partners before marriage are less likely to stay together in the long term – like Kate at the beginning of this chapter, they have practised a lack of commitment and intimacy in sex.[27]

However, located as such examples are within larger families, organizations, networks and communities, the significance does not remain solely within the couple's own relationship and later relationships, but affects many other people too.

Families

Most obviously, families are affected by a sexual relationship – either because they are strengthened by it or disrupted by it. Before marriage, there may be uncertainty surrounding how to treat a cohabiting partner, particularly if the arrangement is long term and based on the 'benefits' of avoiding commitment. Ambivalence towards the couple is carried across to the extended family, and may include concerns about their having children before it is too late.

Father: Cohabitation as a life principle bothers me because the relationship has less permanence; it is a less definite arrangement. However, once the cohabitation began I saw that it had a status and positive aspects that I supported. Because their relationship was strong, good things came from it, but cohabitation in general is not a positive status to promote.

I suspect that David, our son, thought we would strongly disapprove of his decision to cohabit, but that was not necessarily true. Maintaining dialogue with David was very important; he would have done his own thing regardless of what we advised. It would have been unhelpful to try and persuade him otherwise. I had several low-key conversations with him along the lines of 'if you are serious about Emily then you should make it permanent'. David held that their decision was a private affair, and so not anyone else's business. I strongly disagreed with this view. Their arrangement was a public matter; we, his family, were in relationship with them, and so you need a public, contractual step to recognize this wider, involved network.

Mother: David and Emily's cohabitation certainly caused unease. Emily was very reticent, and never felt secure within the family, even though we tried to welcome her and encourage them both. I also believe that David's cohabiting possibly made it easier for his sister to cohabit, which she did for a period before she got married.

When they got married there was a definite change in their relationship. David had thought marriage wouldn't change a thing, but he said afterwards that it had changed everything. Emily was much more secure in the family. She made a concerted effort to get to know the family; she took trouble to invest in little things that are of particular importance or liking to members of the family. She became noticeably more affectionate.

– Parents of cohabitee

We recognize that there are many different types of cohabiting relationship, from the most casual to the most committed, and that this range is not always best reflected by the simple label 'cohabitation'. However, cohabitations do not feature the deliberate and public commitment that marriage does; in most cases, cohabitation is precisely the avoidance of this commitment, temporary or otherwise. Men, in particular, tend to opt for cohabitation's lower level of commitment, and women often acquiesce on the grounds that to have a partner is not as good as marriage, but may lead on to marriage and in any event is better than nothing.[28] This 'all of the benefits with few of the responsibilities' approach that predominantly men enjoy often does not extend to them wanting to have children, which may explain why almost half of cohabitations break up within five years of the first child's birth; when the relationship becomes too much trouble, many fathers tragically decide to cut their losses and leave. Often women in a cohabiting relationship want children but lack the stability and support to have them – a situation that can take up a significant proportion of what is, biologically, a relatively narrow child-bearing window.

In cases of adultery the harm is easier to trace. Affairs can destroy families and, crucially, do not just set husband and wife against each other. Parents, siblings, children and the extended family find themselves torn between conflicting loyalties. For relatives of one or other spouse, usually 'blood is thicker than water', despite the friendships they may have built up with members of the other family. Grandparents and grandchildren may be prevented from seeing each other, or forced to side with either the mother or father. Aunts, uncles, cousins and other friends and relatives may also lose previously close relationships. One study found that over half of extended family members reported difficulties in visiting and maintaining contact with their grandchildren, nieces and nephews after their parents' divorce.[29]

If the affair leads to the divorce of the married couple, the presence of the new partner is frequently a source of bitterness and a powerful deterrent against maintaining original networks of relationships. For the partner who is 'left behind' to care for the children, financial problems are often another threat. In popular culture, the wide-ranging pain caused by affairs and broken relationships is often minimized or of secondary concern. But it cannot be totally hidden and is evident in films from *The Graduate* to *Brokeback Mountain*.

Walk the Line *is the award-winning biopic of the love story between the country singers Johnny Cash and June Carter. In the film, the two are depicted as soul-mates, clearly always supposed to be together, as they finally are after twelve years and numerous adversities.*

The song 'Walk the Line' is a reference to Johnny Cash's resolution to stay faithful to his first wife, Vivian Liberto. However, she and the family receive little attention, despite the fact he was married for thirteen years and had four children by her. His daughter, Kathy Cash, was so upset about this that she walked out of a screening of the film, claiming her mother had been dismissed as a 'mad little psycho', and that the children's suffering during Cash's drug addiction and divorce had been entirely overlooked, as well as the extent of her mother's devotion to him and his career.

It goes without saying that children are often the ones who lose the most in these situations. The 'wicked stepmother'[30] theme of fairytales epitomizes the fears of, and occasionally real dangers posed to, the children of parents who remarry. Although many step- and blended families are supportive and loving, and do an excellent job of childcare, it is still a difficult situation. By definition, it was not the first choice. Statistically, violence against stepchildren by stepparents and stepsiblings is significantly higher than abuse within the biological family.[31]

The 'ripple effect' of such relational injuries cannot be underestimated. The pain and loss of divorce and separation is not confined to those directly involved, but is passed on in a myriad of different ways. Loss of contact – between parents and children, with friends and neighbours – interrupts nurturing relationships and disturbs attachments. Education suffers – school marks typically nose-dive when a child's parents divorce, and may be accompanied by discipline problems.[32] Children are affected in different ways by divorce but through losing at least one parent and role model, ongoing emotional development can be frozen – although married homes can be an even worse environment if there is constant trauma.

The effects of this spread throughout a child's current and future relationships – at school, with friends, dating, in their sexual development. It impacts how they approach all relationships – what their needs are and what they are looking for. Under these circumstances, relationships of pseudo-intimacy may become common. As a result, children of divorce are more likely themselves to divorce or never marry and, as parents, have difficulty forming intimate relationships with their own children.

The local community

Local communities are also likely to be affected, whether this means relationships at work, at a college or university, or in a small geographical community like a village. Once a sexual relationship has been formed, the interaction between the two individuals is unlikely ever to be the same again, which naturally impacts those around them. A minority of companies still ban sexual relationships between workmates altogether due to the potential for compromising productivity and fostering unprofessional approaches to work. Whereas 'office romances' are not as taboo as they once were – in fact, people have come to realize that the workplace, containing a range of people with similar interests, motivations and often ages, can lead to strong partnerships – they still affect the couple's co-workers. At worst, casual or failed affairs may mean that couples can no longer work together. In many cases there may be a 'power differential', in which one or the other side can exploit or take advantage of the difference in status.

One survey found that around a third of people had had sex with a work colleague, and that almost one in five would do so to further their career (including 10% of married people).[33] In colleges, businesses and villages, groups of friends, loyalties and rivalries are shaped by both ongoing and failed relationships. Sex has the capacity to undermine communities, lessen company productivity, and distort relationships between faculty and students. All this may seem obvious, but it is starkly against the popular understanding of sex as being no one's business except that of the 'consenting adults' most directly involved.

Society

At the greatest remove, sexual relationship changes the shape of society. Recent reports have highlighted the part that family breakdown plays in creating situations of poverty, drug and alcohol abuse, welfare dependency, crime and educational problems.[34] It is no exaggeration to say that there is no one who remains unaffected in some way by the sexual choices of the rest of society, whether that choice was to sleep with someone or to end what the Bible expects to be a permanent relationship. And yet we have no opportunity to 'consent' to the vast majority of these choices, and might not do so if we were asked. The consequences of family breakdown includes the growing problems of gang culture in inner city areas, which have been linked to a lack of father figures for young males.[35] Many old people are afraid of venturing outside at all at night, and there are 'no go' areas which many others avoid because of the high risk of being mugged to pay for a drug or alcohol addiction.

At least part of the individualistic approach to life which drives these problems has resulted from the social changes that took place after the Second World War. The welfare state has made great advances in addressing issues such as health, education, employment and social security. But one unwelcome effect of this has been to reduce the responsibility of fathers outside of marriage. 'Many of the high numbers of unwed births in recent decades have . . . [occurred] where the man is tardy when it comes to accepting responsibility for the mother and child and there is the prospect of them being thrown onto public funds . . . comprehensive support is now available for dependent children, whose low-income mothers are able to marry the state instead.'[36]

Whereas single-parent families are now given some degree of protection, this has done nothing to decrease their numbers and means that many fathers have few qualms about simply walking away. It is estimated that there are 200,000 cases of unpaid child maintenance in the UK, with the total debt standing at around £3.5 billion. Around 60% of this is likely never to be recovered from absent fathers.[37] The burden falls instead upon the taxpayer.

The benefits situation means that some low-income families are actually financially better off after separation.[38] Increasingly, politicians have come to criticize the existing tax credit system on the grounds that some couples with children actually *choose* to live apart because their income drops when they move in together. The penalty can be as high as £8,500 for a low-income family.[39] There are around 1.2 million couples 'living apart together' (LAT) in the UK – some because they want to keep their own space whilst enjoying a committed relationship, but others who would like to live together but cannot afford to.[40]

In many cases the effects of sexual relationship are 'absorbed' into the culture and only register slowly, in levels of taxation, child poverty and certain types of crime, when a critical mass of people adopt the behaviour. In other cases, the effects are immediate, visible and serious. Research suggests that family breakdown, partly due to the high divorce rate but now chiefly down to a much larger number of cohabitations that fail while children are still young, costs the country £37 billion per year.[41] A significant proportion of this sum – which equates to around 6% of total government spending or an equivalent of around £1,200 for every taxpayer – goes on benefits for single parents and their children, picking up the tab for absent fathers. That was around a third of the entire NHS budget for 2007, a half of spending on education, and over six times the prison and probation budget. Our cultural approach to 'consent' robs other areas of social need, such as hospitals, schools and care for older people, on which that money could be spent.

Indirectly, we are all influenced by changing sexual standards. In *A Return to Modesty*, social critic Wendy Shalit explores how people take their cues for what is 'normal' from those around them, often with the result that they feel unable to question the received 'wisdom'; women in particular, she believes, are threatened by the so-called ideal of casual sex and disinhibition, which she associates with the greater incidence of stalking, abuse and date-rape. To put it another way, when adultery (or promiscuity, or divorce) becomes normal, only abnormal people avoid adultery.[42]

Faith relationships

Of greatest significance for the Christian, sex also affects a person's relationship with God and his or her faith community.[43] This is something that Paul explains clearly in 1 Corinthians 6:12–20 (see Appendix #4). The believer is united with Christ; the body, as a temple of the Holy Spirit, was never intended for sexual immorality.

In 2 Samuel 12, the prophet Nathan confronts King David after he commits adultery with Bathsheba. Despite the human cost of his actions, which included the murder of Uriah and several other soldiers in his attempt to cover it up, David states in verse 13, 'I have sinned against the Lord.' Psalm 51 is his confession to God after this event. Once again, he sees his sin in terms of his relationship with God: 'against you, you only, have I sinned and done what is evil in your sight' (verse 4).

The spiritual dimension of sexual sin can easily be overlooked. But sexual immorality shows disrespect for the dwelling place of the Holy Spirit, and for God himself – a frame of mind which must surely extend to and affect other areas of our spiritual life. 2 Timothy 2:20–21 reads, 'In a large house there are articles not only of gold and silver, but also of wood and clay; some are for noble purposes and some for ignoble. If a man cleanses himself from the latter, he will be an instrument for noble purposes, made holy, useful to the Master and prepared to do any good work.' How we honour God has implications for how he will use us in his service: sexual morality is not something that Christians can ignore.

The popular idea that sex doesn't hurt anyone else when it takes place between consenting adults is hopelessly blinkered. There are always knock-on effects, which impact on the individuals themselves and their later relationships, on families, communities and society as a whole – and, for Christians, on their relationships with God.

A biblical model of sexual ethics[44]

The Sexual Offences Act 2003, which replaced older and less specific legislation, draws particular attention to the need to protect persons from non-consensual sexual acts. This reflects the widely held view that consensual sex in private is harmless, whereas sex where consent is not given, or legally is not legitimate, is harmful. Whilst both parties must consent to the sex act, consent as the *only* criterion for sex clearly has its problems. For example, the consent of one spouse is not necessary (nor even relevant in modern British law) for the other to begin an affair, no matter how harmful that might be to him or her, their children, parents, extended families, friends and neighbours.

Leviticus, in common with much of the Old Testament, is often avoided by Christians on the grounds that it appears to have little relevance to twenty-first-century life. However, Leviticus 20 is a key text for understanding the biblical approach to sex – particularly in terms of the differences from our modern point of view.[45] There are two general points to draw out from this carefully argued, if neglected passage.

First, *responsibility is corporate.* The introduction to the chapter places great emphasis on the responsibility of the whole community to root out and punish idolaters. There is a sense in which to tolerate such a sin is to take part in it. Throughout Leviticus 20, both God *and* the community are expected to punish offenders. Responsibility alternates, driving home the point that the community cannot ignore these offences, as God does not (Lev. 20:2–5). This theme is carried on through the chapter. In the

first half (20:9–16), the community are charged with the duty to
punish offenders. In verses 17–21, God himself is implied as judge,
though it is fair to expect the community to be responsible for
punishment too. The overall effect is to draw out systematically
both human and divine sides of the situation.

Second, *sexual offence has both spiritual and physical significance.* This
double-sided punishment, by both God and the community,
reflects the seriousness of the crimes – as do the punishments,
which often include a prescription for the death penalty. It also
reflects the two-fold significance of sexual offence in terms of God
and humanity. This is made more explicitly clear by the subdivi-
sions in Leviticus 20, which could be placed under the headings of
Idolatry (verses 1–5) and Respect for Family and Adultery (9–10).
These subheadings recall the sequence and content of the Ten
Commandments in Exodus 20 and Deuteronomy 5. There is the
initial warning against idolatry in Leviticus 20:1–6 which, like the
Decalogue, sets the scene for the following material in terms of
rebellion against God. Aside from the purely human aspect of
damage to the family, sexual sin is seen as a prelude and a part
of spiritual apostasy, hence the frequent references to idolatry as
'spiritual adultery'. (The idea that the unfaithfulness of sexual sin is
a symptom of our unfaithfulness to God is explored in more detail
in chapter 5.)

Leviticus 20:9 recalls the fifth commandment, 'Honour your
father and mother', with a similar command in negative language:
'if anyone curses [treats lightly, contemptibly] his father or mother,
he must be put to death.' This verse suggests that the significance
of sexual offence lies partly in its damage to the family unit; in
fact, many of the following laws are clearly intended to protect
the integrity of the extended family by banning sexual relationships between certain family members, whether related by blood
or marriage.

In early Israel, law encouraged and protected family as the fundamental unit of society. God's gift of the land to Israel was made
to each extended family, who had their own piece of land and
therefore a place of their own; roots, as well as the ongoing ability
to produce food. The Jubilee land law (Lev. 25) was supposed to
ensure this allotment of land was permanent, so it stayed in the

family forever. Many aspects of justice were decided in the family or in small communities, rather than in central courts. People learned about the covenant and its regulations through their families, and many rituals and festivals took place in the home. A threat to the family constituted a threat to the national covenant relationship with God.

Our entirely self-centred approach is a far cry from the biblical model of community. Here in Britain, we might try to encourage people to live a particular way in the hope that – if enough people keep to the right standards – society as a whole will improve, but essentially we start with the individual and allow the shape of society to evolve from what each of us does. Unfortunately, most people do not work out their sexual choices from first principles. Instead, they take their cues from what everyone else is doing: people do what is normal for their culture.

The Old Testament looks at the situation from the other side. It takes a positive model of community as the starting point and lays out guidelines for the individual in the light of that. Sex is one area of life in which this is the case, something that Leviticus 18:29 makes starkly clear with a warning to cut off offenders from the community. It is more a case of 'Now if *that* is the kind of society God wants, *this* is the kind of person you must be if you belong to it'.[46] The Bible does not separate the way we act as individuals from the type of community in which we live.

Deuteronomy 8:1 reads: 'Be careful to follow every command I am giving you today, so that you may live and increase and may enter and possess the land that the LORD promised on oath to your forefathers.' But the force of the verse is lost in modern English translations, which do not distinguish 'you' singular and plural. In Hebrew it switches between the two. The sense is: 'Make sure you [all] keep every commandment I am giving [each of] you [individually] today, so that you [all, collectively] may live and multiply . . .' Responsibility for keeping the law is given both to each of us individually *and* to everyone together.

The Bible consistently combines 'public' with 'private' morality, apparently unaware of our modern distinction and the suggestion that a 'victimless crime' is no crime at all. Ezekiel conspicuously places 'private' sexual offences alongside more visible sins against other people in a way we would hardly think of doing today; adultery is given at least as much weight as robbery (Ezek. 18). The Bible is interested in a person's character and the attitude of the heart, which should be the same in public as in private life. As far as God is concerned, there is no part of life that is 'private'. Similarly, Paul begins his list in 1 Corinthians 6:9–10 with hidden sexual and religious sins, finishing with those that more obviously harm a human third party. This is consistent with an approach that seeks the good of the community and relies on every individual for the outworking of that vision. Paul recognizes this in 1 Corinthians 5, where he criticizes the Corinthians for allowing one man's personal life to affect the entire community: 'a little yeast works through the dough' (1 Cor. 5:6). The biblical view is starkly at odds with prevailing wisdom, which fits our moral standards around our sexual appetites, rather than fitting sex around moral standards.[47]

Consent versus community

The illusion of individualism and the emphasis it places on personal choice is that we live in a moral vacuum and that our sexual choices occur in isolation. It assumes that '"my" history of sexual experience or inexperience is a purely personal and individual thing. It is not and cannot be. Even what I do or think on my own is habit-forming, character building and comes to affect others. What others do affects me; and not only what they do, but how they *interpret* what they do, powerfully conditions my own thinking and practice.'[48]

The biblical authors recognized that sex shapes the community and, where sexual offences do not have immediately obvious third-party victims as in the case of marital infidelity, there are still broader concerns for society in general. Today, this is all too obvious from the widespread incidence of STIs, single-parent families, divorce, abortion and abuse, which have measurable and significant relational and financial consequences.

'Consent' is virtually the only rule of sexual relationships today, but consent is not enough on its own. We need to move beyond consent to look at how we are each affected by the 'private' choices made by every member of the community. In our individualistic culture, this seems an outrageous statement. Surely it is unreasonable to expect a couple to seek acceptance for their relationship from third parties? On the other hand, surely it is unjust to expect these same third parties to shoulder the emotional and financial burden of relationships to which they never consented? We cannot expect to keep sexual liberty without also accepting its widespread consequences. Viewed from the other side, there is a great attraction to living in a society free from the countless complications and consequences of widespread sexual liberty, dysfunction and their resulting pain. If this is the case, we need to expand our view of 'consent' from the individual to the wider family and community.

Before we look further at the case for marriage as the expression of family/community consent and support, we would like to consider some counter-cultural ideas about the opportunities for intimacy and belonging outside of sexual relationship.

Notes

1. Talmudic illustration that the Covenant was with Israel as a whole, not with an individual, found in Leviticus Rabbah, Parasha 4. Shimon bar Yochai was an influential second-century rabbi.
2. See A. G. Weiss, 'The lost role of dependency in psychotherapy' in *Gestalt Review* 6 (2002), pp. 6–17, referenced in *Therapy Today*, June 2006.
3. Nick Totton, 'In Defence of Dependency', in *Therapy Today*, June 2006.
4. 'In Defence of Dependency'.
5. Jean-Francois Lyotard, *The Postmodern Condition: A Report on Knowledge* (Manchester University Press, 1979), pp. xxiv–xxv.
6. Alan MacFarlane, *The Origins of English Individualism* (Basic Blackwell, 1978), p. 170.
7. Dale Kuehne, *Sex and the iWorld: Rethinking Relationship Beyond an Age of Individualism* (Baker, 2009).
8. Anthony Giddens, *Modernity and Self-Identity* (Polity Press, 1991).
9. See also Anthony Giddens, *The Transformation of Intimacy* (Stanford University Press, 1992).

10. This means that two out of five marriages fail, *not* that two out of every five
    people who ever marry will divorce. Gaining accurate figures is difficult,
    as the people who marry in any given year are not the ones that divorce
    that year, or in any single given year down the line; marriages last different
    lengths of time. In addition, this figure rarely takes into account the effect
    on the statistics of second and third marriages, which are progressively
    more likely to break up, skewing the average. What this actually means is
    that *first* marriages in the UK are more than 60% likely to succeed, whereas
    people who have previously divorced are statistically more likely to keep
    divorcing. In 2006, there were 236,980 marriages in England and Wales,
    but 89,360 (38%) involved at least one divorced partner.
11. Office of National Statistics (ONS).
12. For more on the financial costs of sexual liberty, see chapter 5.
13. Christopher Ash, *Marriage: Sex in the Service of God* (IVP, 2003), p. 126.
14. *The State of our Unions, The Social Health of Marriage in America*, The National
    Marriage Project, Rutgers (State University of New Jersey, 1999), p. 13.
    See Patricia Morgan, *Marriage-Lite* (Institute for the Study of Civil Society,
    2000), p. 87.
15. Daniel Heimbach, *True Sexual Morality* (Crossway Books, 2004),
    p. 30.
16. The actual, direct effect is probably impossible to measure above all the
    background 'noise'. The divorce rate did not rise in Clinton's term, instead
    continuing a downward trend (which reflects the declining marriage rate).
    The *net* marriage rate – number of marriages minus number of divorces –
    did dip in 1998, mainly due to a drop in the number of marriages. Overall,
    net marriages declined more slowly under Clinton than during other
    recent administrations.
17. Morgan, *Marriage-Lite*, p. vii.
18. 'Fractured Families' in *Breakdown Britain* (Centre for Social Justice, 2006),
    pp. 56–57. Available at <http://www.centreforsocialjustice.org.uk/
    default.asp?pageRef=180> (accessed 22 July 2008).
19. John Witte, *The Goods and Goals of Marriage* (Notre Dame Law Review,
    2001), p. 76 (footnote).
20. ONS.
21. See 'Secret trial to let GPs carry out abortions' in *The Times*, 5 December
    2007. See <http://www.timesonline.co.uk/tol/life_and_style/health/
    article3001425.ece> (accessed 22 July 2008). Currently, around 87% of
    abortions are performed on the NHS.

22. 'Repeat abortions rise to record levels' in *The Telegraph*, 10 May 2008.
    See <http://www.telegraph.co.uk/news/uknews/1942614/Repeat-
    abortions-rise to record-levels.html> (accessed 22 July 2008).

23. Column in *The Daily Mail*, 29 May 2006. See <http://www.melaniephil-
    lips.com/articles/archives/001720.html> (accessed 22 July 2008).

24. Heimbach, *True Sexual Morality*, p. 34.

25. See Ash's excellent *Marriage*, pp. 45–59 for more on society's moving
    sexual goalposts, and many other helpful insights.

26. See Michael Schluter and David Lee, *The R Option* (Relationships
    Foundation, 2003), pp. 119–126.

27. See Jay Teachman, 'Premarital Sex, Premarital Cohabitation, and the Risk
    of Subsequent Marital Dissolution Among Women' in *Journal of Marriage
    and Family* 65:2 (2003), pp. 444–455. See online at http://www.ncfr.org/
    pdf/press_releases/PRESS%20RELEAS2.pdf (accessed 14 October
    2008). However, premarital sex with only the future husband was not
    found to present a greater risk of divorce.

28. Morgan, *Marriage-Lite*, pp. 55–59.

29. Gordon Andreiuk, 'Access to our grandchildren: court-ordered access'
    in *Canadian Association of Gerontology* 2 (1994), pp. 7–29. See also <http://
    kidjacked.com/family/grandparent_access.asp> (accessed 22 July 2008).

30. The fact that it is usually a wicked stepmother probably reflects the
    comparative likelihood of men remarrying after their wives died in child-
    birth. Though rarer, plenty of examples of evil fairytale stepfathers also
    exist.

31. In particular, the presence of a stepfather is a primary marker for
    increased risk of sexual abuse of female children. (Others markers are
    having few friends, absent or unavailable parents or conflict between
    parents.) David Finkelhor *et al.*, *A Sourcebook on Child Sexual Abuse*
    (Sage Publications, 1986). See <http://www.advocatesforyouth.org/
    publications/factsheet/fsabuse1.htm> (accessed 22 July 2008).

32. US statistics show that 15% of children who live with their mothers and
    have no contact with their fathers are permanently excluded from school.
    Children 'exposed to divorce' are around twice as likely to repeat a grade
    and five times more likely to be suspended or expelled. <http://www.
    divorcewizards.com/divorceclass.html> (accessed 22 July 2008).

33. *Observer Sex Poll*, 2002, see <http://observer.guardian.co.uk/sex/
    story/0,,818356,00.html> (accessed 30 October 2007).

34. See *Breakdown Britain*.

35. Research also suggests that disputes over relationships, whether family, friendship or romantic, are the source of most violence within and between gangs – not turf wars or drug markets. Judith Aldridge *et al.*, *Youth Gangs in an English City: Social Exclusion, Drugs and Violence*, Full Research Report ESRC End of Award Report, RES-000-23-0615 (ESRC, 2007).

36. Morgan, *Marriage-Lite*, p. 85.

37. 'Child Support Agency – implementation of the child support reforms', National Audit Office, June 2006.

38. Jill Kirby, *The Price of Parenthood* (Centre for Policy Studies, 2005).

39. *Breakthrough Britain: vol. 1, Family Breakdown* (Centre for Social Justice, 2007), p. 178.

40. ONS.

41. John Ashcroft and Peter Lynas, *Investing in Relationships* (Relationships Foundation, 2008). See <http://www.relationshipsfoundation.org/download.php?id=218> (accessed 5 August 2008).

42. Wendy Shalit, *A Return to Modesty* (Touchstone, 2000). Shalit also highlights some of the inconsistencies in our approach to sexual behaviour – that the things we normalize in one context may be considered undesirable in others. 'What does it say about *Playboy* that its regular readers are horrified at the thought that their own daughters would appear there?' (p. 78).

43. For Muslims and Jews – though for different reasons – extramarital sex is a major issue. The Qur'an considers extramarital sex (*zina*), whether adultery or sex before marriage, one of the most serious sins, placing it on a par with murder and worshipping other gods (Qur'an 25:68–70). Christians are divided on the subject between liberals (few constraints) and conservatives. Orthodox and Conservative Judaism consider sex within marriage both a *mitzvah* – commandment – and also the only acceptable form of sex.

44. See Jonathan Burnside, *God, Justice and Society: An Introduction to Biblical Law* (Cambridge University Press, 2008), ch. 11.

45. See Burnside, *God, Justice and Society*, ch. 11.

46. Christopher Wright, *Old Testament Ethics for the People of God* (IVP, 2004), pp. 363–365.

47. Heimbach, *True Sexual Morality*, p. 41.

48. Ash, *Marriage*, p. 27.

3. RELATIONAL OPPORTUNITIES

Intimacy without *eros*

Growing up I assumed that everyone had the same kind of friendships I had. I have two friendships which are as old as I am (34 years), and a third which has lasted now for 19 years (we affectionately call him the 'newbie'!). The four of us have travelled far together, metaphorically, geographically, emotionally, and spiritually speaking. As little boys we played together naked; as teenagers we explored the wider world together; as mature men we have debated (rugby vs. hockey!), laughed, and even cried together. Our friendship spans many interests, priorities, character traits, and life philosophies, some held in common, some uniquely our own. Our history affords us the luxury of rarely needing to explain ourselves in depth to each other, even as our life circumstances have changed in small and large ways. Three of us are married, one is dating, and one has a child. All of our partners comment on the same thing – 'you guys have a special friendship'.

This is a common observation, yet it took a while for me to appreciate its truth (some would say that I have yet to realize it). On first appearances we are 'alpha males' and so our 'intimacy' takes other people, especially other guys, by surprise. One friend at university recoiled at the idea of ever sharing a bed with another bloke, instead choosing a hard floor on a weekend retreat; I had no qualms as the 'four of us' had often bunked together on surf trips. There have been several such experiences over the years, when our definition of 'normal' has been challenged by others, and vice versa. We each have other friends and, while our relationship is not exclusive, our other friends have commented that they sometimes feel 'outside the inner circle'. We are not conscious of this demarcation; indeed some of our other friends know details of our lives not known by 'the four'. Nevertheless, when it comes to life's big, difficult, funny, 'family' occasions we gather together.

There is certainly no 'erōs' in our relationship. We are four men, confident in our heterosexuality (even though we all exhibit a penchant for pink shirts!), and very thankful for the intimacy we share, especially as life gets busier, and often stressful. Our friendship affords us a rootedness that facilitates, and informs our highly mobile lives.

– Paul, 34

Changing times

In the last few decades, a combination of changing attitudes has distorted our understanding of the relationship between sex and belonging. The role of sex has been exalted by the sexual revolution, which brought sex out of the bedroom and onto billboards, into magazines, adverts, and almost every arena of life.

Some people claim that marriage interferes with romance. There's no doubt about it. Any time you have a romance, your wife is bound to interfere.

Groucho Marx

TV and film-makers depict sex as a safe, low-consequence activity engaged in by just about everyone – except, oddly, within the context of marriage, where it often seems to serve as an unwelcome reminder of the freedom-curtailing responsibilities that children bring.[1] Advertisers frequently use sexual content – implied or actual – to sell the latest must-have products, which they tell us will enhance our own desirability and lead to sexual and other fulfilment.

Wrapped in only a towel, the man is toned and muscled. The razor, a gleaming, eight-bladed miracle of modern technology, glides over his chiselled jaw with impossible smoothness and accuracy, perfectly removing every hair in its path. He doesn't even cut that awkward bit under his nose. The bathroom door opens and a woman – as flawless and stunning as the body, face, razor and shave we have just been privileged to witness – enters, wrapped in a towelled dressing gown. After the man splashes his face with some water – perhaps from the sink tap but more likely from the pure, ice-cold, refreshing streams of a mountain spring – she puts her arms around him and he smiles.

The message is easy to understand: this is clearly a man who has a lot of high-quality sex, and it's all down to that incredible razor.

The widespread use of sexual themes in advertising is clearly a successful strategy. Products entirely unconnected to sex, beauty or image are frequently accompanied by such material – which may appeal on a conscious or subconscious level – creating an association between the two that is intended to bypass the rational mind.[2] Thus products as diverse and otherwise un-sexual as cars, toothpaste and coffee are sold by juxtaposing them with images and concepts that appeal to our most fundamental biological drives.

Coito, ergo sum?

This tidal wave of sexual media has occurred in parallel to the increasing isolation and individualism of our modern Western lifestyles. People often no longer live with or even near their families, and move around frequently for work or other reasons. The decline in marriage and the rise in divorce rates, along with the length of time people are waiting before they marry, means that the number of single-person households has never been higher – along with the relational isolation and pain which that often brings. Busy lives mean there is less and less time to spend on relationships, and the increasing privacy and inward-looking nature of many homes makes it even harder for single people to form friendships. More people than ever before find themselves alone,[3] and frequently lonely: the cult of the self has left a relational deficit. Nature abhors a vacuum and so, it turns out, does a proportion of the media, which continually takes the line that sex is vital to personal fulfilment. Sex has become popular as a perceived antidote to loneliness.

Sexual activity is seen as the highest good, to know 'who you are', whether this is expressed in terms of casual sex, cohabitation or same-sex attraction; the implicit and explicit sexualization in much TV and film even runs to the promotion of adultery. Who you love, and the right to express that love in sex, are non-negotiable aspects of life. After all, 'the heart wants what the heart wants', as Woody Allen answered to the question of why he married his former girlfriend's adopted daughter. No matter how distasteful its consequences, woe betide the person who tries to repress this fact of life, is the implication. Increasing aloneness and self-sufficiency unsurprisingly seems to spawn an increasingly self-referential morality. The same individualism that has undermined relationships and damaged intimacy has limited our horizons to take into account the consent only of the two individuals who engage in a sexual act.

Lucrative though it is, the promotion of sexual promiscuity and even infidelity by many film-makers and advertisers is at odds with public attitudes surrounding other behaviours such as smoking, drug-taking, drinking and eating junk food, which are perceived to be harmful. These are subject to increasingly strict censure. Even aside from the significant relational costs to those directly or indirectly affected, adultery and other sexual behaviours involve a high price tag for society – yet these themes, implicit or explicit, are accepted, and even promoted, rather than censured.

While it may be argued that 'art holds a mirror up to life' and that all the film-makers are doing is depicting life as it is, the inverse proposition is also true: the media is as much an influence on, as a product of, society. TV and film generally see sex as a universal currency, a way of saying almost anything from 'hello' to 'I care deeply about you'. Small wonder that researchers have found a direct correlation between the amount of sexual content children are exposed to on TV and the age at which they become sexually active themselves.[4]

These factors have promoted the myth that sex is the most important aspect of relationship. To be fulfilled, you must be sexually active; to know and truly connect with someone (usually but not always of the opposite sex) and experience belonging, you must sleep with them. In the last thirty years, has sex suddenly become much more important to us as a society or a species, or is the new emphasis because it provides a counterfeit answer to the real problem: a deficit in intimacy?

Friendship, meanwhile, runs the risk of being demoted – still important, perhaps, but a second-best option on its own terms, if without sex and romance. If sexual relationship – including marriage – has increasingly become overloaded with the expectation that it should fulfil the role of every other kind of relationship, the opposite also holds: friendships are increasingly subject to the expectation that they should fulfil sexual desires too. Convergence (the industry buzzword for the phenomenon that different technologies – mobile phones, cameras, radios, email, Internet access and more – can be combined in a single device) appears to be far less successful when applied to personal relationships. And yet, friendships are vital for wellbeing and do not have the same kind of third-party effects that sexual relationships do, because they do not usually threaten existing relationships in the same way or to the same degree. It is possible and beneficial to have many close friendships; maintaining many sexual relationships tends to cause serious problems.

Aloneness is not the same as loneliness

Humans are not meant to exist in isolation, and the Bible never assumes that we should live outside of relationship with one another. Even biblical characters who sometimes appear to live solitary lives have strong friendships. Jesus, who never married and who often spent long periods of time alone to pray (Luke 5:16; Matt. 14:22–23), was nevertheless close to his disciples, particularly Peter, James and John, and had other friends such as Lazarus, Mary and Martha – who themselves each appear to be single. In the biblical account, if not in popular fiction and speculation,[5] the relationship between Jesus and Mary Magdalene is marked by deep but non-sexual love. Paul, another long-term single, had close friends and travelling companions in his work: Tychicus, Timothy,

Epaphroditus, and many others in the churches he planted around
the Roman Empire.

Love and sex in the Bible

The word 'love' occurs several hundred times in the Bible. Just
how many (from around 300 to 550) depends on which translation
is used, because there are several different words used for our one
English word. Much has been made of the 'four loves'[6] found in
ancient Greek: affection or family love (*storgē*); friendship (*philia*);
romantic and sexual love (*erōs*); and charity or 'unconditional' and
devoted love (*agapē*).[7] The use of these different words in the New
Testament has been influenced by the Septuagint, the Greek translation of the Hebrew Old Testament that was brought together
in the three centuries before Jesus' time. Hebrew, like English,
generally uses only one word (*'ahăbāh*) for love, and it can mean
many things, including both romantic love and charity. The early
translators of the Hebrew Bible used different Greek words for the
different nuances of the Hebrew *'ahăbāh*, which filtered through to
the NT writers.

Two of these words are found directly and frequently in the NT
– *philia* and *agapē*, friendship and charity – and one, *storgē*, only in a
derived form (*astorgos*, 'lacking affection', in Rom. 1:31 and 2 Tim.
3:3). Forms of *erōs* do not occur in the NT at all. Of all the occasions when the church and individuals are told to 'love' in the NT,
the sense is never sexual. In biblical terms, it turns out that there
is far more to love than just sex. 1 Corinthians 13, for all its use at
weddings, has nothing to do with romance and everything to do
with unconditional love and devoted commitment in the community of faith. 1 John 4:7–21 also talks of this serving, sacrificial
love in the church: we are encouraged to love one another because
love comes from God and God first loved us. Jesus said this love
would be the hallmark of his followers (see John 13:34–35).

The Bible – both Old and New Testaments – does not equate
love or relationship with sex, but neither does it separate sex from
relationship. Sexual relationship is *one* part – an important part,
but only a part – of God's relational plan for us. It is not his only
solution to loneliness, or even his first.[8] This may seem an obvious
point, but it is a perspective that still needs stating as it can be one

that our culture barely permits us to hold. The cliché of the couple riding off together into the sunset is categorically not a biblical one.[9]

'A father to the fatherless, a defender of widows, is God in his holy dwelling. God sets the lonely in families, he leads forth the prisoners with singing . . .' (Ps. 68:5–6). The assumption is that what the widow needs is a defender, not a husband. When the widow asks Elijah for help in 1 Kings 17, his solution is not to find her another husband, but to ensure continued financial provision. How would that story have ended if it had been written today? Probably in the same way that *Bridget Jones's Diary* did, along with a thousand other books and films: with the lonely, unfulfilled single blissfully pairing off. The lonely do not merely need a partner, but a family.

Family as the basic unit of society is assumed in the Old Testament. Proverbs, however, recognizes that friendship is sometimes of as great or even greater importance than family. 'A man of [many] friends may be destroyed, but there is a friend [literally 'one loving'] who sticks closer than a brother' (Prov. 18:24, author's translation). And 'Do not go to your brother's house when disaster strikes you – better a neighbour nearby than a brother far away' (Prov. 27:10). Jesus made it clear that family was important (Mark 7:9–13), but that other relationships and concerns could be of even greater importance (Mark 3:31–35).

So friendship, fellowship with both God and other believers, and family all feature as priorities, but not sex.[10] The failure of these 'alternatives' to satisfy today is partly the fault of an over-sexualized society, one that looks first to sex for relationship. In the Bible, aloneness (singleness) does not mean loneliness. This does not rule out marriage as a solution to loneliness; for example, Isaac is comforted by his marriage to Rebekah after the death of his mother Sarah. And, in contrast to the story of Elijah and the widow, marriage was the solution for Ruth, although she shows strong loyalty to Naomi her mother-in-law, and the God of Naomi and of Israel, first and foremost. But there is an emphasis on non-sexual love in the Bible that suggests a balance that is rarely found today. Relationship, and what the Bible calls 'love', is disconnected from sex to a degree which never assumes that the first means or requires the second.

David and Jonathan: intimacy without sex?

As the case study at the beginning of the chapter shows, intimate friendships do not have to involve sex. One of the most striking examples of friendship in the Bible is that between David and Jonathan, the son of King Saul. They shared a closeness that David apparently valued more highly than any other relationship, even including the sexual relationships he had with his wives. Whilst this might be thought inspiring, particularly given that David would eventually be the husband of numerous wives, the story has – in some quarters – been the source of intense speculation. Rather than being taken to demonstrate the value of committed friendship and the deep intimacy which is possible without sex, some have suggested exactly the opposite: David and Jonathan have become biblical poster-boys for the gay movement.[11]

David and Jonathan's friendship begins as soon as they meet, when Saul brings the young shepherd-boy to live in the royal palace after he kills the Philistine Goliath. 'After David had finished talking with Saul, Jonathan became one in spirit with David, and he loved him as himself . . . And Jonathan made a covenant with David because he loved him as himself. Jonathan took off the robe he was wearing and gave it to David, along with his tunic, and even his sword, bow and belt' (1 Sam. 18:1, 3–4).

When Saul tries to kill David out of jealousy at his growing fame, Jonathan intervenes, setting himself against his father. 'Saul's anger flared up at Jonathan and he said to him, "You son of a perverse and rebellious woman! Don't I know that you have sided with the son of Jesse to your own shame and to the shame of your mother's nakedness? As long as the son of Jesse lives on this earth, neither you nor your kingdom will be established. Now send and bring him to me, for he must die!" "Why should he be put to death? What has he done?" Jonathan asked his father' (1 Sam. 20:30–32, author's translation).

Finally, Jonathan dies in battle and is mourned by David. From these verses, some critics have argued that David and Jonathan were lovers. Several features of the text apparently suggest this to the modern reader, at least as a possibility: that 'Jonathan became one in spirit with David' (literally, 'Jonathan's soul became bound to David's soul'), that they 'made a covenant' (sometimes assumed to be a kind of Old Testament civil partnership), that Jonathan 'loved him', arguably Saul's language of shame and nakedness, and particularly that David eulogized the dead Jonathan: 'I grieve for you, Jonathan my brother; you were very dear to me. Your love for me was wonderful, more wonderful than that of women' (2 Sam. 1:26). However, the text never uses the usual Hebrew words for sexual intercourse, *šākab* or *yāda'*. The relationship can be understood in entirely platonic terms:[12] no feature requires a sexual interpretation, and the true significance of the narrative actually lies in terms of the political, not the sexual. In Genesis 44:30, the same language is used of Jacob, whose soul was bound to that of his young son, Benjamin. The covenant is significant because Jonathan has *politically* allied himself with David rather than the house of his father Saul, the king. The language of love (*'ahăbāh*) is best understood as friendship or political alliance, which is often couched in these terms; there are no separate words for erotic love and friendship in Hebrew, as there are with the Greek *erōs* and *philia*. For example, Hiram of Tyre was a friend (*'ōhēb*, literally 'one loving') of David's (1 Kgs 5:1, Hebrew text 5:15), and 'all Israel and Judah loved David' (1 Sam. 18:16). Are we to assume that these, too, were all gay relationships?

The context makes it clear that Saul's language of Jonathan's mother's shame and nakedness refers to his son's political betrayal, and the betrayal of his birthright as king-to-be, rather than to his own sexuality, of which there seems to have been little concept in the Old Testament. In addition, if Saul was willing to put Jonathan to death for unwittingly breaking his oath in 1 Samuel 14:24–47, it would be strange for him to allow his son to escape punishment for homosexuality – and strange that the biblical author did not require David to repent, as he did for his sexual sin with Bathsheba (2 Sam. 12). Finally, David praises Jonathan's love as 'more wonderful than that of women'. This does not presuppose that it was of the *same type*, only that David found Jonathan's loyalty and sacrifices more significant than those of his many women.

The overriding significance of the narrative in terms of biblical history is that Jonathan allied himself with David, recognizing and submitting himself to David being anointed king by Samuel, rather than with his father Saul. He assisted David as the future king of Israel to escape and eventually accede the throne, paving the way for the Davidic monarchy and the line into which Jesus was born. Jonathan's loyalty, help and direct intervention saved David's life on more than one occasion when Saul was planning to kill him. The interpretation that sees David and Jonathan as lovers is surely a symptom of an over-sexualized culture, one that reads sex into every possible situation. In a lighter vein, perhaps the same inter-pretation of homosexual innuendo might be suggested of Professor Higgins in the musical *My Fair Lady*, when he sings 'Why can't a woman be more like a man?' to Colonel Pickering. The point is that both King David and Henry Higgins recognized something highly positive and qualitatively distinct about their respective friendships – not that they wanted to sleep with their male friend as a result!

> *'I want to speak with my friend John. I want to speak with him now. I will not go without speaking.' ... I begin to believe what I have been told and suddenly there is something in me I cannot resolve. I know it is over and within hours or days I will not be wearing a blindfold. I will be unfettered. But I feel it build in me, the weight of my imprisonment. For how much freedom can there be for a man when he leaves half of himself chained to the wall?*
>
> – Brian Keenan, writing of his release from his five-year captivity in Beirut in the 1980s, and the friendship he shared with John McCarthy during that time.[13]

The same is true of Abraham Lincoln, whose intimate friend-ship with Joshua Speed extended to sharing a bed with him. Although some later critics have suggested that this was a homo-sexual love affair, the more likely explanation is that sex was so far from Lincoln's mind, or anyone else's, that he and Joshua could 'sleep together' – not an unusual thing for two men to do, by the norms of the day – without fear of their close friendship being misinterpreted.

Singles

Coming from a mentality that assumes that romantic relation-ship is better than singleness and that everyone who is not 'in a relationship' wishes to be (or else, has something wrong with them), it is easy to devalue singles. 'We need to try to get rid of some of our assumptions (prejudices?) about both singleness and single people,' writes J. John. 'For example, just because a man in his forties is not married does not mean that he is "struggling with his sexual orientation". And just because a woman is a widow or divorcée does not mean that she wants to find a new husband. Equally, a single person may not feel at all lonely, inadequate or unfulfilled. They may well be better balanced mentally, emotionally and spiritually than you or me. It is far better to treat every person as an individual rather than as a stereotype.'[14]

'Don't you want to join us?' I was asked recently by an acquaintance when he ran across me alone after midnight in a coffee house that was already almost deserted. 'No, I don't,' I said.

Franz Kafka

Paul, who chose to stay single himself in order to devote himself to God's service, discusses singleness in 1 Corinthians 7. He acknowledges that physical desires play an important part in this matter and that, although he was happy to remain unmarried himself, he was in a minority. 'I wish that all men were as I am. But each man has his own gift from God; one has this gift, another has that' (1 Cor. 7:7). Paul sees his singleness, apparently stated in terms of freedom from the distractions of sexual impulses, as a gift from God – something barely conceivable in today's mindset.

Paul confirms to his readers that marrying is not a sin (1 Cor. 7:28). At the same time, he suggests that those who do not marry will face fewer troubles and will be more able to live their lives in undivided attention to God. Part of Paul's message seems to be motivated by the Corinthians' specific circumstances, the 'present crisis' he mentions, and the fact that the 'time is short'. This crisis meant that it was sensible for single Christians to stay single. 'The world in its present form is passing away', wrote Paul; whatever he meant by this, he takes it as grounds not to get overly engrossed in things that – although not necessarily bad in themselves – could distract the Corinthians from God at this critical time. There are various theories about what the 'crisis' could have been:

- The nearness of Christ's expected return.
- Persecution, present or anticipated.
- Famine, namely the grain shortage in the 40s and 50s predicted by Agabus in Acts 11:28, which led to social unrest, riots and an increase in crime.[15]
- The circumstances brought about by the Corinthians' own sexual licentiousness.

Postal delays in the ancient world would render his advice obsolete if the crisis was on the timescale of anything less than weeks;[16] the situation is expected to last for some time, though not forever, and it did not stop Paul from making further plans to visit them and organizing a collection (1 Cor. 16). Tom Wright suggests that there were two factors: Paul did initially believe that the 'final crisis' would happen in his lifetime, but he is using the immediate crisis of the grain shortage to highlight the fragility and temporary nature of the present situation.[17] Perhaps the most that can be taken away from this passage is Paul's advice to make the most of singleness while it lasts – whether it is voluntary, or due to circumstances beyond our control. Faithfulness to God in difficult circumstances is more important than conforming to society's expectations to marry.

It is easy to view singleness as the temporary state that people pass through before they are married. Whilst this is true, it tends to split the world into singles and marrieds – which is not a helpful division. Everyone has been single, and at least one partner in every marriage will be again later in life, either after divorce or bereavement. A better way to understand it is not to see single people as others, but as ourselves at different stages on our life journeys.

'Just' friends?

The kind of interpretative bias that suggests a homosexual relationship between David and Jonathan as the most plausible interpretation of the story is a symptom of a far wider problem. In her book *A Return to Modesty*, Wendy Shalit convincingly puts the case that the sexual revolution has been good for neither men nor women: that society has become so over-sexualized that we have ended up with a culture of fear, disrespect, damaged quality of relationship, lost childhood and lost innocence – of even the concept of innocence to lose. Consent may have become the only criterion necessary to legitimate sexual behaviour, but consent itself is undermined in a thousand insidious ways as our culture has become saturated with images and ideals that assume sexual licence and all but deny the possibility of restraint: 'a culture in which pornography has been normalized has certain expectations of its girls, expectations that are often hard to meet . . . If our culture always expects young women to be playing with their sexual power, always at the ready for the advances of anyone, this means they never have the right to say "no".'[18] Chastity, once an ideal in itself, has become synonymous with prudery.[19]

A major casualty of this 'hypersexualization' is platonic friendship. This is unsurprising, given our supposed openness to the possibility of sex, or at least a culture of dating that looks for something deeper than 'just' friends. This can be as much a problem in churches as it is outside – perhaps more so, given the Christian ideal of sex only in the context of marriage. The premise of the 1980s romantic comedy *When Harry Met Sally* is that men and women cannot be 'just' friends because sexual attraction always complicates matters. Or, as Anne Atkins writes in a book for a primarily Christian audience, 'It is only when we forget about marriage that we can make true friends of the opposite sex.'[20]

In addition, our 'dating culture' places an emphasis on the couple at the expense of larger groups of friends; exclusive couples involved romantically take the place of other relationships. In fact, this exclusivity does romantic relationship few favours. As J. John comments, dating couples are more self-conscious about their behaviour: what you see is not what you get. In friendship, there is less temptation to impress and 'you get to encounter people, more or less, as they really are'.[21]

Marriage can be overvalued

As discussed above, marriage is not God's only, or even main, solution to human loneliness. The family is the first and often most significant setting for relational support in the Bible, though friendship and relationships with other believers are important and

may take precedence. Everyone comes from a family, no matter
how transient or imperfect this is in practice. In this respect, family
is more foundational than marriage: not everyone gets married,
and marriage is not necessary for relational wholeness. One of the
curious ironies of overvaluing marriage as the height of relationship is that this ends up devaluing marriage, inevitably harming
family at the same time. Marriage becomes subject to unrealistic
expectations, a huge burden which it cannot live up to.[22]

In this respect, it is possible to overvalue marriage. Many couples
today overload their marriage with such expectations; marriage is
given too much responsibility for providing people with a sense of
identity and significance. Often the idea is present that, once you
are married, problems will disappear, self-esteem will improve and
life will get a whole lot better. People expect of marriage what they
expect from the sum total of all other relationships – an intense
demand that can produce serious tensions. Devaluing singles and
singleness is perhaps the other side of this coin.

The principle that relationship is about far more than sex is
simple, but the practicalities and application are not so easy to
work out. The reality is that more people than ever before are
single, whether or not they wish to be. In addition, alongside
our needs for relationship and emotional intimacy which can be
addressed with 'platonic' friendships, there is also a physical desire
for sex.

Here, our culture's obsession with sex is utterly unhelpful. The
Song of Songs repeatedly warns, 'do not arouse or awaken love
until it so desires' (2:7; 5:3; 8:4) – but the media does exactly that
in the name of entertainment and advertising. Although the Song
of Songs addresses the 'daughters of Jerusalem', it is men who are
disproportionately susceptible and therefore targeted by this kind
of visual temptation.

In 1 Corinthians 7:9 Paul writes that it 'is better to marry than
to burn with passion' – a condition that was apparently leading
the Corinthians into sexual immorality. Given that our environment is almost as sexually saturated as was theirs, we can hardly
expect a different outcome. However, ours also has the problem
of a decreasing marriage rate, while the age at first marriage is
rising – from 24 for men and 22 for women in 1970 to 31 and 29

respectively in 2003, a seven-year shift in the marriage age over just three decades. Marriage is not the solution that people are seeking. As if a concession to this, the likelihood of cohabiting before marriage also rises with age of first marriage – from 19% and 23% for 20- to 24-year-old men and women respectively to 63% and 59% for 35- to 39-year olds.[23]

How should Christians respond to this trend? Should we encourage people to marry younger, or should church leaders suggest their congregations do so, as Paul recommended? If so, how do we keep those marriages together, given that very early marriage, particularly teenage marriage, increases the likelihood of divorce later?[24] And how do we tackle some of the practical issues that underlie the decision to postpone marriage – increased time in full-time education, student debt and lack of job stability? Some of these issues will be explored further in chapters 6 and 7. There may also be the natural desire for children which, for Christians, requires marriage first. Realistically, those who accept the biblical teaching of sex only within marriage might have to make that sacrifice: it may mean giving up the hope of a family. Are there ways of addressing this painful issue, too?

Loneliness in the church
Sex and marriage are not in principle God's answers to the problem of loneliness. 'If in our society the unmarried (or those who are not in what are revealingly called "relationships") do experience loneliness (as they undoubtedly do), we are not therefore to point their hopes inevitably in the direction of a sexual relationship, but rather to human relationships of friendship and fellowship. *This is a challenge to churches to be the kinds of loving communities in which real relationship is not coterminous with sexual relationship.*'[25]

It would have been unthinkable for Paul to have dealt with problems of loneliness with suggestions of marriage or romantic relationships. That would be to turn marriage into an idol. In fact, any evidence at all of loneliness would probably have led him to the conclusion that the church was failing miserably. Paul is clear in 1 Corinthians 7. Marriage is unnecessary in our Christian lives, though often desirable; right relationships with the Lord and other Christians are essential.

'Get up to anything interesting this weekend?' Carol asked when Rhian walked into the office on Monday morning.

'I moved house on Saturday,' she replied.

'In a day?' Carol was stunned. 'That must have been horrendous!'

'It wasn't too bad,' Rhian replied. 'Sixteen friends came over from church and helped, so it actually didn't take that long. It was kind of fun, actually. We did all the moving and cleaning and then ordered in pizza and everyone sat around on boxes eating and chatting.'

'Sixteen?!' said Carol, even more amazed. 'I don't think I even have that many friends – especially not ones who would give up a Saturday to help me move house.'

– Rhian, 27

In Acts 2:42–47, the picture we have of the early church seems to be something like a warm extended family. To enjoy the same kind of fellowship with and support from other Christians that we do with our closest friends and family is a great challenge for us today.[26] The popular saying that 'blood is thicker than water' expresses the priority that family relationships are felt to have over friendships and other relationships. But for Christians the water of baptism should be thicker than blood; Jesus himself prioritized relationships within the kingdom of God above those in his family (Mark 3:31–34).

What is intimacy?

Elaine Storkey defines intimacy in the following terms: 'At its most basic *intimacy is knowing that I am not alone in the universe.* But that *knowing* is not simply a cerebral process. It is something I experience, and live within; something which shapes my understanding and acceptance of reality . . . Intimacy is the sharing of closeness, of bonding, of reciprocation. It is the engulfing of warmth and care. It is the experiencing of *Another.'*[27] The effect of this experience of Another is to broaden our horizons, taking us out of our self-centredness and into the lives and experiences of others. It is a desire for authenticity, to know others as they really are, and to be known as we really are – without any of the barriers, masks and props people typically use to disguise their inner self in everyday life.

Intimacy 'includes the ability to experience an open, supportive tender relationship with another person, without fear of losing one's own Identity in the process of growing close'.[28] Although we discuss individualism at length in this book, it is important to stress that we do not mean that individual identity should be sacrificed for the good of the wider community. Stable individual identity is vital for strong relationships; intimacy with others is dependent on knowing who we are in our own right. Problems only arise when we emphasize individual identity at the expense of third parties – a harmful distortion and denial of the reality that we all exist within networks of relationships.

Your body needs to be held and to hold, to be touched and to touch. None of these needs is to be despised, denied, or repressed. But you have to keep searching for your body's deeper need, the need for genuine love. Every time you are able to go beyond the body's superficial desires for love, you are bringing your body home and moving toward integration and unity.

Henri Nouwen, priest and writer[29]

Intimacy is therefore fundamentally not about sex. Although sex should involve intimacy, and sex is designed to reinforce an intimate relationship, it is easy to confuse the two. Sex can be a symbol of intimacy, but like all symbols it can also be empty of meaning.[30] Many people look for sex thinking they will gain intimacy; although intimacy can be the result, sex does not automatically create intimacy, any more than intimacy need lead to sex. And where sex happens outside of intimacy, there is the risk of that vulnerability and openness being seriously abused.

Another type of intimacy that Storkey identifies – one which is part and parcel of our intimacy with others – is intimacy with the self. How well do we really know ourselves – who we are, what motivates and drives us? What kind of self-awareness do we have? Are we strong enough to be self-critical: to shine a spotlight on our own areas of weakness and pain, in the same way that we might view other people – or fear that other people might view us? As Socrates said, 'the unexamined life is not worth living', an idea reflected in the well-known aphorism, found everywhere from ancient Greek temples to the 1999 film *The Matrix*: Know Thyself.

If we do not know ourselves, how can we expect others to know us, or to understand our relationships with other people? If we are not at ease with ourselves – and low self-esteem is a huge problem in our isolating and reference-less world – will we really expect other people to like us?

If we do not truly know ourselves, are we willing to make the costly effort to do so? This may involve the painful process of think-ing about those aspects of ourselves we would rather not, perhaps discussing them with trusted friends, church leaders or a counsellor. Pain is unavoidable in life, but many people have a degree of pain in their histories that prevents them from finding true intimacy with others. Divorce, bereavement, loss of friends, abuse of all kinds, illness or addiction, or sometimes simply misguided or mistaken parenting and force of circumstance – all can cause deep wounds during our so-called formative years and beyond.

If we have never known true intimacy, or have experienced the hurt of separation and the disruption of intimacy, we may have powerful disincentives to forming intimate attachments as adults. We may not even know what intimacy looks like. The psychoanalyst Otto Rank called it 'refusing the loan of life, in order to avoid the debt of death'[31] – never taking the risk of getting too close to anyone because this brings with it the potential for painful rejection or sepa-ration. In doing so, we pass up Jesus' offer in John 10:10 of life in all its fullness for a safe but ultimately unsatisfying and perhaps even cowardly substitute. Rank's insight goes beyond Socrates' maxim and suggests that the unexamined life runs the risk of not being truly lived – experienced, engaged with and enjoyed to the full – at all.

This is the metaphor of Morpheus's red pill in *The Matrix*: the offer of insight and the opportunity to engage with the world as it really is, rather than living in the illusion of safe mediocrity. What is clear is that people today are desperately searching for intimacy – whether in casual sex, singles clubs, speed-dating, social networking websites and all the other ways we have come up with to try to deal with our culture's inherent loneliness and deficit in intimacy. Far fewer people actually know how to go about creating and fostering intimacy, or the reasons that stop them establishing deep relationships. And if we don't know what those reasons are, change becomes almost impossible.

'If you always do what you've always done, you always get what you've always got.' That wasn't quite how Sheila had put it, of course, but it pretty much summed things up. Chris had started seeing the counsellor six weeks earlier after he broke up with Lou, his third relationship to fail in as many years. But it wasn't just relationships with women where he struggled, he now realized. His friendships often felt superficial too, like he was just skating along the surface – going through the motions, meeting up, having fun, talking about fairly trivial things – but never allowing himself to be too vulnerable because then there was always the danger of getting hurt again. The problem was, if you weren't vulnerable with people, they usually didn't take the risk of being vulnerable back, and you never built up trust and never really got close to anyone. He hated the loneliness, but hadn't seen before now that the risks of intimacy had been scary enough to stop him from addressing that properly. It wasn't going to be an easy habit to change, but at least he knew what had been happening now.

Intimate singleness

The search for a romantic partner as an overriding goal and on its own terms often does intimacy and relationship (in the wider sense) few favours. 'A friend of mine in her twenties was plagued with thoughts of finding a partner,' recounts writer and broadcaster Anne Atkins. 'Every possible man was assessed as soon as she met him. This made true friendship with any man next to impossible. Those who were ineligible were dismissed as no good. Those who scored higher were only seen in terms of future partners, not cultivated as present friends. Again it was not until she freed herself from this attitude that she could enjoy the opposite sex. We are all tempted to do this, and it tends to cripple our chances of deep fellowship with either sex. I could have had far better boy and girl friends as a teenager if I had not been trying to pair myself off.'[32] It is an attitude which does not allow for contentment with present circumstances, and for the reality that singleness could actually last far longer than we might regard as desirable.

> *To adopt the frame of mind that you just have to be married . . . is to be a Titanic looking for an iceberg.*
>
> J. John, evangelist and author

Because our culture can be so isolating, we often do not have easy opportunities to build strong friendships. We typically work long hours, which makes demands on the rest of our time. Even at work itself, team-building exercises and social events notwithstanding, if there is a high turnover of staff it can be hard to get to know people. This can be the same at church, particularly if we are meeting in a large congregation only once a week. Under these conditions, close relationships usually do not happen, let alone thrive.

One issue is the quality of the communication and time spent with people. Paul's genuineness, openness and vulnerability is evident in the letters he writes, particularly in his second letter to the church at Corinth. Shared purpose and common interests are important, but only if they add to, rather than distract from, conversation. A common interest might be film, for example, but two hours spent in silence in front of the TV does little to advance relationship, unless it is followed by a conversation of some kind. The question of how to build closer relationships at church is discussed at greater length in chapter 6.

Although telephones, email, texts, instant messaging and social networking sites have given us many new ways of staying in touch with each other, none of these can be full substitutes for face-to-face meeting. Direct communication – open, honest and real conversation – is vital for relationships to grow. Only a fraction of information exchanged in a conversation is conveyed by the actual words themselves. Body language, tone of voice, eye-contact, facial expressions and many other non-verbal forms of expression make up the large amount of the message. All of these are lost in an email, and many in a phone message. Of course, we take this into account in our various communications; an email isn't a simple transcript of a conversation we might have in person, any more than this book is. Neither can we understand what someone is saying in a foreign language merely by observing their tone and body language. However, the fact remains that a vast amount of information is lost, or never provided, outside of face-to-face communication. The potential for misunderstanding is greater, and the likelihood of communicating with the detail, nuance and accuracy we might expect in person is greatly reduced – however many emoticons or 'smileys' we use online ;-).

A return to innocence

Sex-centred thinking, so firmly entrenched in our culture, is contrary to Christian culture and lifestyle. The Bible sees relationship in a more colourful, whole sense than we do now. Although sex and marriage are good, these are not the only or even the main solutions to the question of belonging and identity. The Bible points to a *dis*connection between love/relationship and sex that is not often heard today. None of this changes the fact that being single can be difficult and often lonely. But the church, especially those members of it who are married, has a responsibility to recognize the importance of non-sexual friendship. The challenge is to foster and promote those friendships for everyone, single or married.

Notes

1. For a detailed discussion of how the church interacts with cinema, see John Coffey's 'Engaging with cinema', *Cambridge Papers* 1 (1) (Jubilee Centre, March 1999). Available at <http://www.jubilee-centre.org>.
2. See, e.g. Tom Reichert, 'Sex in advertising research: A review of content, effects, and functions of sexual information in consumer advertising' in *Annual Review of Sex Research*, 2002. Available at <http://findarticles.com/p/articles/mi_qa3778/is_200201/ai_n9032366> (accessed 22 July 2008).
3. Around 7 million people (13% of the population) lived alone in England in 2006, four times more than in 1960 and almost a third of all households (Office of National Statistics). 'They consume 38% more products, 42% more packaging, 55% more electricity and 61% more gas per person than an individual in a four-person household.' Charlotte Moore, 'Solo living's eco threat', *Guardian Unlimited*, 1 August 2006. See <http://www.guardian.co.uk/environment/2006/aug/01/money.ethicalmoney> (accessed 22 July 2008).
4. At least, for white children. See 'Sexy Media Matter: Exposure to Sexual Content in Music, Movies, Television, and Magazines Predicts Black and White Adolescents' Sexual Behavior', *Pediatrics* 117 (4), 2006, pp. 1018–1027. Available at <http://pediatrics.aappublications.org/cgi/content/full/117/4/1018> (accessed 22 July 2008).
5. For example in Dan Brown's *The Da Vinci Code*, and a vast library of secondary literature.

6. C. S. Lewis, *The Four Loves* (Harvest Books, 1960).

7. Though *agapē* can also be used of intense, uncompromising devotion to something bad, e.g. the world in 1 John 2:15.

8. See Christopher Ash, *Marriage: Sex in the Service of God* (IVP, 2003), pp. 115–122.

9. Where this does occur, as with Isaac and Rebekah in Genesis 24:62–67, it is the exception rather than the hackneyed rule. The camels are also an original touch.

10. Cf. Ash, *Marriage*, pp. 116–119.

11. E.g. Tom Horner, *Jonathan Loved David: Homosexuality in Biblical Times* (Westminster Press, 1978). Oscar Wilde famously used them as an example of 'the love that dares not speak its name' in his defence during his trial for homosexual offences in 1895. A sexual relationship has also been suggested of Ruth and Naomi, and even of Daniel and Ashpenaz. In Ruth and Naomi's case, the friendship is all the more striking in that it spans the generations – Naomi is Ruth's mother-in-law. It also spans cultural boundaries: Naomi was an Israelite woman, whereas Ruth was from Moab, a country with which Israel had historically had a difficult relationship (see Deut. 23:3–6).

12. Robert Gagnon, *The Bible and Homosexual Practice* (Abingdon Press, 2001), pp. 146–154.

13. Brian Keenan, *An Evil Cradling* (Vintage, 1993), pp. 291–292.

14. J. John, *Marriage Works* (Authentic Publishing, 2002), pp. 78–79.

15. Cf. Bruce Winter, *After Paul Left Corinth* (Eerdmans, 2001).

16. Cicero once took a fortnight to make the 250-mile sea journey, but this was extreme (*Epistulae Ad Atticum*). It probably took only a few days under normal circumstances.

17. Tom Wright, *Paul for Everyone: 1 Corinthians* (SPCK, 2003), pp. 89–93.

18. Wendy Shalit, *A Return to Modesty: Discovering the Lost Virtue* (Free Press, 2000), p. 54, see pp. 49–57 for context.

19. Prudery itself is a word that has undergone an unfavourable change in meaning. It originates from a shortening of the Old French *prode femme*, meaning a worthy or respectable woman. By the time it came to England in the eighteenth century the word had taken on the meaning of being overly observant of decorum.

20. Anne Atkins, *Split Image* (Hodder and Stoughton, 1998), p. 179.

21. J. John, *Marriage Works*, pp. 146–147.

22. Michael Schluter and David Lee, *The R Option* (Relationships Foundation, 2003), p. 90.

23. ONS, *Social Trends* 31 (1996-99).

24. Other risk factors include premarital births; premarital conceptions/ short first birth intervals; premarital cohabitation; previous cohabitation with someone else prior to marriage; previous partnership breakdown; parental divorce; and poor economic circumstances. Lynda Clarke and Ann Berrington, 'Socio-Demographic Predictors of Divorce', in *High Divorce Rates: The State of the Evidence On Reasons and Remedies Volume 1* (Lord Chancellor's Department, 1999).

25. Ash, *Marriage*, p. 122, italics mine.

26. J. John, *Marriage Works*, p. 80.

27. Elaine Storkey, *The Search for Intimacy* (Hodder and Stoughton, 1995), p. 4, italics hers.

28. B.M. Newman and P.R. Newman, *Development Through Life: A Psychosocial Approach* (The Dorsay Press, 1984). Thanks to Sharon Willmer for this reference.

29. Henri Nouwen, *The Inner Voice of Love* (Dartman, Longman and Todd, 1997).

30. Kathleen Fisher and Thomas Hart, *Promises to Keep* (Triangle, 1992), p. 13.

31. See Irvin Yalom, *Love's Executioner* (Harper, 2000), p. 100.

32. Atkins, *Split Image*, p. 179.

4. RELATIONAL ORDER

Guidelines for a flourishing society

A man will leave his father and mother and be united to his wife, and they will become one flesh.

Genesis 2:24

When the Bolsheviki came into power in 1917 they regarded the family, like every other 'bourgeois' institution, with fierce hatred, and set out with a will to destroy it. 'To clear the family out of the accumulated dust of the ages we had to give it a good shakeup, and we did,' declared Madame Smidovich, a leading Communist and active participant in the recent discussion. So one of the first decrees of the Soviet Government abolished the term 'illegitimate children.' This was done simply by equalizing the legal status of all children, whether born in wedlock or out of it ... At the same time a law was passed which made divorce a matter of a few minutes, to be obtained at the request of either partner in a marriage. Chaos was the result. Men took to changing wives with the same zest which they displayed in the consumption of the recently restored forty-per-cent vodka.

'Some men have twenty wives, living a week with one, a month with another,' asserted an indignant woman delegate during the sessions of the

Tzik. '*They have children with all of them, and these children are thrown on the street for lack of support!'*

The peasant villages have perhaps suffered most from this revolution in sex relations. An epidemic of marriages and divorces broke out in the country districts. Peasants with a respectable married life of forty years and more behind them suddenly decided to leave their wives and remarry. Peasant boys looked upon marriage as an exciting game and changed wives with the change of seasons. It was not an unusual occurrence for a boy of twenty to have had three or four wives, or for a girl of the same age to have had three or four abortions.

– from *The Atlantic Monthly*, July 1926[1]

Relational order

In chapter 1 we briefly introduced the concept of 'relational order' – an idea that has enormous importance in our understanding of biblical sexual ethics. Relational order reflects the qualities of the relationships within the Trinity, in whose image our humanity is cast.

We recognize that the word 'order' could be misleading. It is worth reiterating that 'relational order' does not refer to a prescriptive pecking-order of relationships; 'order' here is not a synonym for a diktat or a rigid system of hierarchical relationships. We mean order as opposed to chaos. Any social animal will tend towards some kind of order – a group cannot remain a group if it is completely disordered. The question is therefore what kind of order we want. Is it survival of the fittest, rule of the strongest, or an order that also protects and includes the weaker members of the group? Relational order refers to the kind of stability and patterns of healthy human interaction that lead to the social harmony in which communities and individuals can thrive: this kind of 'order' is a life-giving concept.

Relational order is dependent on right relationships, both sexual and non-sexual. Sigmund Freud wrote that civilization is built on the renunciation of instinct,[2] and that chief amongst these is the sexual instinct. Social chaos therefore tends to result from sexual chaos. For example, it is no surprise that there is a direct correlation between family breakdown and crime levels. Proverbs also warns against the direct violence that often goes hand in hand with broken relationships: 'jealousy arouses a husband's fury, and he will show no mercy when he takes revenge' (Prov. 6:34).

> *Of the twenty-two civilizations that have appeared in history, nineteen of them collapsed when they reached the moral state the United States is in now.*
>
> Arnold Toynbee, historian

Other historians have noted the link between moral collapse, including sexual liberty, and cultural decline. J. D. Unwin studied 86 different societies spanning 5,000 years.[3] He found an unexpected and direct correlation between sexual restraint and 'expansive energy' – the ability of a civilization to grow and remain healthy. He concluded, 'In human records there is no instance of a society retaining its energy after a complete new generation has inherited a tradition which does not insist on pre-nuptial and post-nuptial continence.' Although we need to treat these opinions carefully, we can see from our own culture that when a society values sexual freedom so highly, the effect on the family is disastrous and can lead to society-wide tensions and the danger of eventual collapse – as in the case study of 1920s Russia at the beginning of this chapter.

Why is relational order important?

Relational order is fundamental because it enables relational support to be established. Aspects of this include promoting clarity – understanding who is related to who, and on what basis – and maintaining stability. Together, these factors ensure that we have adequate networks of supportive relationships, which are vital for our wellbeing.

Clarity

Key to the concept of relational order is the idea of roles and boundaries.[4] The question posed, at its most simple, is 'Who is responsible to whom, and on what basis?' Knowing whom we are dealing with – and who is involved with whom, and in what way

– impacts on a number of areas. To start with, it helps to establish our identity. Indeed, at the beginning of our lives, we have no awareness of an identity apart from the mother who gave birth to us and the family which nurtures us. As the child grows older, he or she learns autonomy and gradually forms a separate identity. Establishing this separate identity is an important prerequisite to forming intimate, trusting relationships.

This autonomy goes hand in hand with our emotional wellbeing. Autonomy means being able to contain our own emotions and anxiety, to develop to the point where we are not, like the young child, entirely dependent on another person for our peace of mind. It means becoming a separate person, behaviourally and financially as well as emotionally. Paradoxically, this is fostered by the kind of close relationships that encourage individuation within a safety-net of emotional closeness; learning who we are is a complex and difficult process which requires a safe environment. We need to know where we belong. Attachment is arguably the greatest human need and it is hugely important that we know who to attach to safely, whether as a child or later in life in our friendships and other relationships.

Physical safety is another aspect of the clarity that relational order brings. If a child is found playing in the street at midnight, we need to know who is responsible for him or her. One of the tragedies of our current situation of family breakdown and fluid partnerships is that this question cannot always be answered with certainty.

Although the effects of this question may be seen most strikingly in the family, where we learn our patterns for all later relationships, it is equally true across society as a whole. People need to know who it is they are dealing with, and on what basis. A family doesn't work if the father is acting like a child, any more than a school will work if the teachers take on the role of the pupils. In chapter 2 we used the case study of the parents of cohabitee, whose uncertainty around how to treat their son's girlfriend reflected the uncertainty of the cohabiting relationship. Marriage meant that the relationship was clarified and therefore changed, because they knew there was commitment. Boundaries are important; it is not a teacher's job to write a student's essay, nor a young child's responsibility to provide emotional and financial support for a parent, except perhaps in the most exceptional circumstances. This is not to say that people can never change roles; an IT technician could become a manager, or a pupil could eventually become a teacher. What is important is that there is clarity in the new role and that people act accordingly. Where there is relational order, the answers to questions of identity and boundaries are clear.

Stability

Another dimension to knowing who we are responsible to and for, and for what, is stability of relationships over time. As argued above, I am more secure – and therefore less anxious and happier – when I have clarity about my relationships. But I am also more secure if I know that the answer is going to be the same tomorrow, and the day after that, and next year. My wellbeing is likely to be greater if I know that the wife I have today is going to be the same wife I will have in twenty years time, if I will still have my job next month, and if my friends and relatives will still be there when I return from my summer holiday – provided I am happy with the respective relationships. Stability does not mean that these relationships never change and that I am stuck with any dissatisfaction I may have. It means that I have security within that relationship without the anxiety that it may collapse if I try to seek change – we will argue below (chapter 6) that growth is actually fundamental to long-term relationship. This stability is key to building trust, which typically requires some time to establish, and in guiding personality development, which best takes place within stable relationships. Without trust, our relationships tend to be superficial and self-centred; it is hard not to be selfish towards others when there is the risk they won't care about us (in return) for very long. Without personality development, we remain naïve and immature and cannot reach our full potential as human beings.

Together, clarity and stability in our relationships are the foundation of the support that we need to help nurture, facilitate and maintain our personal wellbeing. They are at the heart of relational order.

Relational order and biblical marriage

We turn now to consider briefly the ideal pattern for marriage set out in the opening chapters of the Bible. Amongst other concerns, Genesis 1 and 2 narrate God's vision for marriage; it is this definition of marriage that the remainder of the Bible seeks to affirm, protect, and re-establish amidst a broken humanity. At the outset it is useful to clarify that nowhere in Genesis chapters 1 and 2 is the word 'marriage' used. However, this text sets out the characteristics that constitute the ideal human sexual relationship.

> God created humankind in his image, in the image of God he created humankind, male and female he created them. God blessed them and God said to them, 'Be fruitful and increase, and rule over the earth and fill it.' (Gen. 1:27–28a, author's translation)

Genesis 1:27 states a staggering reality: human beings bear the image of their Creator. Both unity and diversity are evident here: the man and woman are same-but-different partners. Underpinning this is the inherent relationality of human beings, who bear the image of their relational Creator. Verse 28 spells out further what this blessing of male and female image-bearing includes. Human beings are to spread over the earth, filling it and ruling over it. So far, then, it is clear that human beings, male and female, are equally blessed and charged with God's creation mandate.

Genesis 2:18 introduces the only 'not good' of the creation story – the aloneness of the human creature ('ādām):

> The LORD God said, 'It is not good for the human to be alone; I will make a suitable counterpart for him.' (Author's translation)

A companion is sought amongst the animals and the birds, but no suitable creature is found, so God sets about creating one. The concise phrase 'ēzer kĕnegdô, translated above as 'suitable counterpart', describes God's intentions for male and female partnership. The usual translation of 'ēzer is 'help' or 'helper'. Despite the English overtones of 'assistant' or 'subordinate', the word places a far higher value on the helper. It is a term used elsewhere in the

Old Testament to speak of God. In Psalm 33:20 the psalmist's hope rests in 'YHWH, our *'ēzer*'; Exodus 18:4 records the name of Moses' son – 'Eliezer', 'God is my helper'.

The word *'ēzer* is further qualified by *kĕnegdō*, literally, 'like/ according to' (*kĕ*) 'opposite/corresponding to' (*negd*) 'it/him' (*ō*). The helper corresponds to – is like, is face to face with, is opposite to – the alone creature of Genesis 2:18. The two are complementary: pictured for us is a human being, who shares the imprint of God with, who is equal to, but who is different from the person described in Genesis 2:18.

Humans are relational because God is relational; our relationships image the relationships of the Trinity (see chapter 1). But there is more to it than this. In addition to the 'image of God' bestowing a general capacity to relate to others, there is something special about the male-female sexual relationship. The unity has a spiritual quality, as Paul argues in 1 Corinthians 6:12–20. What we do with our bodies – which are members of Christ and temples of the Holy Spirit – has spiritual and eternal significance.

The male-female nature of human sexual differentiation bears the imprint of the Trinity (Gen. 1:27). Sexual love is an image of the unity and love of the Trinity. It is also used as an image of Christ's unity with the church and his redeeming, self-giving love for creation.[5] 'For we are members of his body. "For this reason a man will leave his father and mother and be united to his wife, and the two will become one flesh." This is a profound mystery – but I am talking about Christ and the church' (Eph. 5:30–32). The body and sex are meant to proclaim God's mystery of love within the Trinity and for us. Needless to say, this 'profound mystery' is absent in our culture's approach to sex.

Complementary helpers

To 'complement' means to complete something that is not complete by itself. It does not mean that each 'side' is exactly the same. God's solution to the 'single human' problem was not to create another identical single human; this difference does not necessarily involve hierarchy, as both sides are equally necessary to make the useful whole. For the whole to work as one there is a shared identity between its two parts. In short, 'complementary' holds together the ideas of 'difference', 'similarity', 'mutuality' and 'equality'. The male-female relationship described in Genesis 1 – 2 is 'complementary' in this sense of the word.[6]

This image is continued and expanded in Genesis 2:23, where the man meets his *'ēzer kĕnegdō* or complementary helper:

> Then the man said, 'This one at last is bone of my bones, and flesh of my flesh. This one shall be called woman, for from man was she taken.' Therefore, a man will leave his father and his mother and cling to his wife, and they will become one flesh. The two of them were naked, the man and his wife, but they were not ashamed. (Gen. 2:23–25, author's translation)

Although God did not create Eve solely for the man's benefit, Adam's response suggests that he appreciated God's choice: 'bone of my bones and flesh of my flesh'. Essentially, this 'helper' allows the man to be fully human. Their joint humanity depends on both their similarities and differences.

'One flesh' (*bāśār 'echād*, Gen. 2:24) is another concise phrase that conveys several images. First, the sexual intimacy of this ideal relationship, this 'oneness', is a physical expression of the joy of this relationship, as well as the union necessary for the outworking of the creation mandate. While sexual intercourse involves or even creates 'one fleshness' (see Appendix #4–#5), Genesis 2 is clear that 'one flesh' is much more than sex. Sex must fit within the framework already set out, and even in Genesis 2:24 sex is properly placed within a committed relationship. The man will leave his family and 'cling' to the woman, forming a new family unit. The image of clinging is presented as an ongoing action; the commitment is an active, continuous choice of the one male and the one female to remain one flesh. The one flesh of Genesis 2:24 evokes the 'flesh of my flesh' of 2:23. The male-female *kĕnegdō* (complementarity) is a prerequisite of one flesh.

Living in our broken world, the ideal is difficult for human beings to attain. Rather than allowing our brokenness to determine our relationships, however, we must in God's grace seek healing and right relationships. Each person will struggle with the conditions of the Creation mandate in different ways – whether in its ongoing commitment, its exclusivity, or its inherent heterosexuality. As Christians, we must hold them all together, because to lose one is to opt out of the blessings of the Genesis ideal.

This still leaves the question of what the man needed a helper for. On reading the Creation narratives, many people assume that God created a second human being primarily because the first was lonely. But this is not the main point suggested by the biblical text. In fact, 'The Lord God took the man and put him in the Garden of Eden to work it and take care of it' (Gen. 2:15). While we should not overlook the importance of the companionship and intimacy found in marriage, the interpretation that the only reason the human being in Genesis 2 needed a partner was because he must have been lonely is typical of our over-sexualized society.

The woman was created to be a 'helper' to the man in their task of stewardship. Granted, 'it is not good for the man to be alone' (Gen. 2:18), and the Song of Songs and other biblical texts make it clear that there are relational benefits to erotic love, which is treated as a good gift. But the picture of Adam and Eve as joint stewards is a useful corrective to the idea that sex is primarily supposed to serve 'me' or even 'us': marriage is not supposed to be based solely on the companionship of the couple. In those terms, any reasons for marriage are moved into the sphere of the self and away from any idea of outward service.[7]

The relational good of marriage must be balanced with the job-related, outward-looking task of stewarding creation, which includes cultural and social as well as economic responsibilities. Marriage is not an end in itself but the means of continuing the creation process. The newly created family unit of Genesis 2:24 must not be detached from the commission to fill the earth and steward it. It is clear from the wording of the account of Adam having a son 'in his likeness, in his image' in Genesis 5:3 that procreation is explicitly intended to echo God's own act of creation in 1:26 and 5:1. Adam also takes part in the task of naming his son, as God had earlier named him, further linking the two roles:[8]

> And God said, 'Let us make man in our **image**, in our **likeness**.' (Gen. 1:26, author's translation)

> He made him in the **likeness** of God... And he *called their name 'man'*
> on the day he created them. (5:1b–2, author's translation)
>   Adam ... had a son in his **likeness**, in his **image**. And he *called his*
> *name 'Seth'*. (5:3, author's translation)

However, the church has often neglected the wider task of stewarding, or failed to set procreation within an appropriate framework, and so placed too much emphasis on childbearing – which causes confusion or stress for couples who cannot have children. In addition, Genesis' outward focus corrects the self-serving language of 'Mr and Miss Right'. The authenticity of a relationship is not based on what suits 'me' or 'us' best, but on our ongoing commitment to each other and to our created responsibilities.

Why marriage?

One of the clear purposes of marriage historically has been to ensure that children were brought up in as stable a family as possible. Because (in biblical times and until very recently) contraception was unreliable at best and often non-existent, it was important that sex took place within marriage: avoiding pregnancy could not be guaranteed. In the public consciousness, therefore, sex and childbearing were far more closely associated than they are today. Now, with (technically) reliable contraception, the popular understanding of sex tends to relate more to personal pleasure and quality of (inward-looking) relationship. The past view was arguably more holistic as it combined sex, relationship and possible childbirth, all within the context of marriage.

Studies consistently show that the biological family, with parents married, is the best setting in which to bring up children.[9] This stability arises from the nature of the marriage covenant, which is a legal agreement and a declaration of faithfulness. In comparison with cohabitation, it appears that this express commitment is a major factor in the stability of marriages – against the perceived wisdom that marriage is simply a 'piece of paper' and that having a family out of wedlock is likely to be just as successful as having one within marriage.

In terms of relational order, marriage plays a key role in mobilizing relational support, creating enduring networks of nurturing relationships. The promises of marriage reflect this aim both implicitly and explicitly. In the Anglican marriage service, for example, the families and friends of the bride and groom are asked if they will 'support and uphold them in their marriage now and in the years to come?' They are expected to answer, 'We will.' Needless to say, this public pledge of relational support by two extended families to the couple and their children is absent in the situation of an informal cohabitation. The role of family and friends in supporting the couple is at best unclear, and at worst non-existent. Again, the Russian example at the beginning of the chapter demonstrates what can happen when third parties lose their expectations of marriage.

The counter-argument goes something like, 'That's all very well and it's a nice ceremony for everyone, but saying "We will" is different from doing it.' However, the very nature of marriage facilitates this relational support – not simply by what it gets people to say, but by the structures it establishes in terms of family. Marriage is an exclusive sexual relationship between two people and is strongly connected with raising children and the creation of family. But it is also a joining of two wider families. It is a creation of one from two, both at an individual and corporate level. This union is witnessed by the wider community who, by their presence and assent, promise to support and uphold that union. There is no better way of resolving the issue of clarity we discussed earlier: who is responsible to whom, and for what.

Marriage is also intended to be a permanent relationship: a promise of stability. These two qualities, clarity and stability, mean that marriage is inherently designed to mobilize the relational support from the two extended families, as well from friends and the wider community. The fact that those present are asked to support the couple in so many words is an outward confirmation of the values that are built into the very nature of lifelong, exclusive marriage.

At this point it is worth making a brief digression into the community aspect of marriage. Quite simply, the declaration 'We will' by the congregation is incompatible with the mindset that says that my sexual choice is no one else's business. This understanding of sex as 'just my choice' has many consequences. Marriage has been undermined, with couples either choosing to divorce or never getting married in the first place. But also we should realize that many couples no longer recognize the importance of their own marriage vows. Neither do the friends, family and community who also pledged both to support and effectively police that marriage at the wedding service. We should consider the implications carefully next time we promise 'We will' at a friend or family member's wedding.

> *Gary brought the last of Jane's things in from the car. Fortunately, it had only been an overnight stay in hospital: 'just for observation', the doctor had said. Her blood pressure and pulse rate were back to normal now, but it had been a nasty scare when he'd needed to call the ambulance.*
>
> *Settling Jane on the settee with a cup of tea and a book, Gary's thoughts turned to his wife's grandparents. They had had plans to travel in their retirement, to see the world when it wasn't at war — which was the last time her grandfather had been overseas, serving with the navy. That was before her grandmother had got Parkinson's, twenty-five years ago. Now they were both in their 80s.*
>
> *Twenty-five years! That was nearly half their married life and almost as long as Gary had been alive, but neither of them had ever complained. He would have to take care of Jane for a few days or weeks. Howard had been caring for his wife for a quarter of a century. Gary wondered how he would handle that if it was him.*
>
> *It didn't matter, he realized. That was one of the reasons you got married: 'for better or worse, in sickness or in health'. Howard had made those promises sixty years earlier and stuck by them ever since. Otherwise, what was the point of promising in the first place?*
>
> – Gary, 30

Emotional poverty

That 'personal' sexual choices have consequences beyond ourselves is probably something that many of us have always recognized at some level, even if we have not considered how enormous and far-reaching those consequences are. The problem is that our culture shouts in a much louder voice that what consenting adults do in private is none of anyone else's business: this freedom to act as we want is an inalienable right. We hope that we have supplied enough evidence by now to prove beyond doubt that our culture has got it wrong. As a result, our society and families are witnessing what has been described as a 'never-ending carnival of human misery'.[10]

The extent of this misery was recently highlighted by the case of Shannon Matthews, a nine-year-old girl whose disappearance in February of 2008 sparked a major police investigation. She was found alive, more than three weeks later, hidden in the house of Michael Donovan, her mother's boyfriend's uncle. One of the most telling aspects of the story was the sheer confusion of family relationships. Her mother had seven children by five or six different men. Shannon had little contact with her biological father, who nevertheless lived close by. Her maternal grandparents have alleged that Shannon's mother – their daughter – was unfit to care for her, and that her boyfriend, Craig Meehan, was violent to the children. He denied this. He was later found guilty of possessing indecent images of children. Shannon's mother was arrested for child neglect and for perverting the course of justice. Craig Meehan's sister was arrested on suspicion of assisting an offender. Meehan's mother – Michael Donovan's sister – was also arrested on suspicion of perverting the course of justice.

Central to our idea of relational order is the question: 'Who is responsible to whom, and for what?' The chaos of relationships in the Matthews case means that this question is almost impossible to answer. This problem was picked up by the newspapers, which also commented on the 'emotional poverty' in which so many children are being raised – a new form of social deprivation, more insidious and arguably more serious than material poverty.

'[The Shannon Matthews' story] has revealed that what devastates the lives of modern children is something altogether much worse – inner poverty; poverty of the soul. Although clothed and fed, often with a parent or a stepparent in work, children in Shannon's world have to exist in a state of pervasive, low-level psychological chaos that is beyond the remedy of any social worker. There are no state palliatives for emotional neglect; or an endemic lack of emotional stability. There is absolutely no cure for the horrors of growing up with adults who exist in a state of permanent volatility . . . Their parents are not adults we would recognize as adults. The children do not come home from school to someone to ask them how their day was. Many are denied anything but fleeting attention, interest and stimulation. Many, furthermore, spend their lives trying to be invisible in order to cope with the adults in the house – hostile boyfriends; stressed, angry mothers. Any children's charity will tell you that the biggest threat to children comes from violent boyfriends and lovers; from mothers, in other words, who prioritize their own relationships over their children.'[11]

One of the awful facts of this situation is that it is not an isolated case. Although the disappearance and police investigation were extreme, the same emotional volatility and deprivation are not unusual, existing in many thousands of fractured households across the country. Amidst this ongoing chaos, stability, trust and reassurance are virtually impossible, as is learning the basic life skills that are essential for development and for the health of future relationships. All too often the problem is never solved, only handed on to the next generation.

The benefits of marriage and relational order

The biblical ideal for marriage is in stark contrast to the contemporary perception of sexual relationship in terms of personal fulfilment and inward-looking ends. Of course, this is not always the case; some cohabitations, for example, are stable and committed relationships that bear a strong resemblance to the ideal for marriage. Even in these cases, however, cohabitation usually falls short of the ideal because it does not publicly establish those qualities of clarity and stability. The effect that this has on relational order is all too evident. Single parents and cohabitees generally have less relational support. They tend to be economically poorer, and their children have worse social outcomes.[12]

Marriage, with its promises of permanence, stability and faithfulness, reinforces and promotes qualities that are intrinsically good for relational order. A household in which these qualities are evident is one in which mutual trust is shown and taught, and one in which children are given the skills and disposition to make healthy relationships of all kinds. In terms of roles and responsibilities,[13] it is a household in which there is security and little doubt of who is responsible to whom, and for what.

This is the kind of household in which children are brought up in safety and stability by parents who acknowledge and accept full responsibility for them – but where there is also maximum relational support from the extended family and community. It is one in which parents' care for children is reciprocated with respect, and in which this respect is manifested in care for the older generation as a normal and natural responsibility. There is an understanding that 'I' am not the centre of society, but that we have mutual responsibilities to care for relatives in need. It is the kind of household in which the faithfulness, commitment and kindness that others show us in our earliest relationships is reflected across all of our later relationships. It is one in which strong moral and spiritual development is encouraged, in which everyone recognizes the ways in which their decisions affect other people, and the ways in which everyone is dependent on everyone else. It is an inclusive community into which others are welcomed.

Ultimately, it is the pattern of a society at peace with itself.

'Ideal' marriage . . .

We stress that this kind of relational order is the outcome of strong marriages. Inevitably, there will always be some poor marriages in which these values are not demonstrated – just as there will be some strong cohabitations.

Even in our fallen world, though, it is still clear that marriage generally provides greater relational support for both couples and children, for the reasons we outline above. Marriage in our society is far from perfect; even so, it is demonstrably better for relational order than any of the alternatives. For example, within five years of the birth of a first child, 8% of marriages break up. In the case of those who have married after the child is born, this rises to 25% within five years. In the case of cohabitees, the figure is 52%.[14] It is to the relational damage of the alternatives to this biblical ideal that we now turn.

Notes

1. See <http://www.theatlantic.com/issues/26jul/russianwoman.htm> (accessed 17 July 2008).
2. See 'Future of an Illusion', in *Civilization, Society and Religions* (Penguin Freud Library, vol. 12, 1991).
3. See *Sex and Culture* (Oxford University Press, 1934), and *Hopousia* (G. Allen and Unwin, 1940).
4. See also chapter 1.
5. Robert Reymond, *A New Systematic Theology of the Christian Faith* (Thomas Nelson, 1998), pp. 736–39 has a useful survey of biblical texts on the believer's union with Christ.
6. 'Headship' issues are a separate debate which is not tackled here.
7. Martin Richards, 'The Companionship Trap', in C. Clulow (ed.), *Women, Men and Marriage* (Sheldon Press, 1995).
8. Christopher Ash, *Marriage: Sex in the Service of God* (IVP, 2003), p. 114.
9. E.g. Jill Kirby, *Broken Hearts: Family Decline and the Consequences for Society* (Centre for Policy Studies, 2002), available online at <http://www.cps.org.uk/cpsfile.asp?id=142> (accessed 22 July 2008).
10. Justice Coleridge, see 'Breakdown in families', *The Telegraph*, 7 April 2008.
11. Melanie Reid, 'Shannon Matthews is the new face of poverty', *The Times*, 17 March 2008.
12. See *Breakdown Britain* (Centre for Social Justice, 2006).
13. See Roles: who is responsible to whom, and for what?, chapter 1.
14. Kathleen Kiernan, 'Cohabitation in Western Europe' in *Population Trends 96* (ONS, 1999), pp. 25–32. See further at <http://www.2-in-2-1.com/university/publicbenefit/index2.html> (accessed 22 July 2008).

5. RELATIONAL DAMAGE

How sex outside of marriage disrupts community

Nothing is more noble, nothing more venerable than fidelity. Faithfulness and truth are the most sacred excellences and endowments of the human mind.

Marcus Tullius Cicero

It is horrible to be in a marriage where there is no mutual and permanent commitment. All the years of trust and security are destroyed in the moment you learn of your partner's unfaithfulness. You fear for yourself, and for your children, who are to be denied what every child needs and deserves — a secure, permanent, trustworthy family structure.

My husband Mark and I had worked abroad for a time. We returned home with three young children, and Mark began the difficult search for suitable employment. Used to being the big fish in a small pond, this was a particularly stressful time for him. He found suitable work some way from home; because the children were settled in school and church we decided that he would commute the thirty-mile trip.

I remember Mark's excitement when Sally was recruited, but I didn't think much more about her at the time. Not long after that his behaviour changed. He spent more and more time at work, working closely with

Sally. I became upset, feeling that I was being treated badly. Eventually I confronted him with what I presumed was an impossible option – that he was having an affair. As Christians I believed we were exempt from this 'kind of thing', but his eyes betrayed the devastating truth.

Mark admitted the affair with Sally but assured me that he would not leave me. However, he also stated that he loved her, would not leave her, and would not tolerate anything spoken against her! I was a mix of emotions. My over-riding feeling was sympathy – Mark was in such a mess, and I was convinced that together we could sort it out. I couldn't conceive of a future without 'us'. To protect our children I didn't tell them, figuring they didn't need to know about what I saw as a temporary situation. I was determined not to vilify Mark, as this would only make rebuilding our marriage more difficult.

It became evident that Mark had no intention of making, or owning any decisions, thereby forcing me to make 'our' final decision alone. The church's attempt to help Mark see the consequences of his actions, and ongoing indecision, failed. His family, who had always been extremely protective of Mark, increasingly left me out in the cold. This was an added blow, as I had been very close to them. Mark moved out, telling the children that his mounting workload required him to live nearer his job. Eventually, after much agonizing, I told the children the real reason for his leaving home.

The children hated the idea of their father moving out. We all relied on him to lead, and were emotionally very dependent upon him; we were scared of being left on our own. Mark would visit the children each Saturday; they would try to behave impeccably for him, each desperately vying for his much-desired attention. I sought to calm his anxieties, as he often was very loving towards me, and appeared genuinely confused.

In time I faced the decision of allowing my children to go away to visit their father. I couldn't conceive of them seeing him amidst his new family. However, supportive family, friends, a dedicated prayer group, and a loving church helped me to take the vital step of separating 'the children' from 'our marriage', preventing them being used as a bargaining chip.

Mark still insisted that he might come back, but I realized that he was too weak to make this, or any, decision. He couldn't see that he had already taken a decisive step, and continued in this chosen trajectory. One particularly painful memory was when he arrived unannounced to move back in, only to move out a month later, leaving even more pain and confusion in his wake. It was clear that he was looking for a way out that would absolve him from the consequences of his (their) actions.

Growing emotional and financial insecurities persuaded me to seek legal advice. The uncertainty was destroying me, but I remained adamantly anti-divorce, as divorce would exclude any possibility of reconciliation. A terse letter from Mark's solicitor banished all hope of his return.

Through God's grace I finally accepted that divorce was simply the legal recognition of our already broken marriage. Mark and I agreed to a visiting timetable for the children, to provide a structure for them, but the cracks were evident. They would return from their father's home withdrawn and argumentative. They remained very loyal to him; only much later did they share their hurtful experiences. They were thrust together with Sally's children; while my boys got to play with Mark, my daughter was left to fit in with Sally's girls. She in particular struggled to find her place, and to cope alone with the stressful and resentful dynamics. Mark and Sally's pursuit of absolute freedom trampled upon all in their way. Their marriage eventually fell apart following further affairs by both. Sally moved country; her own children have only a little contact with their mother and have expressed to my children their hatred of what she did to their and our family. The 'collateral damage' is impossible to quantify. However my children, although scarred, have thankfully grown up to rise above their experiences.

– Mary, 52

The 1960s and 70s saw sexual norms and standards redefined. Before the 60s, marriage without previous cohabitation was the general rule. Few couples lived together outside of marriage, and those that did were almost exclusively divorcees. Divorce itself was a comparatively rare event, and children were infrequently born out of wedlock. Same-sex intercourse was illegal until 1967.

Forty years later, the situation is very different. In England in 2000–02, 25% of the non-married population aged 16 to 59 were cohabiting. At the same time, the number of marriages dropped annually, from 352,000 in 1981 to 307,000 in 1991 and 249,000 in 2001, down 29% in just twenty years.[1] Public attitudes have followed this trend; what was once considered 'living in sin' is now actively encouraged on the grounds that 'testing compatibility' is wise. Divorce rose six-fold in the thirty years after 1961 and, although it has now begun to drop, this is largely due to the corresponding drop in the marriage rate. Nearly 2,000 civil partnerships were formed in December 2005, the month in which same-sex unions were legalized. Over 16,000 were formed the following year, though these dropped off to around 700 per month by the end of 2006 and the first half of 2007, after the 'backlog' cleared.

These many and various changes can be broadly summed up in the same concept: the separation of sex from relational order, which is fundamentally connected with family and 'traditional', biblical marriage. This separation, in turn, is an outworking of the individualism that has filtered through every aspect of life, including the sexual. More and more, we believe we are who we are on our own terms, and do not require any validation for our personal sexual choices in the form of formal marriage and community consent. Sex and family no longer go hand in hand – certainly not to the extent that they have throughout human history until fifty or so years ago.

As we stated in chapter 2, we would never argue that the sole purpose of sex is procreation. But in the past, the intimacy-reinforcing role of the sexual relationship tended to go hand in hand with creating a family. We now assume we can disconnect these two aspects of sex – as well as often focusing on sex as intimacy-building, rather than it taking place within an already intimate relationship. But separating sex from childbirth has all kinds of knock-on effects. It has promoted the convenience culture of abortion and raised the divorce rate – because many marriages were childless for some years, divorce therefore no longer affected the family in the same way, reducing the stigma attached. Of course, after the genie has firmly settled outside, returning it to the bottle becomes virtually impossible. Once cohabitation and divorce become socially acceptable and common, the informal social sanctions around having children outside of marriage and so leaving the child fatherless, or leaving a marriage that has children, is also reduced. Reliable contraception originally meant that divorce could take place with minimal damage, as those marriages did not yet have children. But the resulting shift in cultural attitudes now means that thousands more families suffer from that same damage, as married couples with children are more likely to divorce.

We argue in this chapter that what consenting adults do in private *does* affect other people. The case study at the beginning of the chapter is just one obvious example of 'private' choices causing extensive relational injury. Sex before marriage, cohabitation, adultery, divorce and same-sex intercourse all miss the ideal of biblical marriage, and in doing so they also tend to harm those directly involved and third parties in one way or another. Inevitably, that affects the shape of society and deeply impacts the lives of many individuals.

Sex before marriage

The church has traditionally been highly critical of sex before marriage (see Appendix #1–3), as it has of any form of sex outside of marriage. In recent years, with lower levels of commitment expected when couples have a sexual relationship, confused Christians of all denominations have begun to concede some ground in this area.

In *The Scandal of the Evangelical Conscience*, Ronald Sider highlights the depth of the problem in the US church with data from several national surveys carried out by respected statistician John Green. 'He divides those he labels evangelicals into two categories: traditional evangelicals (who have higher church attendance, a higher view of biblical authority, etc.) and nontraditional evangelicals. What are their attitudes on premarital and extramarital sex? Fully 26 percent of traditional evangelicals do *not* think premarital sex is wrong, and 46 percent of nontraditional evangelicals say it is morally ok . . . Of traditional evangelicals, 13 percent say it is ok for married persons to have sex with someone other than one's spouse. And 19 percent of nontraditional evangelicals say adultery is morally acceptable.'[2]

Who we are, what we do
Our cultural mindset suggests that we can compartmentalize our lives into the private realm of 'consenting adults', where anything goes so long as it doesn't hurt anyone else, and the public one in which we have to be a little more careful.

As we demonstrated at the start of this book, politicians like Boris Johnson, Ken Livingstone and Bill Clinton would argue that their personal lives are of no consequence to their public work: as far as we are concerned, we are supposed to view these two facets of them as different people. By contrast, in this book we argue that who we are in private is part of the same public persona the rest of the world sees; what we do when no one else is watching only reinforces that identity. If someone shows a tendency towards dishonesty or unfaithfulness in their sexual relationships, there is no reason to think that they might treat other relationships differently if they can get away with it. Our tendency towards compartmentalization suggests that we expect the answer 'No' to the question, 'If a tree falls over and there's no one there to hear it, does it still make a noise?' Or, in this case, 'If there are no witnesses, is there still a crime?'

The creation principle of 'one flesh' in Genesis 2, and the way that Jesus and Paul use it in the New Testament, logically imply that the biblical ideal for sex is between one man and one woman in a lifelong, exclusive relationship. Premarital sex is only one way in which this ideal is broken, but it is undoubtedly the most common.[3]

A promiscuous person is a person who is getting more sex than you are.
Victor Lownes, former executive of Playboy Enterprises

Promiscuity – repeatedly creating and destroying this one flesh bond – is a further parody and trivialization of the ideal. Although there is an idea in our collective cultural awareness about 'recreational sex' – consequence-and responsibility-free sex, solely for personal gratification – the reality is that promiscuity is damaging relationally and psychologically, both in the short and long term. There are obvious health risks: there were 790,000 diagnoses of STIs in the UK for 2005, up 60% in the last decade;[4] in 2007, half of all newly diagnosed infections (397,990) were in the 16–24 age group.[5] Furthermore, unwanted pregnancies (more than one in five conceptions ends in abortion, or around 193,000 terminations per year) show that casual sex is relationally harmful. It generally reduces sex to a selfish and inward-looking act intended only for 'individual' pleasure. 'Relationship' as a result is reduced increasingly to terms of sex and personal fulfilment.

This factor appears to be one reason why marriages are far more likely to fail when the couple have had previous sexual partners. Casual sex effectively rewards negative habits by basing a relationship on sex – something that provides little practice or incentive for working at solving conflicts and looking to the long term. Instead, there is a relational shallowness to this type of 'sex for pleasure', a tendency that is then carried across to other relationships – even those hoped to be more lasting. It is no coincidence that second and third cohabitations, like second and third marriages, are more likely to break up than the first. Rather than learning from past errors, mistakes are instead reinforced and become part of a person's way of approaching relationships. Put another way, breaking up and moving on ironically may not create a fresh opportunity to do things right. Instead, it generally lowers the standard for next time. That, of course, has consequences for the divorce rate and therefore for relational order. In addition, it undermines the meaningfulness of non-sexual relationship by placing undue emphasis on sex (see chapter 3).

Pornography

Pornography use lacks any relationship. Whilst that might initially suggest that it affects no one, this is manifestly untrue. Most obviously, of course, the people in the images themselves are affected, especially if there is any element of coercion. Even where full consent is given, there are still further third-party consequences.

> Pornography is the ultimate in individualist sexuality. No relationship
> is involved, no other human being to care about with real needs and
> longings. Nor can any disease be caught. It simply exists as an erotic
> visual aid for individual gratification. What is more, sex is reduced to
> an economic category. Pornography does not present sexual activity as
> having integrity in an intimate bonding, full of love and warmth. But
> it is displayed as a cheap commodity which can be bought and sold in
> ever more debasing and dehumanizing forms. The saddest thing is that
> pornography can never be a substitute for relating to another human
> being. It can only widen the loneliness.[6]

It is because pornography is a-relational that it is anti-relational. Like casual sex, the sex-without-relationship nature of pornography means that users become less able to engage in real relationships. 'Men who look at images of models find that afterwards they love their partner less, and feel less satisfied with their lot. If a man looks at a lot of pornography – in which women are essentially slaves – it interferes with their ability to sustain a real relationship. Pornography provides an escape for people who find it difficult to cope with intimacy, but the more they use it, the less they can relate to other people.'[7]

The practical reality of this was hinted at in an appendix to the *Breakdown Britain* report.[8] In a study by Divorce Online, conducted in 2003, around half of the 500 divorce petitions surveyed contained allegations of pornography use, inappropriate online relationships or 'cybersex'. Another study found that those who had had extramarital affairs were over three times more likely to have used internet pornography than those who had not, and that those who had paid for sex were almost four times more likely.[9]

The question arises, of course, of whether pornography use leads to broken relationships, or whether infidelity and use of pornography both stem from the same underlying approach to sexual relationship. Whatever the sequence of events, these factors surely reinforce each other. As Shalit argues, the pornographic society is one in which fidelity is abnormal.[10]

Cohabitation

Marriage is an important social good, associated with an impressively broad array of positive outcomes for children and adults alike . . . economic, health, educational, and safety benefits that help local, state, and federal governments serve the common good.[11]

Institute for American Values

The poverty report *Breakdown Britain* quantified what had long been suspected: that family breakdown creates an 'underclass' left behind by the rest of society, giving rise to further breakdown and further subsequent social deprivation. The divorce rate is high, but has remained relatively constant for the last twenty years and (at least in this area) is a relatively minor concern. The fastest-growing problem in terms of break-up is that of cohabiting parents. In 1980, 12% of children were born out of wedlock. In 2004, the figure had risen to 42%.[12] Half of these cohabiting parents will split up before the child is five years old, in contrast to one in twelve married parents.

Popular misconceptions about cohabitation

Living together is often seen as a sensible option, especially as a possible prelude to marriage.[13] The idea behind this is to treat cohabitation as a 'trial marriage' in order to determine whether the couple are suitable for a permanent commitment. In many cases, cohabitation is seen as a step along the way to marriage. For example, in around three-quarters of marriages, the couples now register from the same address; couples are likely to begin living together when they get engaged, if not before.

This idea of trial marriage seems to have good sense behind it: surely it is smart to live together for a while to gauge sexual and relational compatibility before 'risking' marriage – and therefore perhaps also a messy, expensive and painful separation? In an age when divorce rates are said to be running around the 40% mark, and nearer 50% in the US, cohabitation seems to offer the opportunity to go into the situation with your eyes wide open.

In fact, this is oddly not the case. Evidence shows that cohabitation does not increase the chance of a successful marriage, or reduce the chances of divorce: quite the opposite. All else being equal, *any* kind of cohabiting relationship is less stable than marriage in a similar situation – for any given age, state of pregnancy, number of children, or economic circumstances. Even couples whose cohabitations progress to marriage are significantly more likely to divorce – perhaps up to 50% more.[14] Successful marriage among cohabitees is most likely for those whose first cohabitation ends in marriage, though some surveys have suggested that their chances are still worse than those who have never lived together before marriage; after the first one, later cohabitations are progressively less likely to succeed.[15]

Many people talk of cohabitation as a close approximation to marriage, or claim that they don't require a marriage licence to legitimate living together. In reality, the ideal of cohabitation as an arrangement equal in status to marriage is a myth; cohabitation is almost always short-lived. In many cases, marriage appears to be a goal after all – for at least one of the couple. It is difficult to gain an accurate picture of the immediate situation because a sample population has to be followed over a relatively long period before final outcomes can be assessed. However, past surveys have shown that half of all cohabitations in the UK last under two years, ending either in separation or marriage, and just 4% last for ten years.[16] On their own terms – when they are not a prelude to marriage – cohabitations are around four times more likely to break down than marriages: about 18% last ten years.[17]

A piece of paper?

It could be argued that these results – particularly concerning the relative lifespans of cohabitation and marriage – are only to be expected. After all, many couples claim the reason for living together is to try out a 'marriage-like' arrangement in order to determine whether they are compatible and ready for the real thing. On these grounds, parting ways is as much a 'success' as getting married: the cohabitation has met its avowed aim. And there are many different types of cohabitation, from casual relationships of convenience to the most committed couples.

However, there appears to be more to it than this. The evidence suggests that the lower level of commitment becomes a habit: it actually serves as bad practice for later relationships. This is supported by the fact that prior cohabitation and particularly repeated cohabitations appear to be a specific risk factor for divorce.[18] Demographer Linda Waite summarizes: 'Cohabiting changes attitudes to a more individualistic, less relationship-oriented viewpoint. Live-ins become less committed to marriage and that affects the quality of their married life later.'[19] Cohabitation rewards a shallower form of relationship which is then typically carried across into marriage.

Apart from the relative stabilities of cohabitation and marriage, surveys have consistently shown significant differences in terms of health, wealth and happiness. Once again, the selection factor is partly to explain; simplistically, those from broken homes are more likely to be cynical of marriage, and those with lower incomes are more likely to avoid the cost of a wedding. But, as before, there is more to it than this: cohabitation itself is part of the problem.

One counter-argument to this is that the couples who cohabit before marriage are typically more likely to break up anyway; they may be more individualistic, risk-taking, 'Bohemian', or perhaps simply do not expect relationships to last in the first place. Therefore, any subsequent divorce would be a result of these pre-existing factors, not caused by the cohabitation itself. However, the sheer number of people now cohabiting, and the rise in the divorce rate, suggests otherwise. This explanation does not take into account the way that couples are influenced by the prevailing cultural trends; it also assumes that the cohabiting period – which may last months or years – has no effect on the couple's approach to their subsequent relationship.

Typically, cohabitations are based on sexual and economic grounds and tend to bypass the long-term commitment aim of marriage. In many cases, the cohabitation is preferred precisely because of the uncertainty of the relationship: 'If it may not work in the long term, it would be better not to get married. But right now, living together is better than being apart.' Even when a couple moves in together as an alternative to, not trial for, marriage, the ethos and very 'strength' of the arrangement is that it can be dissolved easily at any time. Cohabitation is frequently marked by an intrinsic uncertainty, especially where it is a 'trial' marriage, and this has consequences for its stability and overall health. Despite sharing a living space and sleeping together, each partner knows that the other can leave with a minimum of inconvenience. Keeping that in the back of the mind does nothing for a relationship's long-term prospects. Couples often go into a cohabitation to practise for the commitment of marriage; in reality, what they are practising is lack of firm commitment. Genuine commitment changes the tone of the relationship: faithfulness is a fundamental good that has positive effects on marriage.

Knowing there is a greater possibility of break-up, cohabitees have a vested interest in keeping things simple and so tend to live life more like two singles. Possessions are thought of in terms of 'mine' and 'yours', not 'ours'; those living together are less likely to feel responsible for supporting a partner economically; awkward or long-term subjects may be avoided – partly because of the awareness that the relationship is provisional and that this might be presumptuous or offensive. So the ability to leave easily can become a self-fulfilling prophecy.

The commitment factor

The popular understanding of marriage as a 'piece of paper' is understandable. After all, marriages do break up all too often, and what often distinguishes the successful ones is the commitment to the relationship. This commitment can sometimes be a feature of cohabitations, too – at least a few of which appear to be similar to stable, long-term marriages.

'Marriage' in the Bible is difficult to understand, mainly because there is little information about it. It was apparently arranged between families on a personal level, rather than being registered centrally as it is today. A concern for a 'proper' wedding, either in church or a registry office, is relatively recent. In medieval Europe, for example, a marriage could be contracted without a ceremony or witnesses, if the couple simply promised to each other that they were married. The community enforced the man's responsibilities, particularly in the case of pregnancy.[20]

But marriage must be a public commitment between the couple. Even if the ceremony itself might be private, as in medieval Europe, the man and woman still openly lived together as a married couple. Part of marriage's success is down to the public recognition of the union, and the fact that the legal commitment requires the effort of a legal dissolution before the partners can fully go their separate ways. However, another aspect of the success of marriage over cohabitation is probably down to the selection factor: those couples in committed relationships are more likely to show their commitment by getting married. Alongside raising the marriage rate, then, there is the question of how to foster emotional maturation and committed relationships – encouraging people both to develop the skills and to enter the setting that best enable fulfilling, long-term partnerships. These issues are covered in chapter 7.

Adultery

*My message to businessmen of this country when they go abroad on business is that
there is one thing above all they can take with them to stop them catching AIDS, and
that is the wife.*

Edwina Currie, former Conservative MP[21]

As far as the Old Testament is concerned, adultery is the archetypal
sexual sin. It appears in both versions of the Ten Commandments
in brief, stark and uncompromising form: 'You shall not commit
adultery' (Exod. 20:14; Deut. 5:18). Its position in Leviticus 20:10,
incurring the death penalty and introducing the other sexual
offences, indicates its fundamental importance as a crime against
both God and other human beings.

From another perspective, Proverbs criticizes the adulterer for
his lack of sense. The Wisdom tradition is not concerned primarily
with righteousness in terms of the Law, but with sound advice for
a godly, successful and content life. Proverbs chapters 5 to 7 hold
up the adulterer as the paragon of foolishness, and contrast the
adulteress with the personification of wisdom in Proverbs 8. The
adulterer leaves the 'wife of his youth', spending time, money and
effort on unjust and often trivial relationships at the expense of
his own family, not to mention risking the husband's anger (Prov.
6:30–35).

Faithfulness, a fundamental good
Throughout the Bible, adultery and prostitution[22] are consistently
paralleled with idolatry. That is to say, not only is adultery used as
a *metaphor* for worshipping other gods (sometimes quite graphically
and extensively, as in the Ezekiel 16 allegory of Jerusalem running
after other gods as a prostitute pursues her clients) but, more
fundamentally, sexual sin and idolatry *by nature* tend to go hand in
hand. Part of the reason for this is because many of Israel's neighbours were engaged in the worship of fertility gods and goddesses,
and a significant aspect of these cults was sacred prostitution. In
1 Kings 14:22–24 or Hosea 4, for example, adultery and idolatry
are quite literally committed in the same act.

But there is more to it than this. In Leviticus 20, the connection is made more obliquely; the list of sexual offences is introduced by idolatry, of a type that probably did not involve prostitution – though child sacrifice still places Molech worship in the common context of sin against the family. Even consulting mediums and spiritists (20:6) – again, almost certainly non-sexual in nature – is called 'prostitution'.

Adultery is a 'sin against God' as well a spouse or any other human, as is made clear by Joseph's description of his potential adultery with Potiphar's wife in Genesis 39:8–9. Marital faithfulness excludes sexual rivals, as our faithfulness to God should exclude religious rivals. Faithfulness is one of the characteristics of God, and it is unthinkable that we should try to emulate this good characteristic in our relationship with him but discard its importance in our sexual relationships. To put it another way, the God-like quality of faithfulness is *always* good. It is unrealistic to think that someone could be unfaithful in one area of life, and this character trait might then be absent in another – public or private. The 'vice lists' of Ezekiel 18 make no distinction between what we would now understand as public and private offences – a compromised morality is compromised, regardless of whether anyone actually discovers it. Adultery and idolatry are different manifestations of unfaithfulness; anecdotally, we often see the connection in the number of young people who turn away from their faith when it starts to conflict with newly found sexual relationships.

In his book on marriage, Christopher Ash explores the theological characteristics of adultery, bearing in mind the frequent sexual/religious overlap of the biblical metaphors.[23] Adultery is a turning away from a pledge: an abandonment of someone we have promised ourselves to. Its aberration is in this broken promise. 'Although it might seem (and often does in people's hopes) to be a turning away from one partner *to* one other partner, nevertheless because it is fundamentally a turning *from* rather than a turning *to*, it introduces into life not a replacement loyalty so much as a terrible plurality, instability and dissipation.' Adultery is inherently secretive, with a tendency towards deceit; 'marriage is inherently a public institution, so adultery is addictively private.' Adultery is self-destructive, compromising an individual's moral integrity. Its 'inherent dynamic towards self justification' inevitably impacts the individual's wider character and sexual attitudes. Lastly, it is destructive to others – to husbands and wives, and especially children (see Mary's story at the beginning of this chapter). On a wider canvas, it is deeply damaging to society, as evidenced by its contribution to the high divorce rate and the ongoing consequences for families of the original marriage.

> *Marriage has a unique place because it speaks of an absolute faithfulness, a covenant between radically different persons, male and female; and so it echoes the absolute covenant of God with his chosen, a covenant between radically different partners.*
>
> Rowan Williams, Archbishop of Canterbury

Adultery is a violation of the creation principle of one man, one woman in exclusive, lifelong union. Faithfulness in this relationship is a fundamental good: the covenant promise is what gives marriage its relative stability over cohabitation. Adultery robs marriage of this stabilizing factor and is a major cause of divorce.[24] Even where the marriage does not break down, there are often significant and long-term tensions in the family as a result. Adultery undervalues sexual relationships and overvalues the individual, at the expense of the covenant marriage relationship and the family.

Divorce

> *'I hate divorce,' says the Lord God of Israel, 'and I hate a man's covering himself with violence as well as with his garment,' says the Lord Almighty.*
>
> Malachi 2:16

In some ways, it might seem strange to include divorce here. After all, we are addressing different types of sexual relationships in this section, and divorce is not a sexual relationship. It may be the result of an extramarital affair, but adultery is by no means necessary for divorce to occur.

We have stated earlier that sex is a symptom, as well as a cause, of social problems – in the same way that sexual behaviour can be an indicator of a healthy society as well as contributing towards it. The root cause is the lack of intimacy fostered by high mobility and fractured family relationships. We expect to fill this relational gap with sex. But ours is an individualistic, materialistic and con-sumeristic society, and we have imported these attitudes into our sexual relationships. The problem is circular: lack of intimacy encourages sex without stable relationship, and sex without stable relationship further undermines our capacity for intimacy.

Divorce fits into this downward spiral as both cause and effect. Divorce is one of the major factors that has damaged relational order and left our culture lacking in supportive family relation-ships. It therefore contributes to the lack of intimacy that many people believe they can fix with sex. However, individualistic attitudes towards sex and marriage inevitably lead to high divorce rates, because they are inherently self-centred. Me-centred, iWorld relationships are incompatible with lifelong, faithful marriage.

Relational order is a prerequisite for healthy relationships, and faithful marriage is a prerequisite for relational order. Divorce undermines relational order and leads to much of the sexual and relational brokenness that caused it in the first place.

Biblical divorce

An often-quoted statistic is that 40% of UK marriages end in divorce – 50% in the US.[25] Sadly, in the US this is just as true within some parts of the church as it is outside, and perhaps even more so.[26] This is in spite of clear teaching by Jesus about the nature of marriage and divorce: 'Therefore what God has joined together, let man not separate' (Matt. 19:6). It is inconsistent for the church to be up in arms about homosexuality (for example) without addressing this striking trend for heterosexuals to divorce and practise sex outside of marriage.

Although the Law of Moses permits divorce, this was intended only as a concession (see Appendix #7–13 for background). 'Moses permitted you to divorce your wives because your hearts were hard. But it was not this way from the beginning' (Matt. 19:8). Divorce, like polygamy and slavery, was allowed by God in the Old Testament, though very much as a second-best option, and for a limited number of reasons. In the New Testament, Jesus makes it clear that divorce is against God's will (see Appendix #9).

Biblical divorce was always expected to be fault-based (Appendix

#8). In recent reforms, fault has been all but removed as a basis for divorce. The changes were made because of the difficulties of establishing who was at fault and the burden of proof. For example, was it the partner who was caught committing adultery, or the one whose years of unproven neglect undermined the marriage to this point? Fault-based divorce is messy and expensive. But no-fault divorce destroys marriage before it even starts by undermining the significance and accountability of each person's vows.

Generation 'ex'

For centuries, marriage was considered a sacrament by the church and divorce was practically forbidden – although there were provisions to 'annul' a marriage, which could be exploited to greater or lesser extent to the same ends. Once the Protestant church separated from Rome, divorce was permitted in increasing degrees.

Since 1961 divorce has risen six-fold. In 2004, the divorce rate was 14 per 1,000 marriages per year. It has been suggested that one reason for this rise seems to be the increase in lifespan. A typical 30-year-old marrying today might reasonably hope to spend 50 or 60 years with a new partner before death does them part. A hundred years ago, life expectancy at birth was less than half what it is now, although high infant mortality rates meant that anyone surviving early childhood had a better prospect. All the same, the average couple could expect only a fraction of the time together that we might today, especially as death in childbirth was so common. This has led some critics to suggest that the high divorce rate simply reflects the number of couples now living long enough to grow tired of each other. Social historian Lawrence Stone called the trend for divorce 'little more than a functional substitute for death'. However, the chance of divorce increases during the first few years of marriage to a peak after around just four years, gradually declining after that. The majority of divorces happen to couples married less than 15 years,[27] suggesting that the longevity of a marriage is not the problem.

Remarriage

The issue of remarriage is a difficult one.[28] Taken at face value, Jesus' statement in Matthew 19 suggests that only sexual immorality is grounds for divorce, and that *both* of the couple commit adultery if they divorce and remarry for any other reason. This effectively means that a woman whose husband leaves her against her will after twenty years of marriage, seeking a unilateral divorce which she is unable to contest, is prevented from remarrying as this would be adultery – assuming the husband had not himself committed adultery. The suggestion is that the conditions of the marriage bond hold, even after the divorce formally dissolves the union. To the modern mind (and probably to the ancient one, too) this seems terribly unfair. The woman would be denied another marriage due to a situation beyond her control. In the light of the complexities of the biblical texts – not to mention the painful realities of relationship breakdown – it is insensitive to be prescriptive about divorce and remarriage. The full biblical picture suggests that a case-by-case approach is required (see Appendix #8–13).

What can be said is that the easier divorce is, the less incentive there is for couples to work out their differences. No-fault legislation makes divorce a first stop, not a last-ditch solution. Divorce has to be obtainable, but the sheer ease with which a couple can currently dissolve a union brings the stability of marriage increasingly into line with that of cohabitation: a potentially low-commitment relationship that can be exited with a minimum of effort.

Same-sex intercourse

I always start my talks on sexuality by stating that we are on opposite sides of the fence but we need not caricature each other. Not all Christians are Fred Phelps (the independent pastor well known for his hatemongering towards homosexuals). And not all gays wear dog collars, march in gay pride parades and have hundreds of sexual partners each year. My aim is to bring us closer to the fence so we can talk face to face rather than from the distance of a cultural divide.

Mario Bergner[29]

Seeing the wood for the trees

Before we look at some of the third-party impacts of same-sex relationships – many of which are broadly similar to the impact of heterosexual relationships outside of marriage – we first need to make sure we are able to deal with the issue fairly and on its own terms. This is not as easy as it sounds. Dialogue between some conservative Christians and some parts of the gay community has been characterized by intense dispute and antagonism. What is more, the outside world views both groups as minorities, which means that they struggle to legitimate their views to each other as well as to wider society.

The upshot of this is that the focus of the whole argument has been shifted away from rational debate and is instead framed in terms of discrimination, prejudice and, increasingly, accusations of hate crime.[30] If nothing else, this book will have advanced dialogue if it tilts the argument back towards a level playing field and encourages open and rational discussion.

Pride and prejudice

While its current status as the church's number one hot potato lends immediacy and relevance to the gay debate, there is another side to the apparent bias towards same-sex attraction as the favoured discussion topic in terms of sexual practice. The fact is that other perceived sexual sins do not get the same press – despite the fact that they are surely more common, both in the church and the wider community.

> *I am reminded of a colleague who reiterated, 'all my homosexual patients are quite sick' – to which I finally replied, 'so are all my heterosexual patients'.*
>
> Ernest van den Haag, psychotherapist

Biblically, homosexual sin is regarded as no worse than any kind of heterosexual sin. This is clear from the lists of offences in both Old and New Testaments, which always place homosexual practices alongside heterosexual sins. Yet it is frequently treated as worse by Christians today, if only in the sheer proportion of discussion time it receives. Promiscuity among heterosexuals tends to be ignored in a way that homosexual promiscuity – or homosexual monogamy – is not. Adultery, both within the church and outside it, almost certainly causes far greater relational injury – damage to relationships with God and other people – than same-sex

partnerships. Given that only a small percentage of the total population identify themselves as gay/lesbian,[31] why are we not more
concerned about the far greater number of straight churchgoers in
terms of cohabitation, premarital sex, adultery and divorce?

Morality is simply the attitude we adopt towards people whom we personally dislike.
Oscar Wilde

Many people have immediate, instinctive and strong reactions to
certain situations. This, of course, is the origin of the word 'prejudice': to pre-judge something, to have a preconceived idea about it
before engaging with the reality. In more recent years, 'prejudice'
has come to be used particularly in terms of civil rights; to be
prejudiced typically means pre-judging a person on the basis of,
for example, their gender, age, (dis)ability, race or skin colour. The
evil of this kind of thinking is that it can lead to individuals being
unfairly denied certain rights, privileges or benefits: not on the
basis of balanced information but on that of a one-dimensional
caricature. All too often, this prejudice is accompanied by a post-
hoc justification – a rationalization of the pre-existing bias.

The sad fact is that, when it comes to the debate raging around
the subject of homosexuality, many people are capable of display-
ing this kind of prejudice. The 'conservative' side is frequently
guilty of speaking from instinct and justifying their pre-existing
arguments, without allowing questioning of the presuppositions
themselves. '. . . Christians have often responded to the issue
of homosexuality from fear and prejudice, rather than with the
understanding, graciousness and compassion of Christ.'[32]

*I don't think gay people should defend pushing everyone who disagrees with them into
a homophobic corner. That's like me saying because I'm black anybody who disagrees
with me must be racist.*
Joel Edwards, general director of the Evangelical Alliance

But Christians and the socially conservative are not the only ones
guilty of overreaction. In part owing to this lack of intellectual
honesty, but also in the interests of their own agenda, gay rights
proponents are equally capable of jumping to the conclusion that

anyone who disagrees with their beliefs and lifestyle is prejudiced. The situation has now come to the stage that many people are legitimately concerned about 'Christophobia'. 'What we are now faced with is not equality but a hierarchy of equalities,' writes Christian MP, Ann Widdecombe. 'When any human right comes up against homosexual rights the latter must always win. The human right to express a religious or conscientious view or to hear religious teaching must give way to a homosexual's right never to feel offended.'[33]

A biblical theology of the body

In chapter 4 we explored the idea that God created humanity male and female in his own image, that of the Trinity (Gen. 1:27). In his *Theology of the Body*, Pope John Paul II argues that the union of male and female in sex is a reflection of God's Tri-unity, and that the union of Christ with the church (Eph. 5:31–32) is symbolized in our unity with Christ.[34]

From a Catholic perspective, unity with Christ occurs in the Eucharist; most other Christians generally understand unity with Christ as occurring through faith. John 17:21–23 compares the believer's unity, both with others in the church and with the Trinity, to the unity within the Trinity itself. If sex and sexual difference in the creation narrative are pictures of the Trinity and of communion with God, then this suggests that there is a profound significance to heterosexual marriage. Same-sex intercourse – like the temporary union of casual sex – is a distortion of that relationship and of the image of the Trinity that God, in his love, has built into humans. This understanding of our very sexual identities imaging God's own nature lies at the heart of the Christian theology of sexuality.

It follows that Scripture should be remarkably consistent about homosexual practice, as is indeed the case (see Appendix #14–20). Its contexts in Old and New Testament offence-lists alike are unambiguous, and there is no strong hermeneutical argument for discarding homosexuality alone from these lists.[35] If homosexual sex is accepted, other barriers have to fall too. Commentators usually have to resort to some form of textual gymnastics, or an unconvincing appeal to other 'compromises' the church has made, to look for biblical endorsement of same-sex practices.

The Bible contains six admonishments to homosexuals and 362 admonishments to heterosexuals. That doesn't mean that God doesn't love heterosexuals. It's just that they need more supervision.

Lynn Lavner, comedian and musician

If the church is to remain true to the Bible, it has to engage with the often awkward reality of what it says, both on superficial and more critical readings. This is just as true of divorce, promiscuity and premarital sex – not to mention materialism, pride, anger, giving to the poor and loving our neighbour – as it is of homosexuality. There will be many Christians who experience same-sex attraction who find this challenging, as there will be Christians who are divorced (or experiencing marital problems and considering separation), unmarried and sexually active (or wondering whether to be), wealthy and concerned about the relative influences of God and money in their lives, angry and unwilling to forgive, and many others who find the Bible's teaching in various areas difficult. Although careful interpretation of Scripture is the first step in order to understand exactly what the Bible really has to say about various areas of Christian life, what offends and upsets many people is not just the 'what', but the 'how'. In other words, the church's pastoral approach – to homosexuality in particular – is crucial.

Orientation or attraction?

One of the major reasons why the gay debate is being fought so fiercely is that it apparently involves issues of identity. Because being gay is seen as part of a core identity – which, like race, cannot be altered – it is argued that to discriminate on the grounds of sexuality is unfair. It is seen to concern not only what people do, but who they are. Some people have gone so far as to suggest that being gay is innate, inborn and unchangeable, perhaps even a genetic characteristic like hair or eye colour.

In fact, research has repeatedly failed to verify the existence of a 'gay gene'. Broad surveys of the scientific literature suggest that same-sex attraction is only possibly, and then only in part, due to genetic factors. Hormonal, psychological, cultural and behavioural influences are far more important, and play a different part in each individual case.[36]

One point to draw from this is that sexuality – hetero-, homo-, bi- or any other form – is far more complicated than most people assume. There are many complex and interwoven factors that appear to determine a person's sexual behaviour. In this respect it is more accurate to speak about homosexualit*ies*, rather than one uniform 'homosexuality'. The factors that draw a person to a same-sex attraction may be very different, even if the end result superficially looks the same. In the same way, the strength of those attractions, how fundamental they are and how easy they are to change, vary enormously. One writer uses the analogy of a basketball player to examine the different influences that go into making up a person's sexuality – or any behavioural trait.[37] There may be a genetic component, but there is no such thing as a 'basketball gene'. Instead, someone might have a physique – tall, muscular – that means, given the right conditions, they might be good at basketball. It does not force them to play basketball, although it might point them in that direction.

The complexity and often fluidity of sexual identity calls into question the use of 'rights' language. There may be some individuals for whom sexuality is a fixed and unchangeable identity that they have experienced from a relatively young age; equally, there are others who change their sexuality and who would not want to be pigeonholed as gay, straight, bi, or anything else.

'Gay', 'straight' and other terms referring to 'sexual orientation' are part of our cultural vocabulary. Although these are a useful shorthand for describing sexual attraction and are hard to avoid, there is an unhelpful implication that sexual 'identity' is part of our core being – that sexuality somehow defines us as humans. This is part of the same tendency towards over-sexualization that was discussed in chapter 3. We are not defined by our sexual attractions: we are defined by our relationship with God. Although we are sexual beings, how we express this is only one small aspect of what it means to be made in God's image.

Further, if sexuality is not an orientation, then there is less of a case to treat it as a rights issue – although obviously the human being involved must be treated and dignified as such, because of their inherent value as creatures made in God's image. Similarly, particularly if it is not genetic in the same way as race or eye colour, there should still be accountability if sexual behaviour causes harm to other people. As a parallel example, it is arguable that humans – men in particular – have evolved to be promiscuous, since in evolutionary terms the genes that are selected are the ones which are best at passing themselves on to the next generation. That does not mean that promiscuity is beneficial for society – far from it. Society and relational order are dependent on people's willingness to curb their instincts and desires. The mere fact that someone experiences a strong same-sex attraction – or any other kind of attraction or compulsion, sexual or otherwise – tells us nothing about the moral validity of acting on that impulse. A 'promiscuous orientation' does not change God's standards, or the harm that it might do others. Just because we want to steal, lie, commit adultery or sleep around does not make it right, even though these things seem to be a part of our human nature.

Ideally, however, we would not want to focus on sexuality as a civil rights category, or as a criterion for deciding one or other public policy at all. Aside from the complexities of sexuality, which are still not properly understood, an emphasis on sex tends to mean other issues are overlooked (see chapters 3 and 7). If public policy is sufficiently robust, it should be able to protect and benefit everyone, regardless of what they do or do not do in the bedroom.

Third-party consequences

The primary significance of homosexual sex is, like premarital and extramarital heterosexual sex, in its disruption of the person's relationship with God – in this case, in its distortion of the divine imprint inherent in male and female, and the way that this reflects God's love within the Trinity and for us. But there is likely to be injury to human relationships, too.

Many of the third-party consequences of same-sex intercourse are the same as for heterosexual sex outside of marriage. The pain of broken relationship is similar, although in some cases it may be more difficult for the individuals involved if one partner is not 'out', and therefore cannot talk openly about the effect on them. Married men and women who have affairs with members of the same sex do just as much harm to their families as if it had been someone of the opposite sex – a frequently-overlooked aspect of such relationships, which are typically justified on the grounds that the person is fulfilling their true identity. In the film *Brokeback Mountain*, the marriages of both men suffer because of their affair, but this theme is treated as much less significant than the romance between them.

Sexual health

Although there is not always a qualitative difference, there are areas in which same-sex relationships do have quantitatively different effects. Sexual health is one. Although this was probably not uppermost in the minds of the biblical authors,[38] it is a factor of which we must be aware when we look at third-party effects. The moral status of a sexual act cannot be judged by its health consequences, but risky sex of any kind causes relational injury. The health risks of gay sex are down to the fact that gay relationships tend, on average, to be more promiscuous, and because the nature of many common gay sexual practices means that STIs are more readily transmissible.[39] The incidence of STIs is an order of magnitude greater among gay men than among heterosexual couples. This is particularly acute in the case of HIV; although the general rate of infection is around 1 in 1,000 in the UK, among gay men it appears to be at least twenty times higher, and probably more.[40] Obviously this has an enormous impact on others – which, for bisexual men, extends to women and potentially to unborn children too.

As stated, these are quantitative differences and do not demonstrate an absolute difference between same-sex and opposite-sex sexual sin, which is another reason for Christians to view homosexuality in the context of heterosexual failings. Heterosexuals can also be promiscuous and can also engage in unprotected, high-risk sexual practices. It should also be noted that the incidence of HIV among lesbians is much lower than for heterosexual couples, and that faithful same-sex partnerships do not involve this risk – although even these carry significant health risks.[41] We need to be aware that risky sex of any kind is part of a package of individualistic behaviours that ignore other people's wellbeing.

A *cultural* mindset

Whilst most Christians would accept that promiscuous sex – gay
or straight – is against God's will, many disagree that long-term,
faithful and stable same-sex relationships are contrary to Christian
teaching.[42] Where these are sanctioned by gay marriage, they may
find even fewer grounds to object.

Obviously, if a spiritual impact of sex is accepted, then legiti-
mizing the relationship with a marriage ceremony makes no
difference to the disruption of the relationship with God. On a
human level, same-sex practice must be understood in the context
of our culture's overall sexual brokenness. Gay sex is just one of
many messages – premarital sex, cohabitation, divorce – we are
given, which tell us that individual choice is more important than
our wider relationships or family form, and that our subjective
'needs' and desires matter more than relational order.

The Western mindset has developed so that sexual relationship
is assumed to be a right: part of an entitlement to self-fulfilment.
Whilst the 'traditional' arguments that homosexuality is wrong
because there is no scope for childbirth fall down as soon as they
meet questions of sterility or contraception, separating parenting
completely from sex is the opposite error. Same-sex relationships – particularly in the form of gay marriage – are part of this
picture. 'Gay marriage might be an effect of an increasing cultural
separation between marriage and parenthood. But how could gay
marriage be a product of this cultural trend without also locking in
and reinforcing that same cultural stance?'[43]

Those societies which place a low value on traditional marriage
– countries where the marriage rate has dropped significantly,
which have high rates of cohabitation, divorce and single parenthood – are also the ones in which support for gay marriage is
strongest. This does not imply that gay marriage actually causes
a drop in heterosexual marriage: correlation does not necessarily
point to causation. However, it is a sign of poor support for traditional marriage as a whole and one of a package of attitudes which
minimize its importance.

> Certain trends in values and attitudes tend to cluster with each other and
> with certain trends in behavior. A rise in unwed childbearing goes hand

in hand with a weakening of the belief that people who want to have children should get married. High divorce rates are encountered where the belief in marital permanence is low. More one-parent homes are found where the belief that children need both a father and a mother is weaker. A rise in nonmarital cohabitation is linked at least partly to the belief that marriage as an institution is outmoded. The legal endorsement of gay marriage occurs where the belief prevails that marriage itself should be redefined as a private personal relationship. And all of these marriage-weakening attitudes and behaviors are linked. Around the world, the surveys show, these things go together.[44]

We have argued above (chapter 4) that we need to strengthen marriage in order to restore relational order; there is no evidence that creating gay marriage will achieve that.

Biological parents

This issue of marriage has recently become inextricably linked to that of gay rights. We stress here that issues of gay sex and gay identity must be kept separate from those of gay marriage and parenting. We do not believe that homosexual practice should be made illegal, or that men and women in same-sex relationships should be excluded from the financial benefits made available by civil partnerships. But marriage, which we have argued is specifically an institution designed for the protection and wellbeing of children, family and overall relational order, is not a 'right' to be won.

Marriage is found in almost all cultures and exists for the creation of stable family: the couple who conceive are the same couple who bring up the child and support each other in the process. However, every child brought up by a same-sex couple must be lacking either a mother or father. Critics might respond that the same is true of any single parent, whether through choice, bereavement or separation. But it is equally clear that these are also not ideal situations. Gay marriage and parenting appear intrinsically at odds with a near-universal understanding of marriage as providing the greatest possible combination of relational support and parental responsibility for a child: it divorces parenting from its biological roots.[45] Again, the same is true of adoption, but this is also a response to an imperfect situation.[46]

The future of 'marriage'?

Finally, there is an argument against creating gay marriage, in that
it represents a landmark development which opens the door to
other forms of civil union or marriage-like arrangements. Once
marriage is no longer about one man and one woman commit-
ting themselves to parenting, family and relational order, then
potentially any combination of men and women could be called
a marriage – three men, four women, two men and two women.
The kind of argument used by the gay lobby in favour of gay marriage is already being applied to the rights of individuals proposing
group marriage – polygamy or polyamory.[47]

Logically, there is no reason not to endorse this alongside same-
sex marriage: if the opposite sex requirement is no longer valid,
why should non-monogamy be a bar to marriage? Polyamorous
marriage is, for bisexuals, a broadly equivalent right to gay marriage
for homosexuals. In September 2005, the first trio – two women
and a man – were 'married' in a polyamorous civil union ceremony
in the Netherlands.[48] This went beyond even polygamy, in that the
women were married to each other, as well as to the man.

The same is true of the incest laws that prevent close relatives
from marrying. These, like objections against gay or polyamorous
marriage, can be seen as no more than outdated, subjective or
'moral' arguments. If there are no children from the relationship,
who would risk disease or disability due to inbreeding, then it
becomes harder still to say what is wrong with incest. A German
brother and sister couple recently compared incest law to the
Third Reich's racial hygiene laws in their attempt to change the
law.[49] The argument for legalizing consensual incest is gaining
ground.[50] At least part of the biblical rationale against incest (Lev.
18 and 20) was surely protection of women, and a desire to maintain boundaries in the family. If incest is no longer a crime, sex
between relatives becomes a matter of consent only; the home
ceases to be a safe environment if women have to prove that they
did not give consent to sex.

A distinctive relationship?

The recent shifts in our centuries-long understanding of marriage
turns it into something quite different. In this new definition of

marriage, children and family are not fundamental, though they
may be appropriated secondarily. Permanency is not fundamental
– or even the intention of permanency. Male and female parents
are not fundamental. Monogamy is not fundamental. Marriage
becomes a barely recognizable flexible and temporary arrangement
of legal convenience. As a result, its crucial role in underpinning
relational order is all but destroyed.

The financial cost of extramarital sex

Whilst the real tragedy of extramarital sex is the emotional toll, set
out in chapter 4, this goes hand in hand with very real financial
costs too – costs shared by everyone. These are likely to be far
higher than anyone has so far recognized.

In assessing deprivation, the *Breakdown Britain* report identifies five key drivers: drug and alcohol abuse, worklessness, family
break-up, failed education, and debt. It estimates that the total
cost of social breakdown is around £102 billion, of which family
breakdown is estimated at £24 billion per year, including direct
costs such as lone parent benefits and other, indirect costs. The
five factors are interrelated and reinforcing. So, educational under-
achievement costs around £18 billion per year: children who have
suffered family breakdown are 75% more likely to fail in education.
Crime costs around £60 billion per year: 60% of prison inmates
come from a broken home.

The Relationships Foundation has gone further in quantify-
ing the costs of family breakdown in a recent report, *Investing in
Relationships*.[51] Including the cost of tax credits, incapacity and
housing benefits (£14 billion), criminal justice costs (£5.6 billion),
health impacts (£12 billion), education (£3 billion) and other areas,
the cost to the taxpayer totals around £37 billion.

But these figures are not the end of the story. They only take
into account government spending, not the impact that the lack
of sexual norms has both on people's earning capacity, and on
the ways in which they are able to spend the after-tax proportion
of those earnings. For example, family breakdown, divorce and
mobility mean that more houses have to be built for ever-smaller

family units. In 1971, the average household size was 2.9; in 2008 it was 2.4. It is expected to stabilize at 2.1 by 2020. The number of people of working age living alone in the same period has more than trebled, from 1 million to 3.5 million.[52] Even allowing for remarriage, there are 100,000 extra households every year as a direct result of relationship breakdown. The average deposit for first-time buyers is £34,000 – before regular mortgage payments and bills are taken into account. For the average home in 2007, these totalled over £11,000 per year, with around £6,600 going on the mortgage.[53] Relationship breakdown makes for expensive living patterns.

Relationship breakdown affects not just living costs but earning capacity in the first place – for businesses as well as individuals – in absenteeism, 'presenteeism' (when people are physically present at work but not functioning properly due to stress, depression or illness) and staff turnover. Lost working hours following break-up have been estimated to cost £15 billion, before lost productivity and other factors are taken into account.[54] A US study suggests that employees lose an average of 168 hours in presenteeism following a divorce, or the equivalent of a full working month. The high marital stress before a divorce costs an additional 38 working days.[55] These are not trivial proportions of time or amounts of money when you consider that the average full-time income for the UK is £498 per week for men and £394 per week for women[56] – each divorce alone, excluding the stress leading up to it or any 'official' absenteeism, costs businesses an average of £1,500 to £2,000 in pay that effectively has not been earned. That figure alone is roughly ten times the cost of marriage preparation (see further in chapter 7).

Balancing lone parenthood and work is difficult, particularly for women, who tend to suffer more than men as a result, becoming on average 18% worse off after divorce.[57] A further factor is the decrease of future earnings by children whose education is disrupted by family breakdown. In both cases, this reduced spending power then has further effects on the economy.

The government has calculated the total annual costs of domestic violence at £23 billion per year, including human and emotional costs.[58] The proportion of the total cost of crime (£60 billion) that might be attributed to relationship breakdown is estimated at £15 billion.

The total economic knock-on effects are probably incalculable, but must total close to £100 billion per year. To put this into context, the global economic problems of 2008 – rising fuel and energy costs, household bills and rates rises – mean that the average UK household is 15% worse off than five years earlier.[59] That amounts to £140 per month less, or £1,680 for the year. There are around 25 million households in the UK, giving a total of £42 billion. In other words, the cost of sexual liberty to the average household is double that of the Credit Crunch – but is being paid every single year.

Notes

1. Office of National Statistics (ONS).
2. Ronald Sider, *The Scandal of the Evangelical Conscience* (Baker Books, 2005), pp. 23–24.
3. At least 95% of Americans across all age groups. Cf. David Crary, 'Most Americans Have Had Premarital Sex', *The Guardian*, 6 December 2006.
4. Health Protection Agency, see also <http://news.bbc.co.uk/1/hi/health/5144482.stm> (accessed 17 July 2008).
5. 'Young people urged to have fewer sexual partners and more tests as infections rise', in *The Guardian*, 16 July 2008. Available at <http://www.guardian.co.uk/society/2008/jul/16/health.youngpeople> (accessed 22 July 2008).
6. Elaine Storkey, *The Search For Intimacy* (Hodder and Stoughton, 1995), pp. 24–25.
7. Oliver James, quoted in Sophie Goodchild and Severin Carrell, 'Sex.com: We are a nation addicted to porn. And nearly 11 million of us got our fix on the net last year', *Independent on Sunday*, 28 May 2006. Available at <http://www.independent.co.uk/news/uk/this-britain/sexcom-we-are-a-nation-addicted-to-porn-and-nearly-11-million-of-us-got-our-fix-on-the-net-last-year-480091.html> (accessed 22 July 2008).
8. *Breakdown Britain* (Centre for Social Justice, 2006), appendix 5, p. 144.
9. S. Stack, I. Wasserman, and R. Kern, 'Adult social bonds and use of Internet pornography', *Social Science Quarterly*, 85(1), 2004, pp. 75–88.

10. Wendy Shalit, *Return to Modesty: Discovering the Lost Virtue* (Free Press, 2000), p. 54.

11. *Why Marriage Matters, Twenty-Six Conclusions from the Social Sciences* (Institute for American Values, 2005).

12. ONS.

13. Other reasons often given are to make some commitment to bring up children born into more casual relationships, economic considerations, or (occasionally) out of ideological aversion to marriage.

14. Patricia Morgan, *Marriage-Lite* (Institute for the Study of Civil Society, 2000), p. 27.

15. There is an argument that religious values prevent couples from cohabiting and also from divorcing, suggesting that this, rather than premarital cohabitation, is the relevant factor. There may be a selection factor at work here – those who are more committed to each other are more likely to marry in the first place – but this does not fully explain the statistics, especially given the high rates of cohabitation and divorce amongst US Christians (figures for the UK are harder to collect).

16. John Ermisch and Marco Francesconi, *Cohabitation in Great Britain: Not For Long, But Here To Stay* (Institute for Social and Economic Research, University of Essex, 1998).

17. Morgan, *Marriage-Lite*, p. 14.

18. Larry Bumpass and James Sweet, 'Cohabitation, Marriage and Union Stability: Preliminary Findings from NSFH2'. *NSFH Working Paper No. 65* (University of Wisconsin-Madison: Center for Demography and Ecology, 1995).

19. Linda Waite and Maggie Gallagher, *The Case for Marriage* (Doubleday, 2000).

20. S. Parker, *Informal Marriage, Cohabitation and the Law 1750–1989* (Macmillan, 1990).

21. Quoted in *The Observer*, 15 February 1987 – during, as it happens, her four-year affair with John Major. On the other hand, she didn't specify *whose* wife.

22. In biblical times, the line between the two was perhaps thinner than it is today. Cultural considerations mean that, even if adultery is forgivable or understandable to many people now, paying for it in cash is often another matter. In the patriarchal societies of the ancient world, there was less social stigma around prostitution, whereas adultery was harshly punished.

23. Christopher Ash, *Marriage: Sex in the Service of God* (IVP, 2003), pp. 358–361.

24. Adultery is given as the grounds for around 20% of divorces today (ONS). This does not include the instances where adultery was a major factor, but could not be *proven* – requiring that other grounds (such as 'unreasonable behaviour') be used instead.

25. Though there is some debate around the strict accuracy of this, as it is only based on the ratio of marriages to divorces recorded.

26. Sider, *Scandal*, pp. 18–20.

27. The average length of marriage for divorcees is just 11.5 years (ONS).

28. 'Remarriage' here and throughout means 'further marriage after divorce', not remarriage to the same person.

29. 'Interview with Mario Bergner', *The Ivy Jungle Report*, vol. 8, Winter 2000. Available at <http://www.anglican-mainstream.net/interview-with-mario-bergner> (accessed 22 July 2008). As a young adult Mario Bergner was heavily involved in a gay lifestyle, later leaving it altogether. He is now married with four children, and the founder and director of Redeemed Lives Ministries, an organization offering pastoral care for individuals struggling with same-sex attraction.

30. This kind of smokescreen of vehement opposition is not as recent as many people like to think. In the fourth century BC, Plato argued against what he considered some of the socially destructive sexual norms of the day, including both heterosexual promiscuity and same-sex intercourse: 'I can imagine some lusty youth who is standing by, and who, on hearing this enactment, declares in scurrilous terms that we are making foolish and impossible laws, and fills the world with his outcry. And therefore I said that I knew a way of enacting and perpetuating such a law, which was very easy in one respect, but in another most difficult.' Plato, *Laws*, book 9.

31. The incidence of homosexuality is extremely difficult to quantify, for various reasons. It is likely to be under-reported, and statistics differ according the criteria used to define homosexuality. The second National Survey of Sexual Attitudes and Lifestyles (NATSAL II), carried out in 2000, found that 2.6% of both men and women over 16 had had a same-sex sexual partner in the last five years. This reflects actual sexual experience; a larger number have felt attraction, but not acted on it. On the other hand, the number of people practising exclusively or predominantly homosexual behaviour is likely to be lower. Kinsey's infamous '1 in 10' statistic has been discredited for too long now for it to be worth discussing.

32. Martin Hallett, founder of True Freedom Trust.
33. 'What about the basic rights of Christians?' in *The Daily Express*, 12 July 2006.
34. Christopher West, *Theology of the Body for Beginners* (Ascension Press, 2004), p. 9.
35. William Webb's *Slaves, Women and Homosexuals* (IVP, 2001) is a clear, unbiased and thorough examination of which scriptural laws are cultural, and which are meant to be permanent.
36. See Simon Burton, *The Causes of Homosexuality* (Jubilee Centre, 2006). Available at <http://www.jubilee-centre.org>.
37. Jeffrey Satinover, *Homosexuality and the Politics of Truth* (Baker Books, 1996), pp. 93–108.
38. Some writers suggest that sexual health is something that Paul has in mind in Romans 1:27b: 'Men committed indecent acts with other men, and received in themselves the due penalty for their perversion.'
39. Satinover, *Homosexuality*, pp. 49–70.
40. The Terence Higgins Trust estimates that at the end of 2006, 31,100 men who have sex with men were living with HIV in the UK. See <http://www.tht.org.uk/mediacentre/pressreleases/2007/december/december4.htm> (accessed 22 July 2008). The rate of twenty times greater HIV infection assumes that 5% of the male population is gay – almost certainly a higher figure than the reality.
41. These include physical trauma, amebiasis, giardiasis and shigellosis, amongst others (the so-called 'Gay Bowel Syndrome'). See Thomas Schmidt, *Straight and Narrow* (IVP, 1995), pp. 100–130.
42. See, e.g., Jeffrey John, *Permanent, Faithful, Stable* (Darton, Longman and Todd, 1993).
43. Stanley Kurtz, 'Dutch Debate', *National Review Online*, 21 July 2004. <http://www.nationalreview.com/kurtz/kurtz200407210936.asp> (accessed 22 July 2008).
44. David Blankenhorn, 'Defining Marriage Down . . . Is No Way To Save It', *Weekly Standard*, 2 April 2007.
45. See, e.g., *Breakdown Britain*, pp. 30, 38 and 56.
46. See also David Blankenhorn, *The Future of Marriage* (Encounter Books, 2007).
47. Cf. Elizabeth Emens, 'Monogamy's Law: Compulsory Monogamy and Polyamorous Existence', in *New York University Review of Law and Social Change* 29, 2004, pp. 277–376.

48. 'First Trio "Married" in The Netherlands', *The Brussels Journal*, 27 September 2005. See <http://www.brusselsjournal.com/node/301> (accessed 22 July 2008).

49. 'Brother and sister fight Germany's incest laws', *The Guardian*, 27 February 2007. See <http://www.guardian.co.uk/world/2007/feb/27/germany.kateconnolly> (accessed 22 July 2008).

50. See, e.g., 'Man Convicted in Incest Case Plans to Appeal to Supreme Court', *New York Times*, 25 March 2007, <http://www.nytimes.com/2007/03/25/us/25stepdaughter.html>; 'Forbidden Love', *The Guardian*, 9 January 2002, <http://www.guardian.co.uk/Archive/Article/0,4273,4331603,00.html> (accessed 22 July 2008).

51. John Ashcroft and Peter Lynas. See <http://www.relationshipsfoundation.org/download.php?id=218> (accessed 5 August 2008).

52. Guy Palmer, *Single Person Households* (JRF 2006), p. 2. <http://www.jrf.org.uk/bookshop/ebooks/palmer-9781859354759.pdf> (accessed 5 August 2008).

53. Research by Sainsbury's Bank, found in '£11,000 a year to run the typical house', *Daily Mail*, 23 April 2007. Available online at <http://www.mailonsunday.co.uk/news/article-450228/11-000-year-run-typical-house.html> (accessed 29 July 2008). Since the 'Credit Crunch' these figures will be significantly higher though the resulting recession may mean subsequent decreases.

54. 'The Cost of Family Breakdown', *Family Matters*, 2000.

55. Glenn Cohen, 'Why Employers Should Take an Active Role Helping Employees Improve Their Personal Relationships' ('I-TO-WE' Relationship Coaching, 2007). See <http://www.i-to-we-relationship-coaching.com/Successful-Relationships-Improves-the-Bottom-Line.html> (accessed 10 June 2008).

56. Median incomes, April 2007 (ONS).

57. Institute for Social and Economic Research; see Jackie Ashley, 'Dumping your wife is now as easy as trading your car', *The Guardian*, 6 February 2006. See <http://www.guardian.co.uk/world/2006/feb/06/gender.lifeandhealth> (accessed 22 July 2008).

58. Sylvia Walby, *The Cost of Domestic Violence*, Women and Equality Unit, September 2004. See <http://www.lancs.ac.uk/fass/sociology/papers/walby-costdomesticviolence.pdf> (accessed 5 August 2008).

59. 'UK spending power "in heavy fall"', 4 July 2008. <http://news.bbc.co.uk/1/hi/business/7488613.stm> (accessed 22 July 2008).

6. RELATIONAL CHURCHES

Christian approaches to building community

*Generally, being single sucks! I am frequently excluded from couples'
dinner-parties. At a friend's wedding the photographer was instructed to
take photographs of the couples; I was in a solo shot. Too often people
ask the unanswerable questions 'When will you get married?', 'Why are
you not dating anyone?' Family and friends seem to enjoy reminding me
that I am not getting any younger – a fact that I am perfectly aware of!
Encouragement to 'randomly date' or 'Go travelling, you are bound to meet
someone then', compounds my confusion and frustration.*

*Church has its own inimical way of highlighting my 'different' status.
When I expressed interest in joining a house group I was consigned to the
single girls group – 'a special cell for special single people'. Speakers in
church often use marriage scenarios as analogies for their theological point,
alienating us marriage 'outsiders'.*

*In addition to the external pressure, I feel an increasing inward struggle
with my status. I am acutely aware that my biological clock is tick-tocking.
An inspirational man seems increasingly difficult to find. Church and
Christian friends are adamant to pair me off with one (any) of the few
remaining single Christian men. If I date men who are not Christian the*

common lecture begins, 'It is easier to pull someone off a table than to pull them up onto it!' I dread being lumped into that tragic Christian category of 'single, really nice girl, desperate for husband'.

I long to be part of, and contribute to, an intimate, committed relationship. I enjoy varying levels of intimacy with friends, but get frustrated with the often complicated arrangements necessary to spend time with someone. There is also the need to explain myself much of the time. I would love to be in a relationship of mutual commitment, investment, and understanding. I want to know, and be known by, one person – achieve the level of intimacy made possible by a good marriage.

In such a marriage both have committed to share the highs and the lows. This assurance facilitates trust, assisting the development of fuller human beings. The thought that I may never get married scares me a lot – never to have someone who you know loves you for who you are. The intimacy I experience with friends is real, but, I imagine, of a different 'sort' than that in marriage.

I know that sex is no replacement for intimacy. However, in the past I have attempted, unsuccessfully, to foster intimacy with casual sex. But, having such temporary physical closeness with someone is deeply hurtful, leaving feelings of lasting shame and embarrassment. I hope that these memories will prevent me from making similar mistakes in the future; but, when I think about still being single ten years from now ... who knows? I guess I should talk to my church leaders about this, but I am not sure how they can help me. Being single is not my first choice, but I need to accept the possibility that I may never marry or have children (or have sex again).

I know I shouldn't feel 'less important' as a single person because 'God loves me the same as everybody else', but there are times when I think 'If I was going out with someone, people wouldn't look at me differently, and I would be more accepted'. I should stress that I enjoy aspects of singleness, such as the freedom to choose what I want to do, and when to do it. However, as more friends get married (not to mention have children) change is inevitable; I dread being increasingly left out, or people over-compensating, to be inclusive of, or sensitive to, my singleness. To reiterate what I said at the beginning – for me, singleness sucks!

– Laura, 32

Engaging with others

Whilst the Bible seems clear about sexual ethics, there is a difference between the response appropriate for the church, and that
expected for the rest of society. However sensitively the message
is communicated, and whatever the realities of fallen humanity and
the nature of pastoral care, the bottom line for Christians is that the
Bible does not endorse sex – of any kind – outside of marriage.

Israel was a theocratic state. There was no difference between
religious and state law; God had a particular kind of society in
mind and his laws were intended to ensure its protection. By
contrast, the situation in the New Testament was very different.
Paul's churches, for example, were small groups in an otherwise
pagan society – hence the problems in Corinth. Both Jesus and
Paul warned that the community of believers would struggle to
stay distinctively different from the surrounding culture – being 'in
the world, but not of the world' (John 17:13–15). Paul recognized
that it was no business of his to judge those outside the church,
but maintained that Christians are called to be different from those
around them (1 Cor. 5:9–13). Our modern situation, living in a
society of many faiths and often none, is effectively the same.

At the same time, Christians are called to be 'salt and light' to the
world, not simply to protect the integrity of the church and give up
on the rest of society. One of the challenges for Christians living
in a secular society is to defend the relevance of the biblical ideals
they try to live out. If the Bible says something is always wrong,
then it is not an arbitrary command from God, made for no better
reason than to see whether we will keep it. We expect there to be
reasons for it, whether we agree with them or not, and whether
we like it or not. And, although we cannot possibly hope to know
fully the mind of God, we should have some understanding of
what those reasons are. Not to know, or even to try, is to make a
blind appeal to authority – an unhelpful approach for those who
do not share the same beliefs, or who have not yet decided.

It is a reality of our society that most churchgoers will either
have been involved in sexual relationships outside of marriage,
or have been harmed by them in some form or another. The task
of pastoral care is to work for healing, relational wholeness and

intimacy, without underplaying the significance of the sin and its effects on both those directly involved and those who suffer the knock-on consequences. We address some broad principles about pastoral care in this chapter, after exploring some ways in which our churches can be an antidote to the prevailing cultural mindset.

Church vs. culture

Faced with a sexually permissive culture, Christians are frequently at a loss to know how to react. As a result, some have adopted the values of the 'iWorld' wholesale. Some, perhaps, maintain their own beliefs, but avoid offending anyone by not commenting on their lifestyles. Others have gone too far the other way, proclaiming fire-and-brimstone judgment on sexual sinners.

The question is, how do we react to sexual brokenness as Christians, both individually and corporately? How do we deal with the fundamental cause, which is a crisis in intimacy brought about by the rise of individualism, without ignoring the symptom of sexual sin and dysfunction itself? How do we establish and model intimacy and relational wholeness in a way that is both helpful to Christians and attractive to those outside the church?

Individual responses

When it comes to saying how Christians should *not* react to our culture of sexual licence, unqualified acceptance and unqualified condemnation both come high on the list. Love does not have the mentality of unqualified acceptance, although it is too easy to caricature Jesus' refusal to throw the first stone (John 8:1–11) as this kind of timid apathy. Matthew 7:1, 'Do not judge, or you too will be judged,' is often a proof-text to which Christians cling in order to avoid making any kind of moral distinction. In fact, the word translated here as 'judge', *krinō*, carries the connotation of harsh-spirited condemnation that should be out of place on Christian lips. We are allowed and encouraged to judge in the sense of discerning what is right; we are only warned against self-righteous demeaning of those who do not meet that standard.[1]

When it comes to unqualified condemnation, none of us have grounds for self-righteousness. Indeed Matthew 7:2 teaches us that we can expect that attitude in return: 'For in the same way as you judge [self-righteously condemn] others, you will be judged, and with the measure you use, it will be measured to you.' Jesus taught that lust is already adultery in the heart (Matt. 5:28); how many people could honestly claim they have never committed adultery in their thought-lives?

When speaking about sexual ethics, style is as important as message. How Christians address the issues is as important as what is said. Too often the truth or importance of the message is lost in language perceived as judgmental. This does not mean that we should ignore sin, any more than Jesus ignored the woman's adultery in John 8. But we have to be aware of any planks in our own eyes before we try to remove the speck from our neighbours' (Matt. 7:3). To do otherwise is to invite the same kind of condemnation from others as we mete out to them.

Even when we manage to come to sexual issues from a position of humility and recognition of our own failings, Christians still have a duty to understand the Bible's teaching on sexual ethics. If we do not understand biblical norms, and are unable to articulate the reasons for our beliefs, how can we expect others to respect our views? Here, as in our deepening relationships with other people,[2] self-awareness is crucial. Many people do not really know why they believe what they do. Whilst some things are simply a matter of faith – getting on and doing what the Bible says just because it says it – we have a duty to understand as much as we can. If we do not make that effort, can we really be sure that 'faith' – at least in this area – is not just a convenient label that we use to justify our own prejudices?

The first aim of this book is to explain to Christians and the wider culture what the Bible's message is, properly interpreted and understood. Secondly, we ask why that message is still relevant today. The understanding of Christianity as a religion that is fundamentally about relationships provides a framework for unpacking issues of justice in the area of sexual ethics. There is a strong argument that sex affects many third parties and therefore society as a whole. This provides an answer to the prevailing culture's case for permissiveness: it is an answer for Christians themselves and for their non-Christian friends, for parents to give children, and schools to teach pupils – an alternative to the 'free condoms' answer which only encourages a relationally shallow expression of sexuality and deepens the crisis of intimacy.

> *The greatest single cause of Atheism in the world today is Christians who acknowledge Jesus with their lips and walk out the door and deny Him by their lifestyle. That is what an unbelieving world simply finds unbelievable.*
>
>   Brennan Manning, priest and author[3]

With this clarity, however, comes the challenge of putting our own house in order, individually and corporately. This means far more than merely avoiding sexual sin: the 'thou shalt nots . . .' so familiar and unattractive to those outside the church, for whom, like Bertrand Russell, Christianity appears to require so many sacrifices with so few rewards. 'The worst feature of the Christian religion, however, is its attitude toward sex – an attitude so morbid and so unnatural . . . the church did what it could to secure that the only form of sex which it permitted should involve very little pleasure and a great deal of pain.'[4]

That challenge means not only avoiding the 'thou shalt nots . . .' but also actively cultivating the kind of non-sexual intimacy that is missing from so many lives today, and for which sex is often employed as a substitute. For too long Christianity has been seen as either a kill-joy, or out of touch with the real world. We argue that, as a relational religion with a concern for real intimacy, Christianity is more relevant than ever in the aftermath of the sexual revolution.

Christian love

Of the 'four loves' about which C. S. Lewis writes, *erōs* – romantic/ sexual love – is the one our culture values most highly. Affection or family love (*storgē*) and friendship (*philia*) are bumped down the list, and unconditional love or *agapē* is barely known. And yet *agapē* is the love that should characterize Christian relationships. Generous, unselfconscious *agapē* should be the Christian answer to our culture's promiscuous *erōs*.

The central question is whether Christians are really willing to be the sort of example that would be an antidote to the culture we criticize. Turning our churches into the relational communities they should be will take time and effort. Worship of any kind intrinsically involves some sacrifice, whether of animals, as in the Old Testament, of time, money, or in other ways. Are we willing to make the sacrifices that would speak more to the world than any number of sermons? Our actions are a barometer of our faith (Jas. 2:14–26).

In their book *Total Church*, Steve Timmis and Tim Chester write:

> *'Community has been insightfully defined as the place where the person you least want to live with always lives!' It is human nature to want to choose our companions, rather than live in an inclusive community in which they are chosen for us. 'But it is in such a community that disciples are made. To be a community of light from which the light of Christ will emanate we need to be intentional in our relationships: to love the unlovely, forgive the unforgiveable, embrace the repulsive, include the awkward, accept the weird. It is in contexts such as these that sinners are transformed into disciples who obey everything King Jesus has commanded.*[5]

Relational communities

The need to provide opportunities for intimacy among Christians of both sexes underlines the role of churches not just as places for personal worship, but as supportive and relational communities. Crucially, these must be the outward-looking congregations of Isaiah 58, not solely concerned with their own welfare.

What Christians do is at least as important as what they say. Living according to the vision we preach is a prerequisite for effective witness. The Bible's teaching on sexuality is an unpopular part of the Christian message. How do we communicate the love of God alongside that? The world should be able to see something attractive about the community of faith, living successfully by these principles, that draws them to it rather than repelling them.

Evangelical about relationships

Right relationships are fundamental to Christianity. In John 17:20–21, Jesus suggests that relationships between Christians should be as close as those within the Trinity: 'My prayer is . . . that all of them may be one, Father, just as you are in me and I am in you.' Non-Christians are often drawn to Christianity when they see strong and caring relationships in the church. As Tertullian quoted of the church's pagan observers early in the third century, 'see how they love one another'.[6] Equally, non-Christians are often put off if they see dysfunctional relationships, arguing that if Christians took their faith seriously this would not happen. Either way, cultivating intimacy and good relationships should be a priority.

Where the church gets this right, there is an attractive model to 'export'. One of the reasons the Alpha Course has been so success-ful is the built-in fellowship it offers, with people meeting to share a meal and explore Christianity in the same groups week after week. There is often an understanding of 'mission' as preaching the gospel to a culture that may share little of Christianity's world-view, such as our own. Although there is undoubtedly a place for such 'top-down' mission, another way of looking at it is to work to change the culture from the bottom up, thereby fostering the kind of culture and values in which Christianity makes sense, and is therefore easier to understand and accept. Through relationships education, churches could encourage this relational literacy. The form that such a 'healthy relationships' course could take might be similar to Alpha and would encourage people to consider what it is they are really looking for from their relationships and how to find it. Once we can learn to see the world through that 'relational lens', the message of Christianity falls into focus far more readily.

Good marriage preparation is vital, but a surprisingly small number of churches run a programme for the couples they marry. Obviously, as Christians this reflects poorly on our supposed concern for healthy relationships. One alternative – besides further training for clergy in this area – is to recommend programmes like Engaged Encounter and Marriage Encounter, or to donate to these and similar courses.[7]

What does it mean to love our neighbours?

Hearing that Jesus had silenced the Sadducees, the Pharisees got together. One of them, an expert in the law, tested him with this question: 'Teacher, which is the greatest commandment in the Law?' Jesus replied: '"Love the Lord your God with all your heart and with all your soul and with all your mind." This is the first and

greatest commandment. And the second is like it: "Love your neighbour as yourself."
All the Law and the Prophets hang on these two commandments.'

Matthew 22:34–40

Jesus summed up the Law with the commandment to love God and love our neighbour. Similarly, John 13:34–35 tells us that love for each other will be the hallmark of Christians. But what does it mean in practice to 'love our neighbour'? 1 Corinthians 13 describes some of the characteristics of love, but how do we become the kind of church that produces and grows close, strong relationships?

Relational proximity
In unpacking the question of how to grow strong relationships, we have found the 'relational proximity' model helpful.[8] There are five domains to relationships: communication, time, knowledge, power and purpose, and five dimensions to relational proximity – that is, conditions under which close relationships are most likely to thrive. If we are aware of these, we can both structure our churches around them, and tailor our individual responses to use them at the personal level.

Communication: the importance of directness
Directness is about both quality and quantity of communication. There is greater directness if you hear something from the person yourself, rather than mediated through a third party, via the church bulletin, or through the church grapevine. Communication is more direct when it is face to face, rather than over the phone, or via email or letter; there is generally no substitute for talking to someone in person. You get (or give) the benefit of facial expressions and body language over and above tone of voice and the content of the words themselves.

Honesty and openness are vital aspects of directness; people need to feel they can be honest with each other. They need to feel that they can tell the truth without being criticized for it, which means both a spirit of acceptance in the other person, and perhaps also patience or 'long-suffering', as the King James Version translates it (Gal. 5:22), which neutralizes any negative feelings you receive in your contact with another person.

Needless to say, to communicate directly with someone it has to be possible to get hold of them. Sometimes this may seem impossible, particularly if they are busy and not good at replying to phone or email messages. Sometimes, people may live too far away to make meeting easy. Sometimes, however, the issue may be more about the size and structure of the church; it becomes difficult to interact with several hundred people on a personal level!

> *I spoke with Andrew most weeks after the service for about a year and a half. After a short time away on holiday I came back to church and asked him how he was doing. He asked me my name. After 18 months, it was almost like we were meeting for the first time. I didn't really bother with him much after that.*
>
> *– Tom, 26*

Attentiveness is key to quality of communication – we all know what it's like to have a conversation with someone who is looking over our shoulder, or to be asked on three separate occasions where we live because they weren't listening the first time. Paying attention to the person you are with is vital if you want to develop a good relationship. If our mind is elsewhere, as in the example above, the other person can feel hurt. If we are going to spend time with someone, it is respectful and caring to give them our undivided attention, which may mean looking at how busy we are, or possibly turning a self-critical eye onto how our behaviour in this area affects others.

Time: the importance of continuity
Continuity is about understanding the narrative of a relationship. It is not only about spending regular time with someone, but doing so with the deliberate intent to progress the relationship. So, for example, it is difficult to form deep relationships if there is a high turnover of people at church, because people do not see each relationship as having a future.

Knowledge: the importance of multiplexity
Multiplexity means that we learn more about people when we spend time with them in different contexts. Human beings are

complex creatures and to know someone well it is always helpful to see them in a variety of different settings. Few people behave in the office as they would at home playing with their children! If you don't have this breadth of knowledge, then skills or possible contributions to church life may go unrecognized, problems or pressure points may be missed, and false assumptions about people may sour relationships. Having the opportunity to meet someone in different contexts, knowing something about their life, friends, family, interests and skills outside your sphere of shared experience, is key to moving beyond a superficial relationship. Third parties play an important role in adding to your knowledge of a person, including in terms of trustworthiness and reliability.

Power: the importance of parity

Parity is about mutual respect. It may often feel like there is a gap in importance or power between those in leadership positions in the church and those with no formal role, or between those in paid employment and those (like stay-at-home mums, older people and children) who are not. But close relationships will be built up if there is mutual respect. Parity requires fostering the dignity and self-worth of others, and treating them fairly. If some people are perceived as gaining preferential treatment, there is not parity, which sooner or later is likely to lead to resentment. Parity is also about participating in decisions and feeling that any decisions that are reached are fair to everybody, not just favouring a few.

Shared purpose and values: the importance of commonality

Where we focus on the range of things we share in common, both inside and outside church life, our relationships will be stronger. Having a common purpose, goals, commitment and values helps to bind people together more than anything else. Sometimes these things need to be discovered, sometimes cultivated. Any event that two people go to provides shared experience.

Some people believe it is important for those in the same church to share common beliefs on most things. Others feel more comfortable with a diversity of views. The importance of common beliefs depends very much on how your church handles differences of opinion, whether on issues of church governance (e.g.

baptism, eldership), leadership, theology, church programmes or style of songs or preaching.

Undergirding common goals and objectives, there need to be shared values. However, it is best if these values are freely entered in upon, rather than forced upon a congregation because the church is self-selecting (that is, people come to your church because they share the same values), or because strong disapproval is shown if people don't toe the line.

Organizing church

The first church was a large evangelical church, with two morning congregations exceeding 300 people each. It valued good preaching, and ran a packed programme of activities. Every time I went I met different people (though I sat in a similar place), because of the number and turnover of those attending. I was too busy to go to a housegroup, which made building deep relationships difficult. Yet, after almost twenty years of membership, I was surprised and upset that when I stopped attending, not a single person contacted me to ask why. Did my relationships in the church mean so little to the rest of the congregation?

Eventually my wife and I moved to a different church, where about 120 adults attended on a Sunday morning. Joining a housegroup was not optional, it was required of all members. I came to know almost everyone in the congregation by sight, and have now spoken to nearly everybody individually. I have close relationships with about a dozen, especially those in my housegroup. In 2001, my home flooded: six inches of brown water over the entire ground floor. The church's response was fantastic. Members of the housegroup came and scrubbed the floors, helped fix the electricity, brought meals for three weeks, and even took away the washing. We were even given a cheque to help pay for a replacement fridge, freezer and cooker. The 'body of Christ' was taken seriously. It transformed my understanding of how love can grow in a church community.

– David, 55

The 'five dimensions of relational proximity' do not ensure close relationships in and of themselves. But they do fulfil the conditions under which close relationships are most likely to thrive, providing the possibility of strong foundations. There are various practical ways in which we can organize our churches so that we take account of these values.

Communication. Sometimes the problems surrounding building strong relationships in church are due simply to the sheer size of the congregation. There needs to be time and opportunities for communication and contact. Is there a chance, before or after the service, to meet people and talk? Are there home groups which offer the opportunity to get to know a smaller number of people much better? In any group of above about 150 members, relationships generally are spread too thin and become superficial – one of the problems with the first church in the above case study. Cliques and sub-groups then form as the larger group becomes unwieldy and naturally divides.[9] This is something of which we must be aware in larger churches. Where numbers are too great to achieve close relationships in and after the main services, there will need to be a particular reliance on smaller groups. We need both quality and quantity of meeting: opportunities for open, honest conversations on an ongoing, regular basis.

Continuity. As well as providing opportunities to get to know people, we need to be aware of the nature of our relationships. Meeting is not an end in itself; we have to be more intentional about it than that. Do we have an overall sense of the narrative of the relationship – what has happened in the past, where we think it will go and what we would like to happen in the future? In other words, is the relationship progressing, or running the risk of stagnating? If the latter, are there changes we can consider?

As far as spending regular time with people over a long period, there may be many reasons this does not happen. It could be that people are busy with other priorities, or it could be that they are unwilling to invest time in a relationship they know is unlikely to last. If other commitments are making this difficult, then there may be ways that the church can help – perhaps with practical tasks like babysitting and cooking meals.

Multiplexity. Church itself can facilitate multiplexity by creating different opportunities for people to meet each other in other contexts. These might be lunches – as a group in church or organized by individuals at their houses – outings, parties and other activities such as a 'Besom' project.[10] It might mean inviting someone into our home for a meal, or offering to pray with or for them. It might mean meeting them in a different context – shopping, sports, socially, with their friends or family – to see a different side of them in order to understand their life better. Is our church somewhere that encourages these things, or is it only concerned with what happens on a Sunday?

Making the effort to get to know one another's friends and family is important, but so is getting to know someone's circumstances. It may be that many of us in church have little knowledge about what other members do during the week. Without this it is unlikely that members will be able to understand why some can get more involved in church events than others. Some may be in debt. Someone may have had promotion. A couple may have had a baby. Someone may have had to put down their dog. There may have been a bereavement in the family. When one rejoices, all should rejoice; when one grieves, all should grieve (Rom. 12:15).

Parity. Making sure that people have the opportunity to be actively involved in main services contributes to the feeling that the leadership are not completely removed from the congregation; they are approachable and there is no perceived 'power gap'. This does not mean that their role or even authority is reduced, or blurred with that of the congregation. It means treating people fairly and as having equal importance, respecting and thanking them for their contribution and not taking them for granted.

This means that those who want to should have the opportunity to contribute to the church's activities in some way. Getting to know people's gifts is important, because we then know who is best suited to what and who to ask. The other side of this coin is that people must be able to say no! Openness and honesty as well as availability may be relevant. Sometimes, people may have been in their jobs for so long that there is no room for anyone else to participate. Alternatively, they may not be suited to that job, or may feel taken for granted.

Commonality. Regular teaching on love and relationships is likely to be key to people's sense of the importance of community. Although churches are united under the very general umbrella of their faith, within that people will have different interests and strengths. Enabling people with shared aims to meet together establishes common ground.

Feeling you belong in a church is crucial, even if you don't feel you belong in every group; it is impossible to please everyone all the time! Feeling understood, and that there are similar expectations in ministry goals, is important. And, of course, the practice has to match up to the theory.

Personal aspects

In addition to these organizational factors – how we structure church meetings and groups, and the values we reflect – there is a personal dimension to relational proximity.[11] Paul's description of the fruits of the Spirit in Galatians 5:22–23 give some indication of the personal qualities which also facilitate the five factors we have mentioned:

> But the fruit of the Spirit is love, joy, peace, patience, kindness, goodness, faithfulness, gentleness and self-control. Against such things there is no law.

Love and gentleness, for example, encourage the kind of conversation that is direct without being harsh – enabling us to be honest without hurting another's feelings. Faithfulness is an aspect of continuity because it requires that we maintain our relationships. It is a divine quality that we can try to reflect in our own interactions with others, thereby gaining an ongoing understanding of their lives rather than taking the occasional 'snapshot'. We know that this is how God treats us (2 Tim. 2:13), and again this is a reflection of the divine in our own relationships.

Patience requires that we forgive any negative words or attitudes from others. 'A man's wisdom gives him patience; it is to his glory to overlook an offence' (Prov. 19:11). Obviously, it is hard to work with someone if we still resent them for some past insult, perceived or real.

Kindness, which includes aspects of compassion and sympathy, suggests that we should learn all we can about another person's life so that we can best tailor our responses to their situation. This will inevitably mean understanding how they interact with others in a variety of circumstances and roles.

Gentleness and self-control necessarily affect the power dynamic of a relationship by encouraging us to curb an aggressive spirit, and to think of ourselves as being on an equal footing with another person, rather than raising ourselves above them and treating them as subordinates.

Finally, all of these fruits should be shared aims for Christians. In addition, humility (Phil. 2:1–11) and understanding of these qualities foster an attitude of putting ourselves in others' shoes, learning more about their values and hopes.

Pastoral care

Pastoral care is a huge topic, and not one that can properly be dealt with in as brief a space as we have here. However, this book would be lacking if we did not include at least some examples of frequently encountered situations, and make some attempt to outline a few broad principles for pastoral care of those struggling to come to terms with sexual sin, or one that involves them as a third party.

The unpardonable sin?

Firstly, and perhaps most importantly, it seems that Christians treat sexual sin as worse than any other sin. Whilst Paul's comment that 'he who sins sexually sins against his own body' confirms that sexual sin is serious, the 'unpardonable sin' in Matthew 12 is not homosexuality, or adultery. Pride and deliberate hardness of heart separate the sinner from God more than these – although you wouldn't necessarily know it from the way some Christians talk.

When we over-emphasize the seriousness of sexual sin, we make the problem worse. We have argued at length in this book that our culture focuses on sex as a substitute for lost and damaged intimacy. As such, it is given greater significance than it deserves. It is important that Christians do not lose sight of the deeper problem by doing the same by over-emphasizing sexual sin. In addition, there is the risk that we would prevent people from seeking pastoral care and forgiveness by increasing their feelings of guilt. This can affect their trust in others, encourage secrecy rather than openness, and drive them further into feelings of depression and guilt. Ironically, this can lead to a greater involvement and dependence on the relationship in question, if still ongoing, because they believe that no one else will talk to them about it without being overly harsh and judgmental.

Secondly, Christians have historically concentrated on homosexual sin – a convenient distraction from the heterosexual sin committed by the majority. Where homosexuality is dealt with in Scripture, it is always in the context of heterosexual sin (see Lev. 18 and 20; 1 Cor. 6:9–10; 1 Tim. 1:8–11). Separating it out so as to deal with it in isolation risks clouding the issue: 'all have sinned and fall short of the glory of God, and are justified freely by his grace through the redemption that came by Christ Jesus' (Rom. 3:23–24). Heterosexuals need to remember the maxim that anyone who points the finger has three more fingers pointing back at them. No one comes to this issue from a position of innocence.

Thirdly, with this in mind, we need to start where people are – not where perfection expects them to be. Paul wrote that 'Neither the sexually immoral nor idolaters nor adulterers nor male prostitutes nor homosexual offenders nor thieves nor the greedy nor drunkards nor slanderers nor swindlers will inherit the kingdom of God. And that is what some of you were . . .' (1 Cor. 6:9–11).

But it is equally true that 'that is what some of you *are*' – now, and have been in the past with ongoing consequences. When preachers speak about sexual morality, it often seems that they expect a standard of perfection from their listeners. And yet there will be a proportion of the congregation who have had affairs or are still involved in one, who have had abortions, who are divorced and remarried, who engage in premarital sex or same-sex intercourse. People's lives do not change instantaneously the moment they walk through the church doors, or even when they make a commitment to follow Christ. Some listeners will still be searching; others will be working through the implications of their faith, which may take years. Some will have made mistakes despite a long-standing faith; others will be uncertain about particular subjects and teachings and in need of clarification. We need to accept people where they are, not where they 'should' be.

Sed quis custodet ipsos custodes? (But who will guard the guards themselves?)
Juvenal, Satire VI

Lastly, we should remember that everyone is capable of making mistakes, including church leaders. Some of the most painful occasions of sexual sin are where ministers have had affairs. There may be little or no accountability for church leaders, who are simply expected to be perfect. In some cases, they may be even allowed to continue leading their churches unchecked because the structures to discipline them do not exist. The effects of this can be devastating for the entire congregation, which may be split as a result, as well as for the immediate families of those involved.

Premarital sex
Statistics differ from survey to survey (and university to university), but it seems a reasonable estimate to suggest that around 80% of undergraduates are sexually active.[12] Despite this, many churches with large numbers of students and young people fail to address the subject. One college tutor with a pastoral role consistently finds that there is a tacit approach that amounts to 'just keep quiet about it and it's fine' when she inquires of how the churches in her university city deal with the subject. Although there are exceptions, many churches have taken on the wider culture's idea of the consent of the other party being enough to legitimize sexual behaviour, perhaps truly believing it is none of their business, or that it is too sensitive a subject, or too offensive, to bring up the issue of their congregation's sexual habits. This implicitly gives students and young people permission to pursue sexual relationships outside of marriage without realizing that the Bible has a different vision. In the process, many people are hurt, and hurt others.

There is another side to this lack of engagement by churches. If 80% of undergraduates are sexually active, this means that 20% are not. Although this is a substantial minority, there is tremendous social pressure to have sex; those who do not are often considered strange or 'repressed' in some way. Our culture's 'liberation', for people to choose to engage in whatever sexual relationships they want, apparently does not extend to the choice *not* to have sex. Openly or otherwise, the question about a virgin at university is, 'What is wrong with this person?' Pastoral leaders are having to deal with increasing numbers of people – particularly women – who feel like social failures and have feelings of anxiety because they currently do not want to engage in a sexual relationship for one reason or another (not least because they have not yet found someone they want to have sex with). Churches, in failing to address sexual issues openly, inadvertently fail those who are not in sexual relationships, too, by allowing the myth to propagate that sex is 'normal' and not to have sex makes you 'abnormal'.

Same-sex attraction

Some years back in my church a male friend (N) developed a 'crush' on another man (J). Both men were married with children. N felt an overwhelming desire to spend time with J, to have an intimate, though not sexual, relationship with him. J did not reciprocate N's desire for intimacy, but as a brother in the church family J did not want to give N the brush-off.

This was a period of acute crisis for N. His early relationship with his father had been difficult, and he had never resolved issues of male attachment. He knew his responsibility to his wife and children, but his desire to be with J was so strong that everything else was of lesser importance. He ate, lived and breathed for the time he could next see J.

J, and his wife, showed extraordinary patience, allowing N to visit, often at first, and then gradually reducing the frequency of these meetings. A small group of men from the church, including J, met with N monthly over several years, to study and reflect on the biblical view of fatherhood, particularly the fatherhood of God, and to support one another in their daily walk with God. N also attended a psychiatrist who had counselled him over a decade of struggling with attraction to other men. The meetings ended when there were a number of disagreements as to how they should go forward which could not be resolved. N was left feeling very upset.

As a concerned friend and observer, I learned the extent of the pain associated with same-sex attraction, and the struggle to separate from the person one is attracted to. Let no one suppose they are taking the moral high-ground by condemning gays. The teaching of Scripture may be clear, but to practise it costs everything.

– Henry, 57

Sexuality is more complicated than we typically accept, and it is still not fully understood. There are many factors that influence an individual's sexual attractions, whether same-sex or opposite-sex. Some of these are biological, perhaps including some degree of genetic predisposition and the hormonal environment of the womb. Others are plainly psychological and cultural. Whereas some people's same-sex attraction appears to be fixed, others also have an attraction to members of the opposite sex or may experience some change over the course of time. Some people are concerned by their sexuality; others are not and do not want to change.

Organizations offering 'reparative therapy' – offering people the opportunity to change same-sex attractions – do exist. These can be effective, in certain respects, and in a number of instances, particularly for those who are highly motivated.[13] However, it is equally true that their success rate is limited. As such, these organizations should be recommended with caution rather than automatically suggested as a first option.

Some men and women are able to identify events and relationships in their backgrounds which have contributed to same-sex attractions. These may be bereavement, distant or over-protective parenting, or even abuse. Often there is an 'absent father' theme. In other cases such events are apparently lacking, and biological and cultural factors appear to play more of a part.

With the first group of people – those for whom certain life-events seem to have contributed to their same-sex attractions – counselling may be of some benefit. However, it is our belief that this should, initially, focus primarily on the deeper issues, rather than on their sexual attractions per se. There may be deep hurts, and sexual attractions may only be the tip of the iceberg. Frequently there are or have been problems with the parents; in many cases the attraction seems to be part of a hunger for a caring relationship they lacked from the same-sex parent. Often there are pre-existing issues of self-esteem, which may be compounded by feelings of

shame about their sexuality itself, particularly in a church setting
that is seen (or assumed) to view such things negatively.

Dealing with these underlying issues first is vital, whether or not
this brings about other changes. It is crucial that those with same-
sex attractions feel accepted and loved by the church, not treated as
projects in need of 'healing' of their sexuality but not of other pain.
Apart from anything else, sexuality does not just 'happen' in isolation
to and from all other development; focusing on sexuality as the only
issue is reductionist, possibly offensive and likely to be ineffective.

What about those for whom a same-sex attraction appears to be
fixed, for whatever reason, after any amount of therapy or none,
whether they wish to change but cannot, or are perfectly happy as
they are? As with any group of people, if the Bible's teachings are
taken seriously then there must be limitations on sexual behaviour.
Everyone, whether experiencing attraction to the same or opposite
sex, has a higher or lower sex drive, a greater or lesser temptation
to promiscuity or adultery. The fact that this appears to be 'innate'
and unchangeable does not mean we should argue that the standard is too difficult to keep and should therefore be discarded.

How did it happen?

If we are to take pastoral care seriously, then we need to look at
more than just the end result, such as an affair or another sexual
relationship outside of marriage. We also need to know why people
take the decisions they do – what has led them to that choice. This
gives us the opportunity to address the causes, rather than just the
symptoms. If we do not do this, we risk sending people out to
make exactly the same mistakes all over again because nothing has
changed; effectively, we are complicit in their sin. In the case study
at the beginning of this chapter, for example, we can see that the
church's treatment of singles contributed to feelings of isolation,
which played a part in prompting the woman to seek intimacy
in casual sex. In chapter 3, we argued that pressures of work and
time, loneliness, and emotional and psychological pain, not to
mention the media's unhelpful contributions, have driven our
culture's tendency to equate sex with intimacy. A relational church
should be one which addresses these factors.

One obvious way we can address this loneliness and lack of

intimacy is not to make such a rigid and unhelpful distinction between married and unmarried within our churches. As we have mentioned before, singleness is a normal part of most people's lives at one time or another. When we marry, we do not and should not suddenly leave our old lives and relationships behind. Reinforcing the distinction between married and unmarried in the way church life is organized overvalues marriage as the best option, undervaluing everyone who isn't married in the process. Home groups that contain a mixture of people at all life stages, and couples and families who are willing to welcome single people into their homes – and vice versa – are important ways that churches can show that community does not begin and end with marriage.

As well as this more general background, we need to know about people's specific circumstances. It is no good dealing with the aftermath of an affair, for example, if the problems in the original marriage(s) are not also addressed. In the case of same-sex attraction, as we have argued, there may be many different contributory factors. Often there will be deeper underlying problems. Trying to deal with the attraction on its own terms without first making a serious effort to understand and heal these issues is likely to be painful, humiliating and unsuccessful. We need to treat these kinds of sexual issues as part of their wider context, not isolate them and expect them to be 'solved' quickly and simply.

Drawing a line

Finally, no matter how much we seek to understand a given situation, there is also the need to maintain boundaries within the church. Faced with an extreme situation of sexual immorality, 'a man has his father's wife', Paul urges the Corinthian church to 'expel the wicked man from among you' (1 Cor. 5:1, 13). His concern appears to have been for the overall purity of the church. If this man's adultery had continued to be accepted, it might have encouraged others towards the same behaviour. The question is, how do we apply this teaching today?

One difference we have to take into account is the nature of 'church' in Paul's time and for us. The Corinthian church was a relatively small, pre-defined congregation, which met in members' homes. Our churches are larger with less well-defined membership.

People come and go, and congregations typically meet in public buildings. It is one thing to bar an individual from a private home, it is another to disallow them from a public building. The difference between our situation and that of the Corinthians means that 'expelling the wicked man' from the church building may be impossible, although expulsion from church membership is not.

The point still holds that we need to maintain some kind of standard, even if we use a different means. For example, allowing affairs between church members to go unchallenged, or permitting remarriage without careful scrutiny of why the first marriage went wrong, can run the risk of being seen to endorse adultery and therefore encouraging other church members to do the same: as Paul argues in the context of the influence of negative lifestyle on a church, 'a little yeast works through the whole batch of dough' (1 Cor. 5:6).

The situation Paul addresses was clearly an extreme and unusual one. It is a particularly shocking form of sexual immorality in which a man is having a sexual relationship with his stepmother, presumably either after divorce or bereavement. To complicate matters, this appears to have come about as a result of the Corinthians' own misunderstanding of the gospel and of the importance of sex, which Paul clarifies in the following two chapters. They had apparently extended their freedom when it came to eating food (which either had been sacrificed to idols or which did not meet the standards of the Jewish kosher laws) to sex too, believing that what occurred in the body was of no consequence to their faith. As a result, not only did they accept this man's affair: they were actually proud of their tolerance (1 Cor. 5:2).

So, the extreme situation called for an extreme solution. The whole church was being undermined by the affair and Paul needed to re-establish its boundaries. Where this is not the case, a more measured approach is possible. Elsewhere, Paul does not opt for such decisive action, instead providing opportunities for repentance and reconciliation (Titus 3:10).

In his second letter to the Corinthians, Paul alludes to this teaching in his own approach to church discipline (2 Cor. 13:1–3). In this instance, the witnesses are not different people, but Paul himself on successive occasions. He has warned certain members of the church in person on two previous visits, presumably for the

'impurity, sexual sin and debauchery' that he mentions immediately beforehand (2 Cor. 12:21).

The picture emerges that, in dealing with sin – whether sexual
or otherwise – we are first to approach the people in question
privately, avoiding scandal or humiliation in front of the whole
congregation. Someone having an affair must be barred from
taking communion (1 Cor. 11). They should be excluded from a
leadership role (1 Tim. 3). It is important to draw some kind of
line in the sand: yes, we should show compassion and understanding of circumstances, but also a recognition of the fact that this is
outside God's will and harms others.

As we have argued throughout this book, sex outside of marriage always has harmful consequences for others, directly and
indirectly, and for the person's relationship with God. We therefore cannot ignore it in our churches on the grounds that it is a
'victimless crime'.

Further resources

The material above is necessarily limited. For more information
about issues of leadership, pastoral care and church discipline,
these further resources are suggested:

Graham Beynon, *God's New Community* (IVP, 2005).
Gary Collins, *Christian Counselling* series (Paternoster, 1989).
Mark Dever, *Nine Marks of a Healthy Church* (Crossway Books, 2005). See also
    <http://www.9marks.org>.
Bill Hybels, *Courageous Leadership* (Zondervan, 2002).
J. David Lundy, *Servant Leadership for Slow Learners* (Authentic Lifestyle, 2002).
Derek Tidball, *Skilful Shepherds* (Apollos, 1996).

John Piper's website, <http://www.desiringgod.org>, includes a
large number of sermons and articles.

Notes

1. Randy Newman, 'Why Are Christians So Homophobic?', in *Questioning
    Evangelism: Engaging People's Hearts the Way Jesus Did* (Kregel, 2004).

2. See chapter 3, subheading 'What is intimacy?'

3. Also quoted in the dc Talk song, 'What If I Stumble?'

4. Bertrand Russell, 'Christianity and Sex', in *Why I am not a Christian* (Touchstone, 1957).

5. Steve Timmis and Tim Chester, *Total Church* (IVP, 2007), p. 111.

6. Tertullian, *Apology* 39:6.

7. See <http://www.marriageencounter.freeserve.co.uk> and <http://www.wwme.org.uk>.

8. See Michael Schluter and David Lee, *The R Option* (Relationships Foundation, 2003).

9. Anthropologist Robin Dunbar calculates that the human neocortex is capable of maintaining around 150 stable social relationships in a group, which includes how each member of the group is doing and how they relate to the other members. See Malcolm Gladwell, *The Tipping Point – How Little Things Make a Big Difference* (Little, Brown and Company, 2000).

10. <http://www.besom.com>. These provide opportunities for groups of church members to give money or possessions but often time and skills to help those in need. It might involve redecorating a room or a house for a single mother, doing some cleaning and household chores for an elderly person, or helping to sort clothes and other items in the warehouse. A group of people can achieve an enormous amount in just one morning or afternoon. As well as making a real difference in someone's life, this kind of project both fosters an outward focus and gives people the opportunity to get to know one another better in a different context. It also helps us to get to know each others' strengths and weaknesses, and perhaps therefore the ways different people might most effectively and enjoyably contribute to church life – see Commonality.

11. With thanks to Gordon Dalzell, personal communication, for this material.

12. Based on survey of 1,333 Durham students. See <http://shag.dsu.org.uk/strategy.php> (accessed 24 July 2008).

13. For a summary of the success of, and mainstream reaction to these organizations, see clinical psychologist and Christian counsellor Gary R. Collins' website, Newsletter 266, 15 November 2007. <http://www.garyrcollins.com/index2.php?option=com_lm&task=archive&view=html&id=291> (accessed 27 March 2008).

7. RELATIONAL PUBLIC POLICY

Transforming the culture

As previously noted, the primary cause of our culture's sexual liberty is the lack of mature intimacy fostered by rootlessness and individualism. We cannot simply fix the symptom, but must also address this underlying issue. As we tackle the causes, we can expect people's attitude towards sex to change. Similarly, addressing sexual behaviour will also feed back positively into wider cultural values. With both these ends in mind, this chapter will discuss the role of public policy. In particular we will set out a relational lens for public policy, showing that policy has an important part to play in getting sex back into perspective.

Legislation and morality

In 1978, Russian writer and survivor of the labour camps Alexander Solzhenitsyn gave an address to the graduating class at Harvard University. The topic of his address was the 'freedom' of the modern West, which he argued had been won at the expense of truth and morality:[1]

Two hundred or even fifty years ago, it would have seemed quite impossible, in America, that an individual be granted boundless freedom with no purpose, simply for the satisfaction of his whims. Subsequently, however, all such limitations were eroded everywhere in the West; a total emancipation occurred from the moral heritage of Christian centuries with their great reserves of mercy and sacrifice. State systems were becoming ever more materialistic. The West has finally achieved the rights of man, and even excess, but man's sense of responsibility to God and society has grown dimmer and dimmer. In the past decades, the legalistic selfishness of the Western approach to the world has reached its peak and the world has found itself in a harsh spiritual crisis and a political impasse. All the celebrated technological achievements of Progress, including the conquest of outer space, do not redeem the twentieth century's moral poverty, which no one could have imagined even as late as the nineteenth century.

In our present society, tolerance is valued over truth. We maintain that it is better to respect other people's beliefs than risk insulting them by insisting on a different reality. Solzhenitsyn argues that such a loss in the moral sphere cannot be compensated for by an increase in the legal, however detailed. Legalism simply fosters the attitude that we should do as much as we can get away with – the law becomes a target, not a limit. Speed cameras in towns would be obsolete if motorists viewed 30mph as a limit, not the point at which they needed to start being careful to avoid detection. So, in many cases, law is only necessary when morality fails.

Solzhenitsyn continues:

I have spent all my life under a communist regime and I will tell you that a society without any objective legal scale is a terrible one indeed. But a society with no other scale but the legal one is not quite worthy of man either. A society which is based on the letter of the law and never reaches any higher is taking very scarce advantage of the high level of human possibilities. The letter of the law is too cold and formal to have a beneficial influence on society. Whenever the tissue of life is woven of legalistic relations, there is an atmosphere of moral mediocrity, paralyzing man's noblest impulses.

The relationship between law and morality is complex, as has been recognized from the time of Plato. But for the purposes of this chapter, we accept that blunt lawmaking is an inadequate and even undesirable substitute for morality. Making adultery or premarital sex illegal, for example, cannot fill the gap left by the decline of 'traditional' values. Law can only provide a baseline, albeit an important one.

This raises the question of whether *any* public policy will work. Again, to quote Solzhenitsyn:

> In today's Western society, the inequality has been revealed between the freedom for good deeds and the freedom for evil deeds . . . It is time, in the West, to defend not so much human rights as human obligations. Destructive and irresponsible freedom has been granted boundless space. Society appears to have little defense against the abyss of human decadence, such as, for example, misuse of liberty for moral violence against young people, motion pictures full of pornography, crime and horror. It is considered to be part of freedom and theoretically counterbalanced by the young people's right not to look or not to accept. Life organized legalistically has thus shown its inability to defend itself against the corrosion of evil.

This implies that whatever policies are adopted will really only be a temporary or partial solution – an imperfect 'fix' that must be complemented with other approaches that address the underlying problem of the decline in morality. Whilst lawmaking serves the important purpose of maintaining a base level of fair treatment and carries an implicit message of normalizing certain standards and behaviours, there is a ceiling to what can be achieved through policy change. If we want to see deep and lasting change in private and public morality, we must recover some of the ground that has been lost over the last fifty years or so. Although it is not possible to force people to adopt a particular morality merely by legislating it, carefully designed policies might shift the framework and language of lawmaking to emphasize relational outcomes.

Relational policy

The goal of relational policy is to move beyond the letter of the law and ensure that legislation is informed by a relational viewpoint, rather than one focused on individual rights. This requires shifts in the goals of policy so that public life is reorganized around the theme of relational wellbeing, or at least considers relational outcomes alongside other desirable goals. Whilst stressing relational outcomes, we do not deny either individual rights or individual identity; good relationship fosters strong individuality, and strong individuality fosters good relationship. The two are inseparable and it makes no sense to set them against each other. The overarching goal of relational policy is the development of mature relationships, and the promotion of personal responsibility within these relationships.

From wealth to wellbeing

> *In a 2006 poll for the BBC programme,* The Happiness Formula, *81% of respondents agreed that government's prime objective should be happiness, not wealth.*[2]

When it comes to measuring the health or 'success' of a nation, the scale that was predominantly used before the 1970s was GDP. Poverty was generally understood in material terms. The production of wealth was seen not just as a route out of poverty and towards other ends, but as an end in its own right. Although 'development' is now seen in slightly broader terms, such as access to food, clean water, health, education, and other concerns, we still heavily emphasize financial measurements and lack an understanding that strong relationships are equally important for wellbeing. 'The quality of people's social relationships is crucial to their well-being. People need supportive, positive relationships and social belonging to sustain well-being. Evidence [shows] that the need to belong, to have close and long-term social relationships, is a fundamental human need, and that well-being depends on this need being well met. People need social bonds in committed relationships, not simply interactions with strangers, to experience well-being.'[3]

Relational deprivation or, as one columnist recently called it, 'emotional poverty; poverty of the soul'[4] is a problem that does not improve with a nation's financial prosperity. In fact, many so-called 'developing' or, more accurately, 'low-income' nations show far stronger relationships – in longer marriages or the social inclusion of older people, for example – than 'developed' high-income nations. Measures of life satisfaction in the West show that, despite large increases in GDP over recent decades, on average people are no happier since the 1950s.[5]

'Our approach is to define the goals of society in relational terms. One way to do this is to focus on the theme of "relational proximity". It relies on a shared human appreciation that quality of relationships – issues such as identity, security, self-esteem and interdependence – are key to personal well-being and happiness, and also the key to organizational and business effectiveness.'[6] Political leaders are just beginning to use language of wellbeing in stating their hopes and aims for society, rather than simply doing so in financial terms. We would expect any manifesto for social progress to include a relational agenda – alongside and even above the financial one. This may sound radical, but the question remains: is money serving our relationships, or vice versa? Do we go to work to earn money to support our relationships, or is work where we find our identity and self-fulfilment, with our families and relationships coming second to that?

The triple bottom line

Harsh meritocracy has corroded solidarity, empathy and humanity. We must put people ahead of the market.

Neal Lawson, political commentator[7]

The ways in which government departments and businesses treat their employees has an enormous impact on their wellbeing. Working hours, flexibility and the option to work from home can either support or harm family and community relationships, as can the locations of new offices and factories.

For some businesses, a new awareness of how their corporate ethics affect relationships may require large changes. The availability of cheap credit, for example, has encouraged many people into high levels of consumer debt, which places particular strains on couple and family relationships. There is a fundamental tension here: it is in the banks' interest that we should be in debt. That debt can trap individuals in cycles of poverty, with desperate consequences for them and their families. Similarly, advertising has a major part to play in influencing our expectations and telling us what is 'normal'. Advertisers are often misleading, overtly or otherwise, about the 'satisfaction' or wellbeing that their products will bring; in fact, establishing dissatisfaction – either with an existing product or with life without the product – is a precondition of the advertiser successfully selling the public their goods.

We argue that relational outcomes must become a priority for government, alongside financial and environmental ones: a new 'triple bottom line' for policy. This should apply as much to government decisions as to the decisions of large companies.

Relational order: break-up is avoidable

With regard to specific legislation on sexual issues, we recognize that there is a tension between the rights of the individual and overall relational order. Suggestions for relational policy will seek to protect relational order, without neglecting the entirely biblical principle of respect and dignity of the person. But although policies aim to treat people fairly as humans, this does not mean endorsing particular behaviours. We do not suggest that relationship break-up should be made illegal or impossible, but there are ways in which we can slow its rate – protecting and benefitting the couple, their families and wider society in the process.

Couple education
To date the government has focused its efforts on treating broken relationships, or the consequences of broken families. A preventative strategy would offer relational education before such problems arise. One recent research paper noted, 'Despite spending £20-24 billion each year on the consequences of family breakdown, government spends just £4 million on preventative

and remedial relationship support. In focusing all its efforts on treatment, government is sending the message that mainstream family breakdown is largely inevitable.'[8] Given the more realistic figure for government spending of £37 billion, we can say that for every £1 spent on strengthening relationships, nearly £10,000 is spent picking up the pieces when they fail.

Research indicates that only a small increase in the former figure would bring about a huge decrease in the latter. Volume one of *Breakthrough Britain: Ending the costs of social breakdown*, reported that 'a major study of 3,000 families in the US found that divorce rates were 30% lower over the first five years of marriage amongst those who had completed a well-organized marriage preparation.[9] With UK family breakdown so heavily concentrated in the early years of marriage and parenthood, even modest improvements in family stability at these key stages will still prove highly cost-effective.'[10]

In fact, depending on the exact programme, 30% is a fairly cautious estimate. The best-researched couples skills programme, PREP, can reduce the rate of divorce by half to two-thirds of that in the control sample up to five years later.[11] This short course is vastly more cost-effective than the alternative of waiting for problems to happen further down the line and then offering counselling. The US military already uses PREP, because the financial benefits are so clear. 'About 35,000 soldiers this year will get a 12-hour course on how to communicate better with their partners, and how to resolve disputes without throwing plates. It costs about $300 per family. Given that it costs $50,000 to recruit and train a rifleman, and that marital problems are a big reason why soldiers quit, you don't have to save many marriages for this to be cost-effective.'[12] In a similar vein, we estimate that the costs of divorce and its fallout are so high that housing associations would benefit from employing a full-time marriage counsellor if as few as five marriages could be saved per year. The costs to the Exchequer are between £4,000 and £15,000 per year per lone-parent family.[13]

Relationship inventories highlight those couples most at risk of divorce. Premarital inventories can be used to assess a couple's differences in such areas as communication, approach to finances, dealing with family and friends, and other potential areas of conflict. Ten to 15% of couples taking a premarital inventory in the

UK cancel their weddings;[14] the divorce rate over the first five years of marriage is around 14% and the profiles of the couples who cancel after completing the inventory is similar to the ones who end up divorcing anyway. It appears that the use of this inventory may simply prevent those couples from making the mistake in the first place.

Tax breaks for relationship education
Under the government's Green Transport Plan, businesses can take advantage of tax incentives by encouraging staff to cycle to work. Employees receive up to 50% off the cost of a bike, which is paid for from their pre-tax earnings. The company reduces its Income Tax and National Insurance contributions, employees get a new bike and hopefully a healthier lifestyle, and the government comes a step closer to meeting its greenhouse gas emissions targets by reducing the number of cars on the road.

Given the amount of work days and earnings lost through relationship breakdown (see chapter 5), why should a similar tax-relief scheme not be offered with marriage preparation or relationships skills workshops? These could be paid for in the same way, with businesses reducing their tax contributions and improving productivity, employees enjoying more stable relationships, and the government benefitting from the reduction in public spending that would result. If necessary, the scheme could be further incentivized for the individuals by offering a tax break on earnings for the first year of marriage if they accept the offer. Whilst two days off work for a course and a tax break might seem like a lot, the amount of money this represents pales into insignificance given the costs of divorce to the individual, employers and the government. This money could be better spent reducing the tax burden, or invested in other areas.

Cautious divorce
Although much of the received wisdom suggests that divorce is ultimately beneficial for couples and children, because they are happier living without the stress of conflict, research shows that this is rarely the case. In reality, divorce typically leaves parents and children poorer, less healthy and more at risk of abuse. Only when

there is serious conflict – repeated fighting in front of the children – do they benefit from their parents breaking up. These cases only account for around a third of divorces. Plus, the couple themselves are likely to regret it later on. Around 40 to 50% of divorcees regret the decision after five years. Even more convincingly, around 86% of unhappily married couples who remain together have happier marriages five years later, with 60% saying their marriage is 'very happy' or 'quite happy'.[15]

Much of the pain caused by divorce is avoidable, particularly given that many of the couples who divorce would likely stay together if they were given the right marriage education and/or counselling. We do not believe that divorce should be unobtainable in those cases where the marriage genuinely has irretrievably broken down and where forcing the couple to remain married would cause more harm than separation. (There is, of course, the problem of who decides whether the relationship has reached this point, and how.) However, we do believe that many marriages end unnecessarily. This has the effect of downgrading marriage by damaging its stability and permanence: divorce is such an easy option that there is little incentive to work at making a marriage succeed when it runs into difficulties. Walking away becomes the simplest option for the short term, and the promises of marriage start to look more like the 'until further notice' arrangement of cohabitation.

A few changes in divorce proceedings would allow couples to take a more measured and informed approach, as well as taking some pressure off the overstretched family courts. A 'cooling off' period between separation and divorce, which should include compulsory mediation, would help couples to understand fully the likely implications of their choice. We also suggest renaming 'no-fault' divorce as 'no-contest' divorce, which better reflects the reality of the situation and avoids the loaded question of who caused it.

Reforming cohabitation law
Around 25% of UK adults aged 18 to 49 are cohabiting at any one time.[16] Currently, cohabiting couples who break up have no financial rights, although their children do have some. At the end

of July 2007, the Law Commission published a report detailing recommendations to parliament.[17]

The case for reform was based on the 'hardship for many cohabitants on separation and, as a consequence, their children . . . in many cases relationship breakdown may lead to reliance on the State in the form of claims to welfare benefits and social housing'. The report made a distinction between the 'distinctive legal and public commitment that marriage entails' and the 'broad range of cohabiting relationships, exhibiting different degrees of commitment and interdependence'. The report therefore did not recommend identical remedies for cohabitants as for married couples; their suggestions are 'entirely distinct from that which applies between spouses on divorce'. It suggested that cohabiting couples should have *some* financial rights if they have children together, or have lived with each other for a minimum number of years – unspecified at that stage, but suggested as between two and five.

These rights are given by default to cohabiting couples; those who wish to opt-out must expressly choose to waive them. Because the cohabitation reforms focus on financial and legal matters, which are relatively low down the list of reasons that people choose to get married, the Law Commission suggests that their recommendations will not undermine marriage. These rights aim to provide a degree of protection to partners – and therefore to children – who have made financial sacrifices in the course of the relationship, reducing the burden on the State and taxpayer for benefits in the process. As it stands, the proposed agreement provides a basic minimum of protection for the couple, not full rights or responsibilities.

The Law Commission's recommendations would go some way to strengthening relationships outside of marriage. Crucially, this would occur without actually imposing marriage upon the couples, which would be likely to affect marriage rates since couples who would otherwise plan to marry would postpone, knowing that they would be married by default soon anyway. 'Marriage by default' also completely removes the public commitment aspect of marriage, which we have identified as a major factor in its strength over cohabitation in its mobilization of relational support. In

addition, imposing marriage would lead to more couples opting
out of the agreements out of an aversion for the risk of later
divorce proceedings. As it stands, the Law Commission's interest in justice, protection and responsibility *by default* in the case
of unmarried couples is broadly aligned with the concerns found
in biblical passages dealing with analogous situations (see Exod.
22:16–17). In essence, the Exodus passage aims to provide protection and responsibility for the couple – particularly the woman
– who would otherwise be disadvantaged by a premarital sexual
relationship.

Balancing rights and responsibilities

It may appear unfair that we place so much emphasis on married
couples, apparently 'discriminating' against cohabitees and same-
sex couples in the process. Our central theme has been that
the separation of sex from marriage, and the wider concerns of
parenting and building family, has been harmful to society. We
acknowledge that there are bound to be at least a small number of
what have to be called simply 'bad marriages', which are unstable
and difficult environments for children; similarly, there are some
strong cohabitations which may appear to do just as good a job of
parenting as many marriages. In addition, we would not suggest
that sterile heterosexual couples who do not adopt should not
marry, just because their family form – like a same-sex relationship
– separates sex from parenting.

The aim is not to control or censure behaviour, but to send a
message through what the law says. An analogy is the drink-drive
law. There may be many people who can safely drive with a blood-
alcohol level of more than 0.8mg/ml, the current legal limit. They
are arrested anyway. Another example is the downgrading of the
drug marijuana from Class B to Class C status in January 2004.
This was followed by widespread confusion that use of marijuana
had been decriminalized, resulting in greatly increased use. The
point is that a line has to be drawn somewhere, and where that
line is drawn sends a powerful message to society. The evidence
is overwhelming that marriage has, as a rule, proven the best and

safest environment for raising a family; although there are exceptions, other family forms generally prove much more short-lived and include fewer intrinsic benefits. For children, the results of broken relationships can be a rise in poor educational achievement, poverty and crime, as well as disturbed attachment, all of which prepare the next generation for making exactly the same mistakes.

Removing discrimination against extended family and friends

There is another side to the profusion of forms of couple relationship now current, and their associated legislation, and that is that it places an undue emphasis on sexual relationship. We argue that marriage holds a special place as the strongest family form, and should therefore be privileged due to its importance in creating a stable, healthy context for child-rearing. We have also argued that emphasizing sex over other forms of relationship is harmful (chapter 3). Our culture's over-sexualization in its relationship legislation has created some bizarre and poignant inequalities: sexual relationships are now promoted above all others.

Civil partnerships were created to provide a measure of protection, benefits and equality for same-sex couples that was not available to them through marriage – for example, in terms of inheritance and pensions. Incidentally, many of these benefits will also be made available through the proposed cohabitation reforms, which do not distinguish between same-sex and opposite-sex households. However, these arrangements only apply to so-called 'marriage-like' relationships, and specifically exclude relationships between existing family members, such as an uncle and nephew, or a grandparent and grandchild.[18] Essentially, blood relationship – or other forms of close, caring but non-sexual relationship – is less valued by society than sexual relationship – despite the fact that everyone comes from a family of some kind, but not everyone is in a sexual relationship.

These inequalities would be removed if civil partnerships were opened to a wider range of couples – a kind of 'household rights' bill that could apply to siblings and other family members, or even friends who shared a house. Given the environmental, financial and social costs of building more houses, it would surely be beneficial to encourage more people to live together. There is, of course, no reason why same-sex friends (or elderly people and their carers) cannot become civil partners now to obtain the legal benefits; there is no requirement for sex to take place, and – thankfully – no way for the government to prove it anyway. However, the connotations of 'gay marriage' mean that, in practice, few want to do so. Family members are currently the only group explicitly prevented due to the 'degrees of consanguinity' that also restrict marriage.

A relational culture

Just saying 'no' prevents teenage pregnancy the way 'Have a nice day' cures chronic depression.
Faye Wattleton, president of the Center for the Advancement of Women

Ultimately law cannot take the place of morality. There are underlying cultural and moral values which cannot be altered by passing laws. We need to shift people's frameworks of thinking, to emphasize relational values and to take into account the relational injury that arises from their decisions.

This means viewing sexual ethics as a whole, rather than picking out individual aspects and dealing with them in isolation – an approach which threatens to be like pushing down one or other bubble under the wallpaper. It makes no sense to reform cohabitation law without taking into account other factors, such as the benefits and tax credit system, as well as related concerns like marriage and divorce; there is no point encouraging cohabiting couples into marriage if this simply leads to a higher divorce rate a few years later. We need to encourage people into marriage *and* find ways to keep them there – voluntarily.

The relationally literate society
Some of the changes we detail in this chapter may seem remote from sexual ethics. However, if sexual behaviour is to be understood in terms of relationships and its wider impact on third parties and the community, rather than simply in the narrow terms

of 'consent', then other areas of public life should also be evaluated on these criteria. The shift from the me-culture of the iWorld to the relational values of the rWorld (see chapter 1) will require some extensive changes in our frameworks of thinking.

One tendency of the 'iWorld' is to separate sex from the rest of life and treat it as a value or commodity that can be pursued in isolation from relationships. But as we have argued, our current understanding of 'consent' is too narrow, as sex is closely and intricately linked to many other areas of life. Sexual choices cannot be made without affecting our existing networks of relationships – families, friends, local and work communities, schools, colleges and universities.

It is therefore understandable that a framework for public policy that has healthy relationships as its aim should speak into the wider issues that both contribute to and result from the sexual choices that people make. This vision is based on the Christian faith, with its unique solution to the problems of death, evil and self-centredness. But it does not require belief in the Christian faith to succeed. Instead, it appeals on a broader level. As shown in Britain in the nineteenth century, it is possible to have a swing back towards Christian sexual ethics without everyone in the country becoming a Christian. If people understand the limitations of the 'iWorld', with its me-centred, rights-based, materialistic and relationally shallow worldview, it will be possible to build on a shared foundation that provides a real alternative in terms of organizing society and people's personal lives.

Families and communities[19]

At present, many government policies are either neutral or actively harmful to couple and family relationships. Careful financial investment can strengthen relationships, and therefore wellbeing. There are a number of changes we would like to explore.

The importance of roots
Mobility is a major factor that drives rootlessness, isolation and loneliness – some of the problems for which casual sex and low-

commitment relationship are being treated as panaceas, as people
seek this form of pseudo-intimacy in lieu of stronger, established
networks of relationships. Mobility also contributes to the breakdown of couple relationships and disrupts relationships within the
community for couples and their children. People are frequently
separated from their extended families – those who have the greatest interest and joy in supporting couples and their children.

Other than general education in relationship skills or 'relational
literacy', there are various ways in which we might encourage rootedness and commitment to a place and community. In
Singapore, for example, there are grants for first-time homebuy-
ers who choose to live in public housing near to their parents or
married child. In the UK, some larger employers like BT and John
Lewis are enabling employees to move to a different branch of the
company to be nearer their parents or extended families. In reality,
this benefits everyone, since one of the pressures on employees
is the difficulty and expense of arranging childcare – something
parents and in-laws are frequently all too happy to assist with, if
they only had the opportunity. Unfortunately, it is equally true
that other large employers – not least the NHS – require professional trainees to move around the country on a regular basis as
part of their training, something that plays havoc with intentions
for stable relationships and raising a family. Sometimes mobility is
seen as the solution to regional unemployment, with painful consequences for both the nuclear and extended family.[20]

Facilitating home ownership

A major cause for people leaving their families and hometowns
is that there are few jobs – or few in their chosen careers. This
often happens because money becomes concentrated in particular
areas (such as London) meaning that people have to follow it to
find work. Promoting investment trusts that focus on regional
businesses is one way to correct this tendency. Citylife[21] offers
employment bonds to bridge relational and financial gaps in communities across the UK. The initial investment from individuals
and corporations is repaid, but the interest is used to help people
into employment. Extending Gift Aid to this scheme would make
it far more appealing to local investors. Localizing part of people's

pensions, which would provide funds for investment in local health, housing and education services, would strengthen local economies and provide a source of employment for them and their children.

These factors on their own are not necessarily going to promote rootedness, although they may help. In the end, it comes down to the decisions of individuals and families whether to move or not, and frequently that decision is based on salary. We need to develop a more relational outlook on our careers and finances, understanding how our new roles, locations, and salaries will affect our relationships – and whether any perceived financial improvements are worth the relational costs to our families, friends and other relationships. We also need to consider the effects of our decisions now on our lives and on the lives of our children, grandchildren and communities in another twenty, thirty, forty years, or more.[22]

Debt

Consumer debt in the UK runs to around £1.5 trillion. Over £1.2 trillion of this consists of mortgages, but around £240 billion is unsecured debt in the form of loans and credit card debt. The average Briton owes almost £5,000 in unsecured debt. Every day, 300 people are declared insolvent or bankrupt.[23]

This debt affects relationships more severely than many people realize: nearly 11 million people suffer relationship problems because of money worries.[24] 'Low-income families, especially those who reside in poverty neighbourhoods, are daily exposed to a variety of experiences that place extraordinary stress on the couple and family relationships . . . Domestic violence is more prevalent in low-income households . . . Service providers who work with these couples note how often these accumulated stresses spill over into home, and anger and frustration too often poison their relationships between parents and children.'[25] Debt breaks up families, which in turn leads to the probability that subsequent generations will also struggle financially; women, in particular, tend to be worse off financially after separation.

Whilst part of the problem is Britain's 'buy now, pay later' culture, some of the blame can be laid squarely with the banks and credit card companies who aggressively market their products and services. At present, banks may sign a voluntary code of good practice, but, as stated, the fact is that it is in the banks' interest for customers to be in debt, so long as their own liabilities are protected (as they generally are). Instead of the voluntary code, the government could require that they sign a mandatory agreement which prevents aggressive marketing to those least able to afford it, and pledges to provide transparent information about fees.

Financial education in schools, perhaps as part of maths lessons, is vital; part of the problem is simply that many people do not understand how expensive borrowing money really is. Debt counselling is also effective and should be paid for by those lenders who market credit to customers. Credit card controls, such as restricting limit increases and fixing gradually increasing minimum repayment levels, would also help.

It is important to encourage people to avoid debt wherever possible. Even if it can be afforded under present circumstances, there is always a risk to debt; jobs can be lost, health can deteriorate, housing markets can go down, family situations can change. The apostle James warned Christians not to *presume* on God's goodness in the future (Jas 4:13–14). It is often less stressful to live without the next holiday, car, kitchen or 42" plasma TV if freedom from debt means more secure and less stressful domestic and workplace relationships.

Family finances
Sharing finances is a way of strengthening extended family relationships. Families are major economic units – the UK has three million family businesses with a turnover of more than £1 trillion[26] – and major welfare units, caring for relatives and offering financial and relational support. This should be encouraged rather than undermined. This could be achieved through packages of shared financial interests – multi-generational family insurance, welfare, and savings – which would spread risk and provide privileged access to savings products and other financial services. Pro-family business policy would encourage family businesses and the self-employed; a quarter of couples with children include at least one self-employed parent.

Mutuality in finances

The tax and benefits systems show inconsistencies in their treatment of relationships, and could be overhauled to support relationships rather than force people apart. For example, the benefits system, family law, the Child Support Agency and inheritance laws all assume that family income and assets will be shared among family members; in contrast, the tax system largely ignores the couple and other family relationships. So, although the benefits system would expect one working spouse to support the other unemployed spouse, the tax system does not recognize the marriage. Couples cannot pool or split their income, and a single-income couple earning £50,000 per year would pay £3,000 more than a double-income couple earning the same amount. The tax credit system expects two adults and a child to live on the same amount of money as one adult and a child.

Contrary to myth, the very poorest families in the country are not those headed by single parents: they are two-parent families with a low-paid, single breadwinner, who are paying very dearly for their commitment to the stability of marriage. As things stand, we do not so much fail to 'recognise' marriage – we positively penalise it.[27]

A number of measures would address this couple penalty. Increasing the couple element of working tax credit would help to keep couples with children together, rather than encouraging them to live apart because they would otherwise lose benefits. The UK is currently virtually the only country in the EU in which marriage is not in some way recognized by the tax system. The UK also has the highest rate of family breakdown and the worst social problems in Europe. The cost of these bear repeating again: an estimated £37 billion for the direct consequences of family breakdown to the taxpayer, before emotional costs or personal financial factors are taken into account, and a probable total of around £100 billion. This is nearly a sixth of government spending: a sum that could make an enormous difference to other areas such as care for the elderly or education.

The present tax credit system makes it financially more attractive for many unmarried couples to live apart in the first place, even if they have a child together. On top of that, there is little incentive for couples to stick with a difficult relationship. Quite the opposite, in fact: why should a man stay with his partner and children when he knows that a) the state will pay for them if he leaves and b) he is already paying hundreds of pounds in taxes for similar situations the country over? Current policy is like splitting the restaurant bill equally with a group of friends who each insist on a starter, main course, several glasses of wine, dessert and coffee when you only intended to order a bowl of soup: there is little incentive for restraint.

The best example of this trajectory is seen in Sweden, where marriage and cohabitation are treated equally under the law. State-run day-care starts at age one, and single parents are given generous benefits. '[T]he Scandinavian family has in many respects been replaced by the state.'[28] It is concerning to think where this could lead if ever a non-benign political party was voted into power, as the Fascists were in Germany in 1933. There is a high financial cost, which makes it difficult for women to stay at home and raise the children if they want to. After the first year, when day-care starts, women tend to go back to work full time. Taxes are higher than anywhere else in Europe: government spending is more than half of GDP and the top rate of income tax is 60%. The Swedes even have a special word for this 'tax tiredness': *Skattetrat*.

As an alternative, in America, unmarried and separated couples with children are treated in the same way as a married unit; the choice whether to live together under the same roof is left to them. France takes transferable tax allowances a stage further. Income can be divided between both parents and children, with children counting as half an adult (an earning father and a stay-at-home mother with two children can split their income three ways).[29]

At the very least, to safeguard relationships, policies which are effectively paying families to break apart have to be abolished.

Public services policy

There are a number of ways in which public services could contribute to relational outcomes, including in education, the criminal justice system and the health service.[30] Although a detailed treatment of these is outside the scope of this book, in each case we need to look at the ways in which public services affect other people in our families and communities. In terms of education, this might mean placing more of an emphasis on opportunities for relational development through 'soft' subjects like drama, music and PE, which can be used to promote group co-operation, rather than taking a rather narrow and individualistic view of learning that tends to focus on technical knowledge, not how to apply it.

Because relational education is fundamentally a practical, rather than academic discipline, it will impact the way schools model their relationships to pupils, including teacher/pupil, teacher/parents and teacher/teacher. This would mean treating schools as more than 'retail outlets that sell education', where education means grades in various subjects that grant access to particular forms of employment.[31] In terms of sex education, we would expect the curriculum to include not only issues such as health and protection, but the likely knock-on effects to third parties.

Relational justice means that, as Tony Blair so popularly précised, we need to be tough on crime, and tough on the causes of crime.[32] The Bible does allow for some measure of social exclusion, as in the 'cities of refuge' for those who commit manslaughter (Deut. 19). However, our ever-increasing prison population suggests that we have taken this to extremes. The number of prisoners in England and Wales now stands at over 80,000, the highest rate in the European Union. Around two-thirds of these reoffend within two years of finishing their sentence. A third of prisoners have nowhere to live on release, but stable accommodation can reduce the rate of reoffending by 20%.

Most significantly, around 40% of prisoners lose contact with their families, yet good family ties are a major factor in reducing reoffending.[33] A large proportion of prisoners come from dysfunctional and painful family backgrounds, but this is rarely taken into account. Greater efforts could be made to house prisoners closer to their families; to use meal-times to develop relational skills; to help offenders deal with anger and frustration; to improve literacy and communication skills; to enable them to handle difficult situations at home.

In terms of health, the vast majority of government spending is focused on clearing up when things go wrong, rather than investing in health and wellbeing to begin with. This would appear to be another facet of our materialistic, commercialized and compartmentalized lives. Instead of treating our bodies as an essential vehicle for enjoying and maintaining our networks of relationships, we think of them more as second-hand cars, to be driven into the ground and patched up when necessary.[34] As with couple breakdown, prevention is far better than cure – financially as well as relationally and physically.

Business and finance

Regulating working hours is crucial for relationships. The UK has the longest average working week of any country in the EU and is second only to the US. We need to reduce working hours in line with EU legislation so that parents have more time with children and each other. Perhaps more important is flexibility of working hours. Many parents – typically mothers – would like to go back to work once their children start nursery or school, but are unable to because they cannot work a full day if they have to pick their children up early in the afternoon. Many fathers do not get to see as much of their children as they would like because they have to work long hours.[35]

In many cases it is impractical for mothers to go back to work because the cost of childcare is so high. Many people have family who would love to help out, but who live too far away. National companies could be of assistance here by allowing employees to relocate to branches of the business nearer their families. Similarly, housing policy may make a real difference; giving the parents of a single mother priority in nearby housing might make the difference between surviving on tax credits and going back to work.

Sunday as family and friends day
Our 24/7 culture means that working hours have become extended not only during the day but also across the week. The relaxation of Sunday trading regulations threatens to make Sunday like any other

day of the week, meaning that people lack a shared day off to spend with their families; 1.34 million families have at least one parent working on each of the days of the weekend.[36] Another day off during the week is unlikely to coincide with their partner's day off and, in any case, their children will probably be at school. In addition, complete deregulation is likely to hit small local and family businesses hard, as they struggle to compete with the big supermarkets.[37]

Relational awareness

The way our society is organized means that it is easy for people to make mistakes in their sexual relationships. This is not just true of legislation which, for example, makes little or no distinction between the married and unmarried, and does little to discourage people from exiting what might otherwise prove to be a stable and beneficial marriage. It is also true in terms of the cultural norms that are part of our collective backgrounds.

Parts of the media play a major role in setting and promoting these standards. Campaigning for appropriate programming and censuring TV and film-makers' tendency to normalize and even glamorize adultery and casual sex are therefore important. But there are further initiatives – by the church or by other groups – by which we might seek to shift society's standards and expectations and facilitate stable, committed relationships.

Deliberate relationships

Lots of people in Britain hook up in a bar or a club, but you wouldn't buy a house or car drunk, so why would you expect to find a life partner that way? Then people wake up 20 years later and wonder why they haven't found someone to settle down with.

Aneela Rahman, 'marriage arranger'[38]

As an alternative to the confused loneliness described by Aneela Rahman, many people wake up and realize that a relationship they started on the spur of the moment has somehow progressed, they are living together, perhaps with a child – and are still no more suited to each other than they were on day one. How many failed relationships begin 'by default' in this way? What can we do to discourage this and enable people to go into their life-relationships with their eyes open?

To borrow a popularized maxim of criminal law, sex requires means, motive and opportunity. Means has become considerably easier since the availability of reliable contraception. As a motive, biological drive remains unchanged; loneliness, on the other hand, has encouraged people to seek sex as a form of relational bandage. Opportunity has increased with drinking hours, working hours and practices, and a consumeristic dating culture. Reducing casual and relationally harmful sex means addressing these areas.

Whilst we do not expect or desire businesses to police every potential sexual relationship, once the concept of relational injury is better understood and accepted, organizations might show some awareness by means of voluntary codes of conduct governing, for example, drinking hours and behaviour, dress codes and even single-sex accommodation policies in universities and colleges. Author Wendy Shalit highlights the extent of the discrimination against those with Judaeo-Christian values. 'In the fall of 1997, five Orthodox students asked to be excused from Yale's requirement that they live in coed dorms, and the administration denied the students their request. This is the same administration, incidentally, which approved a Bisexual, Gay, Lesbian, and Transgender Cooperative, an African-American cultural studies house, and a Latina/Latino cultural center. Apparently diversity ends where religious morality begins.'[39]

In many different ways our culture routinely promotes casual sex – and therefore relational harm – above stable, committed relationships. The priority is not to censure behaviour, but to shift our values from promoting harmful relationships to promoting wellbeing through healthy relationships.

Notes

1. 'A World Split Apart' – Commencement Address delivered at Harvard University, 8 June 1978. See online at <http://www.orthodoxytoday.org/articles/SolzhenitsynHarvard.php> (accessed 4 October 2007).

2. John Ashcroft and Phil Caroe, *Thriving Lives: Which Way for Wellbeing?* (Relationships Foundation, 2007). <http://www.relationships foundation.org/download.php?id=171>.

3. Ed Diener and Martin Seligman, 'Beyond Money: Toward an economy of well-being' in *Psychological Science in the Public Interest*, 5 (2004), pp. 1–31.

4. Melanie Reid, 'Shannon Matthews is the new face of poverty', *The Times*, 17 March 2008 – see chapter 4.

5. Richard Layard, 'Happiness is Back', *Prospect* magazine, March 2005. See <http://www.prospect-magazine.co.uk/article_details.php?id=6761> (accessed 24 July 2008).

6. Michael Schluter, 'What Charter for Humanity?' *Cambridge Papers* vol. 15 no. 3 (Jubilee Centre, September 2006). Available from http://www.jubilee-centre.org.

7. 'New Labour has presided over a social recession', in *The Guardian*, 22 February 2007. See <http://www.guardian.co.uk/commentisfree/2007/feb/22/comment.politics> (accessed 22 July 2008).

8. Harry Benson, *Relationship Education in the UK* (2007). <http://www.bcft.co.uk> (accessed 29 April 2008).

9. Scott Stanley *et al.*, 'Premarital education, marital quality, and marital stability: Findings from a large, random, household survey', in *Journal of Family Psychology*, 20 (2006), pp. 117–126, reported in *Breakthrough Britain* (Centre for Social Justice, 2007), p. 49.

10. *Breakthrough Britain*, p. 49.

11. <http://www.prepinc.com/main/research_foundation.asp> (accessed 22 July 2008). Some studies have found the rate drops by up to 80% after three years. K. Hahlweg, H. J. Markman, F. Thurmair, J. Engel, and J. Eckert, 'Prevention of marital distress: Results of a German prospective longitudinal study', in *Journal of Family Psychology*, 12 (1998), pp. 543–556.

12. 'The Frayed Knot', in *The Economist*, 24 May 2007.

13. 'Fractured Families', in *Breakdown Britain* (Centre for Social Justice, 2006), p. 66.

14. Scott M. Stanley, 'Making A Case for Premarital Education', in *Family Relations Journal* 50, 2001, pp. 272–280.

15. Linda Waite and Maggie Gallagher, *The Case for Marriage* (Doubleday, 2000). See Sarah Russo, *The Many Benefits of Traditional Marriage*, <http://academia.org/campus_reports/2000/december_2000_4.html> (accessed 22 July 2008).

16. Office of National Statistics.

17. See <http://www.lawcom.gov.uk/cohabitation.htm> (accessed 22 July 2008).

18. See 'Counterfeit Marriage: how "civil partnerships" devalue the currency of marriage' (The Christian Institute, 2002). See <http://www.christian. org.uk/html-publications/counterfeitmarriage.htm> (accessed 22 July 2008).

19. For more detailed information, see the Relationship Foundation's forthcoming *Finance, Relationships and Well-being* project. See <http://www. relationshipsfoundation.org>.

20. Helen Hayward, *The Impact of Mobility on Personal Relationships* (Jubilee Centre, Cambridge, 1992); Michael Schluter, *Family Roots or Mobility?* (Jubilee Centre, 1986).

21. <http://www.citylifeltd.org>.

22. See 'Roots', in Michael Schluter and David Lee, *The R Option* (Relationships Foundation, 2003), pp. 147–157.

23. Credit Action figures for April 2008. <http://www.creditaction.org.uk/ debt-statistics.html> (accessed 19 November 2008).

24. YouGov reports that 10.7 million people suffer relationship problems because of money worries. See press release from Social Justice Policy Group, 11 December 2006, available at <http://www.conservatives. com/pdf/breakdownpressrelease.pdf> (accessed 24 July 2008).

25. Theodora Ooms, 'Strengthening Couples and Marriage in Low-Income Communities', in A. Hawkins *et al.*, *Revitalising the Institution of Marriage for the Twenty-First Century* (Praeger, 2002), pp. 79–100.

26. Institute for Family Business.

27. Janet Daley, 'Give single parents more incentives so marriage is more appealing', *Daily Telegraph*, 26 February 2007. See <http://www.telegraph. co.uk/opinion/main.jhtml?xml=/opinion/2007/02/26/do2602.xml> (accessed 22 July 2008).

28. Stanley Kurtz, 'No Explanation', *National Review*, 3 June 2004. See <http://www.nationalreview.com/kurtz/kurtz200406030910.asp> (accessed 22 July 2008).

29. 'Marriage, tax reform and better schools: how to repair the social fabric', David Green, *The Daily Telegraph*, 19 February 2007.

30. See Nick Spencer, *Votewise* (SPCK, 2004).

31. Spencer, *Votewise*, p. 56.

32. See Spencer, *Votewise*, pp. 78–87, for an overview of relational justice. For a more detailed treatment, see Jonathan Burnside, 'Criminal Justice', in

Michael Schluter and John Ashcroft (eds.), *Jubilee Manifesto* (IVP, 2005), pp. 234–254.

33. See 'Reducing re-offending by ex-prisoners', Social Exclusion Unit, 2002. See <http://www.cabinetoffice.gov.uk/social_exclusion_task_force/~/media/assets/www.cabinetoffice.gov.uk/social_exclusion_task_force/publications_1997_to_2006/reducing_summary%20pdf.ashx> (accessed 24 July 2008).

34. For more on relational healthcare principles, see Schluter and Lee, *R Option*, pp. 159–169.

35. See <http://www.keeptimeforchildren.org.uk>.

36. Figure provided for the Relationships Foundation by the National Centre for Social Research. See <http://www.keeptimeforchildren.org.uk/NatCen_exec_summary.doc> (accessed 24 July 2008).

37. See <http://www.keepsundayspecial.org.uk>.

38. See 'Arrange me a marriage: Could Asian-style match-making be the way to find a perfect partner?', *Daily Mail*, 8 November 2007. <http://www.dailymail.co.uk/femail/article-492348/Arrange-marriage-Could-Asian-style-match-making-way-perfect-partner.html> (accessed 24 July 2008).

39. Wendy Shalit, *A Return to Modesty: Discovering the Lost Virtue* (Free Press, 2000), p. 61.

8. RELATIONAL SEX

Seeing the consequences of 'my' sexual choices

A voice in the wilderness

Even if the reader agrees with the principles of this book – that sex has consequences far beyond the couple involved and that 'consenting adults' is far too narrow a criterion to legitimate a sexual act – we recognize that some of our other conclusions may be harder to accept. For some people, personal liberty is so important that they may feel that relational disorder and pain are a worthwhile price to pay for it. Some may see this as a hard-hearted book, because it concentrates so much on the thoughts and feelings of third parties to a sexual act, at a personal, family and community level; it may seem there is a risk of becoming disinterested in the rights, pain and desires of those most directly involved in the sexual relationship.

Ultimately, however, this book is the opposite of that. Instead of denying individual rights and identity, we argue that the individual is best understood, nourished and sustained in the broader context of healthy relational communities. Such individuals are themselves more able and likely to create enduring intimate bonds with others, benefitting themselves, their families and their communities. This is in contrast to the behaviours of individuals who enter into casual, chaotic or uncommitted sexual relationships, which often have powerfully negative and painful consequences, on themselves and others. We believe that individuals are best protected and encouraged in their development when these matters are known and addressed.

If the emphasis of the book is too much towards third parties, there is good reason. There is little need to stress the rights of individuals. Our culture places a high premium on personal freedom: as we have argued, this is the root of the problem. On the other hand, the self-referential morality that individualism fosters has had the effect of separating sex from its wider concerns of parenting and family, whilst cultivating a forced association between sex and intimacy. There has been a collective denial about the effects that 'personal' sexual choices have on other people: family, friends, colleagues and wider society. These consequences often go unnoticed and unquestioned, and yet they cause an enormous amount of emotional, relational and financial harm. The aim of this book has been to provide a corrective voice by drawing attention both to the wide-ranging casualties and to the exciting potential of a more holistic approach to relationships. Although we are aware that we need to show grace and understanding, there is also a need to promote a positive alternative which will reduce the direct and indirect knock-on effects suffered by so many.

Personal freedom vs. collective wellbeing

As Freud said, civilization – or, in our terms, relational order – is built on the renunciation of instinct. There is a fundamental tension between the desires of the individual and the overall health of society, and therefore an inherent difficulty in holding the two together. How we deal with this in practice is not clear, although we have made a number of suggestions for public policy, both specifically on sexual issues and to encourage the wider culture to think more relationally.

What we are *not* suggesting is that we should simply legislate against sex outside of marriage. This is too much of an invasion of privacy: we believe that certain freedoms are essential to our

humanity, and that to curtail them would be to invite more serious
problems in the future. It is not government's job to decide what
should or should not go on in the bedroom, any more than it
should decide the contents of our kitchen cupboards, or how
often we exercise. However, people surely have a right to know
about the consequences of their actions. Whilst we should not
prohibit people from eating unhealthy food or drinking heavily,
we would expect that they should be aware of the potential risks
to themselves, and the costs they are likely to impose on other
people, so that they can take steps to protect themselves and
others from the direct and indirect consequences of their behaviour. Public policy might encourage people away from these and
other harmful behaviours by various measures, without ultimately
denying their personal freedom.

So, we do not suggest that we should outlaw adultery and premarital sex, scrap civil partnerships and make divorce impossible to
obtain. Rather, we want to highlight how society has been operating
under a misconception about the consequences of sexual liberty
for the past fifty years. This raises the question of whether sexual
freedom is worth the price we have paid, and are continuing to pay.

'Just' sex?

In terms of sex, our cultural mindset and legislation require little
more than that sex takes place between consenting adults. But
is the agreement of two people an adequate basis to take into
account the interests of those who are affected? The implication
of the case presented in this book is that individual consent alone
is not enough: sex affects far more people than the two directly
involved.

In the case of adultery, for example, if we want to follow the
principle that we should obtain the consent of those who would
be affected by a sexual act, then consent would theoretically be
required from many people. Firstly, and most obviously, it would
be required from the spouse, as well as any children from the marriage. Since the affair is likely to have an effect on the duration
and certainly quality of the marriage, this might also be extended
to children who have not yet been born. Then there are the four
parents of the couple, as well as their friends, relatives and work

colleagues – those people who might be affected in one way or another through their personal or business relationships. At the widest level, there is the taxpayer who may have to pay for additional housing and single-parent benefits as a result.

Realistically, then, there is no way of obtaining consent from all the people who might be affected by a sexual relationship. Even if consent could be obtained from all of these, the Christian will recognize that there is still the problem of obtaining consent from God!

Relational thinking

At the moment, people often start or end a sexual relationship for reasons that are not necessarily clear. They lack information: information about how their relationships will affect themselves and their partners, future partners, their friends, family and community as a whole. These consequences are enormous, yet almost entirely hidden at the moment of making the decision to sleep with someone. We need a more relational framework to understand the effects our 'personal' behaviour has on others, and on ourselves.

Our culture tends to compartmentalize sex from every other area of life, personal and public. But these expressions of our core character and identity surely cannot be separated so neatly. Who we are behind closed doors is not irrelevant: in fact, it is arguably the best indication of who we really are, because it is out of sight of others that we act with least influence from external expectations and pressures. People often claim that what they do in private has nothing to do with the rest of their lives, and is nobody else's business but their own. Nothing could be further from the truth.

This compartmentalization of life occurs on a far wider scale. People might be individualistic in their thinking about their sexual relationships, but they are also individualistic about the rest of their lives. Our culture teaches us to be rapacious. It tells us that material possessions are important. Banks give us cheap credit to buy things now and pay later (and far more than had we paid up front). We are taught to consume, but we are not encouraged to consider the consequences that our consumption has on ourselves and upon others until disaster looms – whether in terms of personal debt, global financial turmoil or environmental crisis.

Almost every message we receive tells us that it is our choice and right to *have*. We are unlikely to stop being individualistic, materialistic and consumeristic in our sexual relationships unless we address the same individualism, materialism and consumerism in the rest of our lives. Sexual attitudes are both a reflection of, and an influence on, the wider culture, and we need to address both: in our personal lives, in our churches, businesses, schools and universities, and at a national level through public policy.

To return to the title and the theme of the book, 'just' sex is never just sex. The idea of 'just sex' – sex that is fair to those directly involved and to all others affected – requires a deeper understanding of sex than the one our culture gives us. There is no such thing as 'just' sex, in the sense of 'only sex', without the strings of third-party impact. So, just ensuring the consent of those directly involved can never be an adequate moral basis to justify a sexual act. We need to find ways of rediscovering and fostering true intimacy, in which people can understand their identities not by trying to look inside themselves in isolation from others, but as individuals who have come to know themselves through relationships, with God and with other people. We need to recognize that the key to our sexual freedom, and indeed to our whole personal development, does not lie within ourselves, but in getting relationships right with God and with other people.

APPENDIX

Sex in the Bible: Twenty questions answered

It is God's will that you should be sanctified: that you should avoid sexual immorality; that each of you should learn to control his own body in a way that is holy and honourable, not in passionate lust like the heathen, who do not know God; and that in this matter no-one should wrong his brother or take advantage of him. The Lord will punish men for all such sins, as we have already told you and warned you. For God did not call us to be impure, but to live a holy life. Therefore, he who rejects this instruction does not reject man but God, who gives you his Holy Spirit.

1 Thessalonians 4:3–8

We have stated in this book that we consider the Bible's ideal for sex is that is should take place only within the context of lifelong, heterosexual, monogamous and exclusive marriage. We recognize that not everyone will agree with this! This may be either because they are uncertain about what the Bible says or because they interpret its teachings differently. In this appendix we provide a brief discussion of some of the arguments from biblical texts about sexual issues. We believe that the Bible's teachings are not arbitrary; both the Bible and our observations from modern life and culture independently point to the same ideals of sexual behaviour if we are to build a truly relational society.

#1. Does 'fornication' really matter?

The fourth-century saint and teacher Augustine believed that marriage was a second-best to abstinence, but still far better than 'fornication' which he placed on a par with adultery. 'Fornication', which translates the Greek word *porneia*, is usually translated in newer versions as 'sexual immorality', a fairly unhelpful and non-specific term. It appears in the 'vice lists' of the New Testament (Rom. 1:29; 1 Cor. 6:9–10; Gal. 5:19–21; Col. 3:5) and in other places. In Acts 15, avoiding sexual immorality is one of the only conditions imposed on new Christians. The New Testament authors therefore viewed it seriously.

#2. But how do we know *exactly* what is and isn't meant by 'fornication'?

The exact meaning of *porneia* – 'fornication', 'sexual immorality' – in the New Testament is not immediately clear, which is unfortunate as it is important in understanding what was and wasn't permitted by the NT authors. Etymologically, *porneia* derives from the Greek verb *porneuō*, from *pornē*, a prostitute and *pornos,* the masculine form, a 'fornicator' (the man who visits them or hires them out to others). Ultimately these derive from *pernemi*, to sell.[1]

Fornication, which translates *porneia* in the older versions, comes from the Latin word *fornix*, meaning an arch (the related verb is *fornicatio*, from which the word 'fornication' comes). Prostitutes would gather under particular arches to solicit clients, and so *fornix* also came to mean 'brothel'.

Originally, then, the words applied specifically to prostitution – as Paul uses them in 1 Corinthians 6:16 and 18. Here, the sexual immorality in question does happen to be sex with prostitutes, which does not *per se* rule out – for example – premarital sex within a committed relationship. But etymology alone does not give us the precise meaning of the word for the New Testament context, only where it originally came from.[2] *Porneia* is elsewhere used in a much wider context than prostitution, whatever the origins of the word. In 1 Corinthians 5:1, *porneia* is a general term for sexual immorality, one form of which in this Corinthian example is that 'a man has his father's wife'. In Matthew 5:32 it is apparently used of a wife's infidelity. Neither of these involve selling sex.

#3. So 'fornication' might not *necessarily* apply to sex before marriage . . .?

There are no absolutely clear occurrences of *porneia* as specifically relating to sex before marriage. However, in 1 Corinthians 7:8–9 and 36–38, Paul indicates that it is better for the reader to marry than to 'burn [with lust]' or 'act improperly towards the virgin he is engaged to'. In any case, both Paul's and Jesus' insights into the significance of 'one flesh' suggests that the nature of sex as both spiritually and physically binding is always significant whoever the partner; it was just that visiting prostitutes was one common vice Paul had to address in the Corinthian church. In the absence of any laws explicitly forbidding premarital sex, this positive principle – that sex creates an enduring bond – is enough to infer that *any* temporary sexual relationship is contrary to biblical norms.

#4. What's this 'one flesh' business that Genesis, Jesus and Paul seem so keen on?

Paul and Jesus both quote the 'one flesh' verse in Genesis 2:24 as fundamental to sex and marriage. Jesus uses it in the context of a discussion with some Pharisees about their views on divorce (Matt. 19:1–12). "'Haven't you read," he replied, "that at the beginning the Creator 'made them male and female', and said, 'for this reason a man will leave his father and mother and be united to his wife, and the two will become one flesh'? So they are no longer two, but one. Therefore what God has joined together, let man not separate.'" In Paul's case (1 Cor. 6:12–20), it is quoted in the context of casual sex or sex with prostitutes. 'Do you not know that he who unites himself with a prostitute is one with her in body? For it is said, "The two will become one flesh." But he who unites himself with the Lord is one with him in spirit.'

In dealing with the biblical concept of 'one flesh', it is helpful to understand exactly what the term means. The ideal that the one-flesh act takes place within marriage is clear, but does it mean that sex *should* be carried out within the context of marriage, or that sex in some way *creates* the 'one fleshness'? Does sex outside of marriage still constitute a one-flesh encounter? Paul's statement that 'he who unites himself with a prostitute is one with her in body' shows that the one-flesh status *can* be made and broken fairly easily, but that this constitutes a shocking trivialization or distortion of the creation principle. Jesus also made it clear that it was not a union that was supposed to be casually broken, though it is open to that abuse: 'So they are no longer two, but one. Therefore what God has joined, let man not separate' (Matt. 19:6).

The language used – Hebrew *bāśār*, 'flesh'; *'echād*, 'one' (the same word used of God's oneness in Deut. 6:4, 'Hear O Israel: The Lord our God, the Lord is one') – suggests the creation or union of 'flesh' or identity where there was none before. The cognate Arabic word *baśar* means 'skin'; the cognate Syriac *besrā'* and Assyrian *biśru* both mean 'blood relation'. Elsewhere in the Bible, *bāśār* is used for the flesh of animals (mcat), but also of the human body itself. In Genesis 2:23, this seems to be the meaning of 'flesh of my flesh': 'body of my body'. This is the sense of 'flesh and blood' in Genesis 29:14, Judges 9:2, 2 Samuel 5:1, and elsewhere. This meaning has the same sense as *śě'ēr bāśār*, 'near of kin', in Leviticus 18:6.[3]

An implication seems to be that 'one flesh' is more than just a close relative – it is the *same* flesh. Perhaps this (as well as the potential damage to the extended family) is part of the reason why some relatives by marriage are treated like blood-relatives in Leviticus 18 and 20. Genesis 2 supports this idea, that a new family is formed where there were previously two separate ones: 'For this reason a man will leave his father and mother and be united to his wife, and they will become one flesh.' The creation of a new family is essential to the nature of marriage.

#5. So in the OT, if you had sex, you were married?

It is quite difficult to know what 'marriage' actually meant in early Israel, because there is little or no explicit information about what was involved in getting married. There are laws governing marriage, and narratives that involve weddings (like Samson's in Judg. 14), but unfortunately no equivalent to our reading of the banns, *Common Worship* marriage service, or signing of the register. Gaining such insights into biblical marriage has been compared to trying to recreate traffic laws by sitting by the roadside and watching the traffic pass. Often, points are only considered noteworthy by the biblical writers because they represent a departure from the norms of the day. In the Bible, knowledge of marriage customs, and the need for them, generally seems to have been assumed. Perhaps the reason for this lack of explicit legislation is simply that there was no need to have a national law for something that was so widely obeyed and highly respected in the culture. In any case, marriage was not centrally recorded but appears to have been arranged within families and clans, and regulated by these and the wider community.

Whatever the details, throughout the Bible it is expected that sex will occur within marriage. Much of the Bible's legislation about sex concerns the consequences of sex outside of marriage. More than that, sex practically *is* marriage; where possible, premarital sex results in the immediate marriage of the couple (Exod. 22:16).

There appears to be a sequence of events usual in arranging marriages:[4]

1. Agreement between members of the two families that the bride will be given in marriage to the groom – it is group, not individual consent.
2. Payment of the agreed *mōhar* (betrothal payment) by the groom, followed by a period of betrothal.
3. Claiming of the bride by the groom on the strength of payment of the *mōhar*.
4. Completion/consummation of the marriage.

Where this sequence is disturbed by premarital sex, a 'shotgun wedding' takes place in order to regularize it as soon as possible (where the seriousness of the offence – for example in violation of an existing betrothal or marriage – does not require the death penalty).[5] Exodus 22:16–17 concerns the case of an unbetrothed virgin who is seduced; the seducer has to pay whatever the father demands and marry her, unless the girl's father considers him completely unsuitable – in which case, he must still pay the bride price. In Genesis 34:11–12, Shechem offers an almost unlimited price to Jacob for Dinah.[6]

The Mishnah (Kiddushin 1:1) understands that betrothal could be achieved in three ways: through money (accepted in the presence of witnesses), through a contract (a written betrothal declaration), or through sexual intercourse. Usually all three conditions would be met for a marriage, but any one was legally binding. In biblical terms, sex could effectively formalize marriage. Even in England, before the Marriage Act of 1753, a couple could be married without witnesses or a ceremony, simply by saying that they were married to one another. Today, the commitment derived from the legal and social impact of the marriage covenant is initiated by the formal wedding ceremony, not by sex (though non-consummation can still be grounds for divorce/annulment).

On these grounds, it could be argued that premarital sex is not unbiblical, so long as it *does* sooner or later progress to marriage to that person, and there is no sex with a third party by either. The problem with this approach is that a future marriage cannot be guaranteed – one or other of the couple could change their mind in the meantime. James 4:13–17 also warns against presuming on God's goodness: we do not even know what will happen tomorrow, so should not base our sexual behaviour on a decision to marry that lies months or years in the future.

The biblical regulations are no doubt shaped by cultural and economic considerations – namely, both the protection of the male interest (to ensure that any children were his) and the protection of the female interest (so that she was not left alone and without provision in the case of pregnancy). However, Genesis 2 and the New Testament texts that refer to it make it clear that the importance of sex is greater than merely social and economic. It is also of spiritual significance. In the eyes of God, as well as in those of early Israel, sex *creates* one flesh-ness. 'So they are no longer two, but one. Therefore what God has joined together, let man not separate' (Matt. 19:6). Paul's warning about sleeping with prostitutes in 1 Corinthians 6:16 makes it clear that this warning is about sex, not the ceremony or practice of marriage.

#6. Wasn't prostitution a normal part of life in biblical and Ancient Near Eastern cultures?

There are numerous occasions in the Bible where characters visit prostitutes, or where prostitutes are mentioned in other contexts (as with Judah in Gen. 38 or Samson in Judg. 16). It is equally clear that this was not condoned by the Law. 'Do not degrade your daughter by making her a prostitute, or the land will turn to prostitution and be filled with wickedness' (Lev. 19:29). Prostitution was closely related to idolatry, and the package was repeatedly denounced (Lev 20:6; Hos. 4:10–19; 1 Cor. 6:9–10). Arguably, the two still are a package, with sex today as the worship of pleasure.

#7. Is divorce allowed in the Bible?

In Matthew 19, Jesus engages with the Pharisees over the interpretation of Deuteronomy 24:1–4, which legislates for divorce (specifically, that the divorced couple could not remarry each other if the woman had remarried and then divorced someone else). 'If a man marries a woman who becomes displeasing to him because he finds something indecent about her, and he writes her a certificate of divorce . . .' Divorce, like marriage, seems to be taken for granted in the Old Testament. By New Testament times, people had started to ask exactly what circumstances make it acceptable.

#8. So, what circumstances made divorce acceptable?

The Hebrew of Deuteronomy 24:1 (*'ervat dābār*, 'something indecent' – literally 'nakedness of a thing') is ambiguous. The Pharisees' question in Matthew 19 surrounds the interpretation of this verse, and what constituted legitimate grounds for divorce. Amongst the Pharisees, who sought to interpret these verses for everyday use, there were different approaches. These were recorded in the Mishnah. Some rabbis thought that only some form of infidelity was cause enough (perhaps suspected adultery or undisclosed premarital sex; proven adultery was supposed to have been punishable by the death penalty, although there is some evidence that divorce was used as a substitute at times when Jews did not have the right to carry out executions). Others thought that any reason for displeasure was enough, or if a man found another woman more attractive. Mishnah Gittin 9 reads:

> Bet Shammai says, a man should not divorce his wife unless he has found her guilty of some unseemly conduct, as it says, 'Because he has found some unseemly thing in her' [placing an emphasis on 'unseemly', presumably some form of unfaithfulness].

> Bet Hillel says, [he may divorce her] even if she has merely burnt his dish, since it says, 'Because he has found some unseemly thing in her' [placing emphasis on 'some . . . thing', that is, *any* thing].

> Rabbi Akiva says, [he may divorce her] even if he finds another woman more beautiful than she is, as it says, 'it cometh to pass, if she find no favour in his eyes' [placing emphasis on the man's displeasure with his wife].

In Matthew 19:3, the Pharisees ask Jesus: 'Is it lawful for a man to divorce his wife *for any and every reason?*' (Greek: *kata pasan aitian.*) This suggests that the context of the discussion was actually the Pharisees' own debate about the legitimate grounds for divorce, and particularly, whether Hillel and Akiva's liberal interpretations above were as valid as Shammai's conservative one. It is quite possible that the Pharisees intended to damage Jesus' reputation with the people in this, as they expected him to side with the stricter – and far less popular – position. Essentially, this was not intended to be a general discussion about divorce, but specifically about *no-fault* divorce, an idea that seems to have been as popular in first-century Judea as it is in the twenty-first-century West. 'No-fault' divorce here is really unilateral divorce; the husband does not need a reason – at least, nothing worse than a badly cooked meal – to sever ties with his wife. She does not get a say in the matter because she has no claim on her husband. The Pharisees never had any question about *whether* divorce was permitted – that was taken as read. The only issue was what grounds were permissible.[7]

#9. So where did Jesus come out on that debate?

Jesus, in answering the Pharisees' question, refuses to engage directly with their implicit options, thereby shrewdly avoiding siding with one or other faction. Instead, he looks to an earlier and better story for a guiding principle: the one-to-one lifelong, exclusive bond of the archetypal couple in the creation narrative. These two become 'one flesh' and are considered permanently united by God. 'Therefore what God has joined together, let man not separate' (Matt. 19:6). The emphasis is shifted away from human desire and towards God's intention for marriage. This does not necessarily mean that divorce is always the wrong option, only that it is not God's will for marriage and, where it does occur, is intended to be a least-worst solution in a broken world.

#10. OK, but precisely what grounds did Jesus allow for divorce?

The Pharisees' interpretation of the Torah often involved 'building a fence around the Law' – creating sets of rules that would keep the people as far as possible from sinning. For example, Deuteronomy 25:3 requires that no criminal should be given more than forty lashes, otherwise 'your brother will be degraded in your eyes'. In New Testament times, 39 lashes was a common punishment (as Paul found out, see 2 Cor. 11:24); the idea was that, even if one lash was somehow miscounted, the Law would still not be broken. Jesus' criticism of this system of interpretation of biblical law was that it led to large volumes of complex rules, which could lay an unnecessary burden on people and result in legalism – following the 'letter' rather than the 'spirit' of the Law (Matt. 23). For example, working on the Sabbath was not permitted. But what constitutes work? How far could a person walk, what domestic tasks could they do, how much weight could they carry? And if healing required 'work' to be done, such as grinding herbs for a cure, then that might be considered unlawful as well – particularly if the illness or injury was not life-threatening (Matt. 12). This 'better safe than sorry' approach led to injustices of its own.

Jesus himself used a kind of 'fence' in interpreting the Torah, though it was a fence around the believer's heart rather than around the Law. For example, in his exposition of the Law in the Sermon on the Mount in Matthew 5, he does not define in detail what acts might constitute adultery and therefore which are permissible. (The Talmud, and therefore presumably Jesus' contemporary Pharisees, did discuss precisely what degree of contact was considered adultery.) Instead, he places the fence around the intention: not only is the physical act of adultery sinful, but so is the thought of lust which leads to it. Not only is murder a sin, but so is anger, which leads to violence. In the same way, his answer to the question of divorce was not to define exactly what was and wasn't just grounds for separation, but to relocate the debate in the *spirit* of the Law. Divorce of any kind is not God's will, as the creation account implies. This is made abundantly clear in Malachi 2:16: '"I hate divorce," says the Lord God of Israel.'

#11. Then Jesus didn't allow divorce for any reason at all?

Some people interpret these verses to mean that marriage is binding for life and that, effectively, there is no such thing as divorce – certainly not remarriage (the Catholic position). This, of course, is the ideal. But it is also clear that God allowed the early Israelites certain concessions 'due to the hardness of their hearts' (Matt. 19:8), perhaps for those cases where sin had already damaged the marriage beyond repair. The ideal was that the one-

flesh bond *should* not be broken, not that it *could* not be. In Matthew
5:32 and 19:9 the exception to the rule is given ('except for *porneia*'
– some kind of sexual infidelity). In this case, the exclusivity of the
one-flesh union has been broken: the damage has already been
done, though it is worth noting that this event only makes divorce
an option, rather than requiring it.

#12. So is adultery the only valid grounds for divorce?

As a counter-example to the principle that divorce is *always* unacceptable in the Bible, Ezra and Nehemiah commanded divorce
for Israelites who had married foreign wives against God's
command after the return from exile in Babylon (see Ezra 9 – 10;
Neh. 13). They even made a covenant before God to send away
the foreign women and included their children. The suggestion
here is that divorce *was* the right option, rather than continuing
in marriages that were going to be harmful to the overall community. Divorce in these circumstances was another least-worst
solution, albeit to a problem that should never have arisen in the
first place.

David Instone-Brewer[8] notes that Jesus apparently allowed
adultery as just cause for divorce (Matt. 19:9); many theologians
add Paul's grounds of abandonment by a non-believer (1 Cor.
7:12–15). There is no mention of abuse or neglect, and Paul
doesn't allow separation (1 Cor. 7:10). So one interpretation is that
Jesus wasn't condemning divorce whatever the reason, as we often
understand these words today, but was condemning the Pharisees'
newly invented 'any cause' divorce. In other words, he was saying
that divorce wasn't wrong *per se*, but that divorce for effectively no
good reason was unacceptable. Exodus 21:10–11 says that even
a slave-wife (and therefore, by implication, every wife) had three
rights within marriage: 'food, clothing and marital rights'. What
was shocking to Jesus' listeners was that he said they couldn't get a
divorce whenever they wanted one – there had to be a legally valid
cause, and these were limited. If this is the case, then Jesus wasn't
rejecting Old Testament teaching on divorce. He was correcting a
misinterpretation of the Old Testament.

#13. Are there other interpretations of Jesus' views on divorce?

As stated in chapter 5, there is a wide range of view on divorce amongst Christians![9] Although the first-century context helps inform the divorce debate, Jesus never actually refers to Exodus 21 and so the argument that withholding food, clothing or marital rights was grounds for divorce is an argument from silence. The confusion over the meaning of *porneia* also affects our understanding of Jesus' statements. If, in Matthew 19:9, *porneia* does not mean 'adultery' but 'premarital sex', this might imply that premarital sex with someone other than the current husband that took place during the betrothal period, or remained undisclosed at the time of marriage, was the only legitimate grounds for divorce (a modification of Deut. 22:13–21).[10] This was what Joseph thought Mary had done, and he would therefore have been justified in divorcing her (Matt. 1:18–19). If that is the case, then divorce would be illegitimate in most instances.

The more legitimate causes for divorce we read into Jesus' words, the less radical his statement: 'What God has joined together, let man not separate' (Matt. 19:6). John Piper writes, 'The deepest meaning of marriage is to display the covenant-keeping faithfulness of Christ and his church (Eph. 5:25). And Christ will *never* divorce his wife and take another.'[11]

#14. What does the Bible say about same-sex intercourse?

Both Old and New Testaments prohibit same-sex intercourse. There are a number of texts that state this clearly (Lev. 18:22; 20:13; Rom. 1:26–27; 1 Cor. 6:9–10) as well as several other narratives that may include or implicitly suggest disapproval (Gen. 9:18–27; 19:1–29; Deut. 23:17–18; Judg. 19; 1 Kgs 14:24; 15:12). Consequently, when Christians argue for the legitimacy of homosexual expression, they have to deal with these verses.[12]

#15. Fine. But aren't the biblical laws about same-sex intercourse outdated – just a product of their times and culture?

Biblical law is often criticized on the grounds that it is no more than a reflection of the broader cultural norms of the time, and when we try to apply it today we are uncritically importing those ideas.

In the case of biblical teaching about sexuality, however, this is not true. There is strong evidence that same-sex intercourse was common in Mediterranean culture – for example, in Canaanite religion in the Old Testament and in Greco-Roman society in New Testament times.[13] At the time, some thinkers were ambivalent towards it, or even openly spoke against it,[14] but there is no doubt that same-sex intercourse was a common feature of pagan culture in Jesus' and Paul's time – both in religious and secular life. So the Bible's teachings in this area are all the more noteworthy for being strikingly counter-cultural. Slavery, as a counter-example, was common in the Greco-Roman empire. Paul does not condone slavery, but neither does he criticize it out of hand – though he does encourage slaves to gain their freedom if they can (1 Cor. 7:20–23). Paul's teachings concerning slaves presuppose slavery as part of the culture; they are not counter-cultural in this respect.[15] But his teaching concerning sexuality is counter-cultural, and what he has to say therefore cannot be explained away as part of the general social background of the times.[16]

#16. Doesn't the Old Testament criticize same-sex intercourse only as part of a pagan religious rite – that is, when it involved idolatry?

Some texts (like 1 Kgs 14:24) do refer to same-sex prostitution, and therefore cannot be used to assess the legitimacy of consensual, long-term same-sex partnerships – any more than the ban on heterosexual temple prostitution would suggest the illegitimacy of marriage. The emphasis in some texts may have a different nuance, but this does not undermine the overall agreement across Old and New Testaments of this main point. Other texts do not relate to temple prostitution. For example, Leviticus 20 appears to be more concerned with maintaining sexual boundaries (between family members, genders, species, etc.).[17] So we cannot argue the validity of same-sex intercourse from this text, so long as it is not part of a pagan rite, without doing the same for adultery, incest and other biblical offences.

#17. Surely this doesn't apply to relationships between consenting adults?

There are no clear biblical examples of same-sex erotic relationships between consenting adults.[18] It is sometimes argued that these would have been (or would now be) acceptable to the biblical writers. Furthermore, critics of the apparent biblical ban on same-sex relationships claim that Paul (see Rom. 1:26–27) and other ancient writers did not understand the concept of sexual 'orientation', and that the texts refer to heterosexual men and women engaging in acts that therefore seemed 'unnatural'. It does seem to be the case that the Bible considers homosexuality as a behaviour, rather than an orientation – that is, it addresses it as an activity, not a disposition.[19] The distinction between the two was probably not fully recognized until much later. The English words 'homosexual' and 'heterosexual' were only coined in the nineteenth century – and possibly, with them, the growing idea of an exclusive sexual preference for the same or opposite sex. The idea of using sexual attraction to describe our identities is a recent one.[20]

Against this, in Leviticus 18:22 and 20:13, homosexuality is found alongside a range of other sexual offences: incest and sex with other close (not blood) relatives, adultery and bestiality. The context suggests that these were intended to have continuing relevance;[21] if not, there is little but (rapidly shifting) cultural mores to stop the others from being accepted too. Because the offences in Leviticus 18 and 20 are all consensual acts in ordinary daily life, it would be odd to single out homosexuality as the only item in the lists relating to issues of consent (or to issues of idolatry).

In the New Testament, the terms that Paul uses in 1 Corinthians 6:9 to describe homosexual acts are *malakoi* and *arsenokoitai*. The terms are rare in the NT, occurring in this form only here and in 1 Timothy 1:10 (for *arsenokoitai*). *Malakos*, 'soft', has been taken to mean just about anything from enjoying a decadent lifestyle with regard to food, fine clothes and aversion to hard work, through 'effeminate', to the passive partner in homosexual intercourse and specifically to male prostitutes. *Arsenokoitas* is a slightly easier term, literally meaning 'men who take males to bed'. Here the discussion tends to surround not the description of the man, who appears to be the active partner in homosexual intercourse, but the circumstances – whether it refers to a pederast or someone who uses prostitutes, or whether consensual sex with an ongoing partner is meant.

The precise meanings of these words are considered more fully elsewhere.[22] However, the context and pairing of *malakos* with *arsenokoitas* suggests a sexual meaning for the former as well as the latter, implying that Paul meant them to apply to consensual relationships for both partners.

#18. We don't keep every Old Testament law today – like not eating shellfish or wearing clothes made from mixed fabrics. So why single out same-sex intercourse?

Determining which laws are still binding, and why, is crucial in understanding the Old Testament's relevance to Christians. A typical response to the suggestion that Christians should accept the Old Testament's laws banning homosexuality is that the Bible has many other laws that Christians today do not keep, including subjects as obscure as avoiding clothes of mixed fabrics (Lev. 19:19), tattoos and particular kinds of haircut (Lev. 19:27–28), or not eating certain foods (Deut. 14; Lev. 11).[23] At the same time, we unquestioningly accept some other Old Testament rules, like the ban on murder. Clearly, not every law still applies; on the other hand, not every law has been abolished either. Most Christians accept this, but – aside from a few examples at either end of the spectrum – many people are uncertain where to draw the line.

The Old Testament – and Leviticus in particular – contains a wide range of law. Rules about what we would consider serious crimes appear alongside others that seem to us to be trivial. Some, like most or all of the Ten Commandments (Exod. 20; Deut. 5), we accept as relevant today; in all cases except the Sabbath they are also unequivocally upheld in the New Testament, adding weight to their importance for Christians (see Mark 2:23–28 for Jesus' treatment of the Sabbath). But in other cases, as with the food laws, we do not keep them. We eat pork and shellfish, rarely worrying that these would have been unclean to Jesus and his disciples, as well as the early Israelites. As Christians, if we reject the Old Testament laws on homosexual sex, must we also reject those on adultery and murder? Or if we keep them, must we also avoid bacon and poly-cotton clothes too? How do we know which Old Testament laws were supposed to be permanent and which weren't?

Jesus said he had come to fulfil the Law and the Prophets, not to abolish them (Matt. 5:17–19). Therefore, the Law is still important in *some* sense – we cannot entirely discard it. But Old Testament laws had many different purposes, and we cannot understand their relevance for today without knowing what they meant in the context of scripture as a whole.[24] Some laws dealt with offences against the interests of the whole community (like murder, idolatry, and many sexual offences). Others concerned crimes against individuals' property or persons (like theft and dishonest trading). Some included discipline, inheritance, marriage and divorce. There were rules about the temple cult (including the laws about when people were 'clean' and 'unclean'); laws about special times surrounding Sabbaths, festivals and other calendar laws; and laws which highlighted and symbolized Israel's distinctiveness as a nation (the food laws, laws about not mixing fabrics and crops), and those forbidding practices linked to, but not in themselves, foreign worship (probably including tattooing and cutting the hair and beard in particular ways; 'cooking a calf in its mother's milk', Exod. 23:19, may also be a reference to a Canaanite religious rite). Some offences were serious and warranted the death penalty; others could be addressed with a fine.

To understand how different laws apply now, we first have to discover, as best we can, their Old Testament context. Then we need to ask whether there are any New Testament principles that explicitly change our understanding of the Law. For example, the NT makes it clear that the food laws (and other symbolic distinction laws) are no longer relevant because there is now, after the Cross, 'no Jew nor Gentile' in Christ (Gal. 3:26–29, see also Mark 7:1–19) – although Christians should aim to be distinctive in many other ways (Mark 7:20–23). Secondly, because Jesus was the perfect sacrifice (Heb. 10:1–18), further sacrifice for sin is unnecessary and the sacrificial laws are no longer binding – though we may still *choose* to make a 'free will offering' (Exod. 35:29; Lev. 22:23) of time or money out of gratitude, and out of recognition that we do not really 'own' these at all. Third, Paul says religious laws about festivals and special days are a 'shadow' of the reality found in Jesus (Col. 2:16–17).

In terms of our sexuality, the Bible states that we are made in God's image, as gendered beings designed for heterosexual marriage (see chapter 4). The creation pattern for sex in Genesis 1 and 2 is reflected in the laws of the creation of the covenant with Israel in Exodus 19 to 24, as well as the new covenant and finally the new creation in Revelation (see 21:8).

Jesus did not speak about homosexuality, but he does affirm the Old Testament's standard for marriage when he condemns adultery (Matt. 5:21–30). Romans 1:26–27, 1 Corinthians 6:9–10 and 1 Timothy 1:10 support Old Testament sexual standards. Nowhere in the New Testament, in fact, are the moral standards of the Old Testament contradicted. This means that the rules about sexual behaviour in the Old Testament are not simply a product of their culture and era: they are absolute.

#19. What about women? The Old Testament doesn't say anything about lesbians . . .

Typically, in any study of biblical teaching on homosexuality, lesbian relationships receive far less consideration than gay male ones. This is partly due to the Bible's own comparative silence. Paul mentions female homosexuality in Romans 1:26 (before male homosexuality) but this is an isolated reference. It does not appear in the standard Old Testament texts that deal with homosexuality, including Leviticus 18:22 and 20:13.

Part of the reason for this may be because the relatively terse Old Testament texts are apparently restricted to offences involving penetration by a male (so that women are included in the bestiality prohibition of Lev. 20:16, but not in the same-sex prohibition of 20:13) – a fairly crude but clear definition of sex. This does not mean that every other form of sexual act was allowed; we cannot logically infer, for example, that adultery or incest which did not involve penetration was considered acceptable. This becomes clearer in the New Testament when Jesus emphasizes the spirit over the letter of the Law in Matthew 5.

Cultural considerations may also have played a part. There was a concern for posterity and lineage which we do not share today. So – in the OT – adultery is always seen in terms of an offence against another man's wife. If a married woman had sex with a man who was not her husband, it was always adultery. If a married man had extramarital sex, it was only considered adultery if the other woman was married. With less freedom, women may not have been able to pursue lesbian relationships, and even if they wanted to they would have been expected to marry a man anyway. It would pose little danger to family structure, inheritance or questions of paternity. In a patriarchal society – which may or may not have acknowledged its existence – lesbianism may simply have not been considered necessary to legislate against. Like Paul, the Jewish writers of the Talmud extend the OT prohibition on homosexual sex to women.[25]

#20. The church doesn't always do what the Bible says – for example, in the case of divorce. So why not just turn a blind eye to same-sex relationships, too?

Although Jesus speaks strongly against divorce, it is common in the church today. He did not mention same-sex intercourse at all, and yet the church is divided on the issue. Some have asked how we can justify divorce but not homosexual unions.[26]

It turns out that divorce is a poor analogy for same-sex

relationships.[27] Jesus did not need to speak about homosexual sex for the same reason he said nothing about incest or bestiality: it was simply not a matter of any doubt to his listeners in the way that it is today, whereas divorce was hotly debated. There is no conflict in the Bible about homosexuality, whereas there is some latitude within the Bible on the subject of divorce. Although Jesus did not allow no-fault divorce, there were circumstances when divorce was regrettably an option (see Appendix #10–13). It is a concession – a last-ditch solution to a problem that cannot be solved another way (Matt. 19:8). And although Deuteronomy 24:1–4 permits it, and other parts of the Torah presuppose it (Lev. 21:7), it is certainly not celebrated in the Old Testament. Malachi 2:15–16 is stark: '. . . do not break faith with the wife of your youth. "I hate divorce," says the Lord God of Israel.' Divorce is also at odds with the creation ideal in Genesis 2:24 (see Matt. 19:6).

So divorce is generally undesirable, even sinful in many cases. It is possible to divorce unilaterally, without the agreement of a spouse; consent need not even be an issue. And repeated divorce *is* treated seriously by the church, though divorce usually only happens once or twice in a lifetime. Accepting same-sex relationships would be like celebrating an ongoing, perhaps daily, cycle of divorce and remarriage. Wrongful divorce is, like a same-sex union, something to be repented of and ideally not repeated – not celebrated and blessed by the church. Jesus did not 'complete' (see Matt. 5:17) the Old Testament divorce law by giving equal rights to women to initiate divorce. Instead, he introduced fairness and upheld scriptural principles by returning to the pattern of Genesis 2 and maintaining that ideally *neither* should seek divorce. In the same way, the answer to an apparent inequality in our church (for instance, the lack of recognition of homosexual couples, when divorce is tacitly accepted) is not to bless homosexual couples in their unions but to work to bring the divorce rate down. Identifying one way in which we fall short of the biblical ideal is not grounds for doing the same in other areas.

Aside from the prohibitions in both Testaments, there is the positive pattern in the creation narratives. The 'One Flesh' union that is God's ideal for human sexuality is intended to be a permanent one between one man and one woman: lifelong, heterosexual, monogamous and exclusive. Monogamy and heterosexuality are both key attributes of 'one flesh' union; promiscuous heterosexuality can hardly be said to be more biblically acceptable than faithful homosexuality. If God created Eve specifically to be *kĕnegdō* – complementary – then a male-male or female-female pairing is intrinsically incomplete. It is sometimes argued on 'natural' grounds and 'structural prerequisites' that God designed men and women exclusively for heterosexual sex (or a similar secular argument). The 'natural' argument contains potential flaws, particularly as homosexual activity is not entirely absent in other species.[28] In addition, the male-female pattern in Genesis 2 is an observation, not a commandment, and therefore its moral significance is harder to judge – though its place before the Fall suggests it is intended to be the norm and Jesus' reference to it in Matthew 19 makes it sound normative in his mind. The argument starts to gain more weight in the light of the suggestion that the male-female human relationship is a reflection of God's divine nature.[29]

As discussed earlier, the Old Testament (most strikingly in Lev. 20) appears to legislate against sex between non-complementary partners – those who do not fulfil the creation principle of *kĕnegdō*, or complementarity (see Gen. 2:18, 20). This includes those who are too similar, as well as too different. Incest involves sex between two people who are already, in one sense, 'one flesh'; they are close relations. Homosexuality involves sex between two people who are also too similar, this time in terms of gender. Paul alludes to creation in the context of same-sex attraction in Romans 1:20–27.

The closest comparison we have for the interpretation of the texts dealing with homosexual sex is not divorce, but precisely other offences that have not changed, and show few signs of doing so – rape, but particularly incest, adultery and bestiality, which are found in exactly the same context as same-sex practice in Leviticus 20. If the Bible's laws really are only cultural mores, it raises difficult questions about these four absolute examples, not to mention any other non-sexual laws we might treat so subjectively, including the remainder of the Ten Commandments. Homosexual sex appears to be proscribed, severely and absolutely, in both Testaments, in the same way as, for example, adultery or incest.[30]

Notes

1. Strong's Concordance 4202–4205.

2. Compare the modern-day example of the word 'nice'. This originally meant 'simple' or 'ignorant', from the Latin 'nescire', 'not to know'. It came to mean 'wanton' or 'lascivious' by Chaucer's time and only gained its present sense of 'pleasant' in the nineteenth century.

3. See F. Brown, S. Driver and C. Briggs, *Hebrew and English Lexicon* (Hendrickson, 1997, third printing).

4. The bride appears to have been 'the object of the agreement rather than a party thereto' – Raymond Westbrook, 'Biblical Law', in N. S. Hecht *et al.* (eds.), *An Introduction to the History and Sources of Jewish Law* (Clarendon Press, 1996), pp. 1–13, cited in Jonathan Burnside, *Consent versus Community* (Jubilee Centre, 2006), p. 21. In practice, the bride may have had some significant input, as in Rebekah's case in Genesis 24:54–60. Nevertheless, this was a family decision – not one made simply between the couple themselves.

5. See Burnside, *Consent versus Community*, pp. 35–45.

6. See Jonathan Burnside, *God, Justice and Society* (Cambridge University Press, 2009), chapter 10.

7. For more on the rabbinic implications for how to interpret the Bible's teaching on divorce, see David Instone-Brewer, *What God Has Joined* (Christianity Today, 2007) – see <http://www.christianitytoday.com/ct/2007/october/20.26.html> (accessed 9 October 2007).

8. Instone-Brewer, *What God Has Joined*.

9. For a different view to the one above see, e.g., Burnside, *God, Justice and Society*, chapter 13.

10. See John Piper's response to Instone-Brewer, 'Tragically Widening the Grounds of Legitimate Divorce' at <http://www.desiringgod.org> (accessed 22 July 2008).

11. See 'Tragically Widening the Grounds of Legitimate Divorce'.

12. For a short, accessible and thorough approach to the different arguments, see Dan O. Via and Robert Gagnon's *Homosexuality and the Bible: Two Views* (Augsburg Fortress, 2003). For supporting material and further articles, see <http://www.robgagnon.net>.

13. For more on the Ancient Near Eastern background, which includes both positive and negative examples of homosexuality, see Robert Gagnon's *The Bible and Homosexual Practice* (Abingdon Press, 2001), pp. 44–56.

14. E.g. Plato, *Laws*, book 9, arguing against sexual liberty in the wider sense as well as against same-sex intercourse.

15. Whilst Paul does not call for an outright ban on slavery, he does address it in a different way. By asking Philemon to accept Onesimus 'no longer as a slave, but better than a slave . . . as a brother in the Lord' (Philm. 16), he tries to change the way the he views his slave. If Paul was successful, we can see that the form this slave/owner relationship took would be very different.

16. Cf. Via and Gagnon, *Homosexuality and the Bible*, p. 42.

17. William Webb, *Slaves, Women and Homosexuals: Exploring the Hermeneutics of Cultural Analysis* (IVP: 2001), pp. 196–201. See also Burnside, *Consent versus Community*.

18. For the suggestion that David and Jonathan were engaged in a kind of Old Testament civil partnership, see chapter 3.

19. There is evidence that some ancient writers did have some understanding of our modern concept of 'orientation'. In his *Symposium*, Plato discusses the original existence of three types of double-faced creatures: men, women and androgynous beings. Zeus decided to humble and weaken humans by cutting these beings in two. The result was men and women, and sexual attraction: the halves were attracted to reunite in their original form. Those who were originally part of an androgynous being were attracted to the opposite sex, whereas those who had been part of a primeval man or woman sought out their own sex.

20. This growing tendency to self-identify by means of sexuality may be a result of the increased mobility and rootlessness of modern life: the need to find an identity and support group when ties to family and kinship networks, communities of birth and role in those communities, are so much weaker than they were in the past.

21. Cf. Webb, *Slaves, Women and Homosexuals*.

22. Cf. Gagnon, *The Bible and Homosexual Practice*, pp. 303–339.

23. Season 2 episode 3 of *The West Wing*, 'The Midterms', includes a character called Dr Jenna Jacobs, who is a thinly-veiled caricature of real-life conservative and anti-gay radio host Laura Schlessinger. In the episode, the President uses similar arguments against Jacobs' attitude towards homosexuality; the arguments themselves were paralleled in a satirical open letter to Schlessinger, criticizing her for her intolerant views and lack of consistency in applying biblical law.

24. See Christopher Wright, *Old Testament Ethics for the People of God* (IVP, 2004), pp. 288–301.
25. Gagnon, *The Bible and Homosexual Practice*, pp. 143–146; see also pp. 299–303.
26. Walter Wink, 'Homosexuality and the Bible,' in W. Wink (ed.), *Homosexuality and Christian Faith: Questions of Conscience for the Churches* (Fortress, 1999), pp. 33–49. See online at <http://www.bridges-across. org/ba/winkhombib.htm> (accessed 25 September 2007).
27. See Robert Gagnon, 'Are There Universally Valid Sex Precepts? A Critique of Walter Wink's Views on the Bible and Homosexuality', in *Horizons in Biblical Theology*, 24 (2002), pp. 72–125.
28. Particularly in Bonobos (Pygmy Chimpanzees), which are closely related to humans. Bonobos show a range of sexual behaviour in contrast to the Common Chimpanzee, the other member of their species. Having said this, 'no evidence has as yet emerged to suggest that any nonhuman primate studied to date would rate at 6 [exclusively homosexual] on the Kinsey scale of heterosexuality/homosexuality.' L. A. Rosenblum, 'Primates, Homo sapiens and Homosexuality', in *Homosexuality/ Heterosexuality: Concepts of Sexual Orientation* (Oxford University Press, 1990), pp. 172–173.
29. See chapter 4. For a more thorough approach to this issue and related ones, see Thomas Schmidt, *Straight and Narrow* (IVP, 1995), chapter 3.
30. Gagnon, *The Bible and Homosexual Practice*, pp. 449–452.

SELECTED FURTHER READING

Christopher Ash, *Marriage: Sex in the Service of God* (IVP, 2003).

Breakdown Britain (Centre for Social Justice, 2006). Available at <http://www.centreforsocialjustice.org.uk/default.asp?pageRef=180> (accessed 31 July 2008).

Breakthrough Britain (Centre for Social Justice, 2007). Available at <http://www.centreforsocialjustice.org.uk/default.asp?pageRef=226> (accessed 31 July 2008).

Jonathan Burnside, *God, Justice and Society* (Cambridge University Press, 2009).

Robert Gagnon, *The Bible and Homosexual Practice* (Abingdon Press, 2001).

Dale Kuehne, *Sex and the iWorld: Rethinking Relationship Beyond an Age of Individualism* (Baker, 2009).

Michael Schluter and John Ashcroft (eds.), *Jubilee Manifesto* (IVP, 2005).

Wendy Shalit, *A Return to Modesty: Discovering the Lost Virtue* (Free Press, 2000).

William Webb, *Slaves, Women and Homosexuals: Exploring the Hermeneutics of Cultural Analysis* (IVP, 2001).

Christopher Wright, *Old Testament Ethics for the People of God* (IVP, 2004).

ABOUT JUBILEE CENTRE

The Jubilee Centre seeks to demonstrate the continued relevance of biblical principles to the challenges facing society today. It believes the Bible presents a coherent social vision, based on right relationships, that provides an alternative to contemporary political ideologies.

The Jubilee Centre has applied this relational agenda to areas as diverse as the economy, criminal justice, care for the elderly, asylum and immigration, and the environment. Its publications include the ground-breaking 'Jubilee Manifesto' and the quarterly 'Cambridge Papers', an influential collection of peer-reviewed studies. The Jubilee Centre maintains an extensive blog and archive of its resources, most of which can be downloaded for free, on its website.

In addition to this book, its full range of resources for the 'Fair Sex Movement' include three short public information bulletins, available on the Jubilee Centre's YouTube channel, together with an accompanying set of discussion questions.

To find out more, please use the contact details below:

Jubilee Centre
3 Hooper Street
Cambridge
CB1 2NZ

Tel: 01223 566319
Email: info@jubilee-centre.org
Website: www.jubilee-centre.org
YouTube: www.youtube.com/jubileecentre

related titles from IVP

foreword by James Jones

Jubilee
Manifesto

a framework, agenda
& strategy for christian
social reform

For any who want to change society or change their workplace, this is a crucial handbook of both theory and practice.

Based on the work of the influential Jubilee Centre in Cambridge, *Jubilee Manifesto* presents a biblically-based alternative to Capitalism, Socialism and other ideologies. It identifies relationships as the foundation stone of any society. Ultimately it is the quality of those relationships, in families and communities, in organizations and between institutions, that holds society together.

Through careful study of the biblical material the contributors explore how a relational society approaches issues of nationhood, government, economics, criminal justice and international relations.

'Many years ago in Nairobi I was privileged to witness the beginnings of what is now the Jubilee Manifesto. I commend this book as a serious and significant contribution by fellow pilgrims.'

Mutava Musyimi
General Secretary,
National Council of Churches of Kenya

ISBN:
978-1-84474-074-1

Available from your local Christian bookshop
or via our website at **www.ivpbooks.com**